MARKETING THE UNORGANISED SECTOR
Issues, Perspectives and Strategies

About the Author

Dr. Kamal Taori belongs to the UP cadre of the 1968 batch of the I.A.S. He had a short stint in the army and has doctorate in Rural entrepreneurship.

He has been with the Khadi and Village Industries Sector for nearly 12 years. This was his opportunity for a deeper understanding of Gandhi, Vinoba, Lohia and Kumarappa and to sublimate his ambition into a mission with holistic action.

A short assignment with the UNDP, and subsequent study of the United Nations system were helpful in the convergence of his lifelong studies, experience and understanding into a world-view and a global vision. He is always concerned about what could have been done, as against what has been done.

A Social Science Scientific researcher and author of a number of books and research papers, he has organized and led many a seminar and workshop on a whole range of socio-economic issues and topics.

Currently he is Adviser, Inter-State Council, Ministry of Home, Government of India.

MARKETING THE UNORGANISED SECTOR

Issues, Perspectives and Strategies

Dr. Kamal Taori, *IAS*

CONCEPT PUBLISHING COMPANY, NEW DELHI-110059

Revised and Enlarged Edition 2003

ISBN 81-8069-009-1

First Published 1995

Published and Printed by :

Ashok Kumar Mittal

Concept Publishing Company

A/15-16, Commercial Block, Mohan Garden,
New Delhi-110059 (India)

Phones: 5351460, 5351794
Fax: 091-(11) - 5357103
Email : publishing@conceptpub.com

Dedicated to all
self-employed entrepreneurs
in the unorganised and
non-formal sector

FOREWORD

The importance of unorganised sectors in the economy of India is self-evident, but it has been only intermittently realized by our economic *pundits* after independence. Before the country attained independence and during the leadership of Mahatma Gandhi the activities of khadi production and the very small-scale industries located in the rural areas were one of the main planks of the constructive programmes of Gandhiji and the Congress Party. But after independence all the emphasis shifted mainly towards bigger industries. Some attention, however, continued to be paid by a few dedicated leaders of khadi for about a decade after independence and consequently the All India Khadi and Village Industries Commission (AIKVIC) was constituted in 1956. Khadi and Village Industries Boards were also established by State governments to coordinate the work in this field. However, from the Second Five Year Plan onwards the focus gradually shifted towards the big industries and even the small-scale industries were in reality medium-size industries mostly concentrated in the urban areas.

This proclivity towards the bigger and urban industries has had some extremely undesirable effect on our body-politic. The rapid growth of urbanization, the tendency of the rural population to shift to large cities, and the increasing incidence of rural and urban unemployment are some of the consequences of this neglect of the very-small-scale sector, and gradually a realization is dawning that the key to the solution for the problems of unemployment and urbanization lies in the development of Khadi and Village Industries alone.

With the emphasis after independence shifting away from the rural industries there has been a dearth of good literature/books dealing with khadi and the small-scale sector. The KVIC and a few individuals have been valiantly fighting a lone battle during the past few decades to fill up this gap but the effort has proved inadequate. Meanwhile there has also been a qualitative change in the problems relating to this sector. Rapid industrialization in the country, modernization of various technologies, availability of electricity in the rural areas are some of the factors which have had their impact on the village industries also. This process has been further intensified during the past few years due to the atmosphere created by the liberalization policy of the Government in the fields of finance and industry. There was therefore a keenly felt need for a book dealing with the problems of Khadi and Village Industries comprehensively, taking into account the changes during the past two decades. This book of Dr. Kamal Taori is a valued attempt to bring into focus these various problems and to suggest possible solutions from a modern point of view taking into account various developments in the fields of advertising, marketing, quality control and relating these solutions to the availability of finance from banks and other institutions in the Five Year Plans.

Dr. Taori is a person with a vast background of a special interest on the marketing side and has been actively associated with the work of Khadi and Village Industries for more than a decade. He was the Chief Executive Officer of the Khadi and Village Industries Board of the large State of Uttar Pradesh and Secretary to the Government also in the same department and later on has been working for the past five years as the Chief Executive Officer of All India Khadi and Village Industries Commission, Bombay. He possesses a wide experience in all the aspects of this sector and is fully acquainted with their problems. He also has an appreciation of the modern techniques particularly of publicity and marketing propagation for this field. It is to be noted that the small scale of the village industries units does not necessarily mean that its marketing also should be on a similar small scale. The modern marketing techniques and the easy availability of an all-India market for the products of this sector make it imperative that a suitable marketing organization be created to handle the products of Khadi and Village Industries in both rural and urban areas. Dr. Taori has a special interest and experience in these technologies and the suggestions made in this book will surely prove of great help in this task.

This book, dealing with these special aspects and problems relating to the activities of Khadi and Village Industries pays particular attention to the problems of marketing and quality control. There are two weak points in the present organization of the very small-scale sector and Dr. Taori has attempted to apply modern means for tackling the special problems and suggested solutions for them. As such this book should prove equally useful to the workers in this field and also to the entrepreneurs who want to start new industries.

J.N.Tiwari
IAS (Retd.)
(Former Secretary to the Government of India)

Note :
Shri J.N. Tiwari was also the Chief Executive Officer of the Khadi and Village Industries Commission, Bombay, for about five years.

ISSUES AND COMPLEXITY OF OUR TIMES

1. Mass awakening all around.
2. Simplicity to Complexity.
3. Introvert to Extrovert.
4. Rural to Urban.
5. Organised *Versus* Unorganised.
6. Grant, Rebate *Versus* Internal Resource Generation.
7. Duplicity *Versus* Simplicity.
8. Self-sufficiency *Versus* Dependency.
9. Small *Versus* Big.
10. Democracy *Versus* Authoritarianism.
11. Interference *Versus* Interlock.
12. Natural *Versus* Artificial.
13. Voluntary *Versus* Mercenary.
14. Craftsman to Entrepreneur (commercial venturist.)
15. Law-maker to Law-breaker.
16. Law-enforcer and Self-regulator.
17. Charity to Creativity and Confidence-building.
18. Right to information.
19. Involving All
20. Delegation, Decentralization and Local Self-Governance.
21. Vision to Action.

PREFACE TO THE FIRST EDITION

The need for compiling some studies on marketing has been felt in the light of the new economic policy. The unorganized sector faces various competitions both internal and external.

By analyzing the SWOT (strengths, weaknesses, opportunities and threats) of the sector, one is able to fully grasp the potentials that the sector processes.

This compilation does not claim to be of an academic value. It is a synthesis of theory and practices rather more weighted in favour of an action-oriented plan development.

This purpose would be served, if we could generate interest in the implementors, evaluators, financiers to fully integrate their efforts for developing a hope-generating, replicable model.

There is much fat accumulated in the various structures created over the past four decades. With better imagination, compulsion to perform and integrated service, culture and development, we should be able to show better results, even without any massive investment.

The "Consumer" is supreme and has to be treated so. Mahatma Gandhi, realized this long time back and put it in these wise words:

> A customer is the most important visitor on our premises. He is not dependant on us. We are dependant on him. He is not an interruption on our work. He is the purpose of it. He is not an outsider on our business. He is a part of it. We are not doing a favour by serving him. He is doing us a favour by giving an opportunity to do so.

The above becomes much more relevant today than it was at that time. The Consumer has to be ultimately considered in totality.

At the end, an innovation is made in the form of charts in the chapter 'Demystification Issues–at a glance' for the intellectual to ponder over various aspects of a number of issues, one by one, at a glance. This will evoke stimulation from within.

I am extremely grateful to Shri. J.N. Tiwari, IAS (Retd.), who was Chief Executive Officer of KVIC for 1974-1978 and also former Secretary to Government of India. Shri Tiwari has seen the organization from multiple angles and over a period of time has seen the areas of comparative weaknesses holding back full exploitation of hidden strengths.

I am extremely grateful to Shri Naval Kishore Sharma, Chairman of KVIC, and other members of KVIC with whom I had good fortune to interact from time to time. Needless to say that views expressed in this book are entirely of the author.

June 29,1995

KAMAL TAORI
(Vidyarthi)

PREFACE TO THE SECOND EDITION

Marketing of the unorganized sector is bound to develop into a very important "hope-generating" area of action and research. With other models of development having failed, it is important to look at the emerging investment opportunities from different sectors. These are difficult and timely areas for action analysis as complexity of our time undergoes a radical change.

Shri J.N. Tewari, former secretary to the Government of India, is no more with us but the intensity of the problem which was explained by him from time to time has become much more serious with the introduction of the liberalization policy in early 1990s.

During the period I had an opportunity to draw some more conclusions based upon observation and analysis.

My assignment of writing a report for the UNDP, a paper for the ILO, Chairmanship of the Textile Corporation, Kanpur, followed by the job of Principal Secretary, Khadi and Village Industries, Textile, and Chairman of Administrative Reforms and Decentralisation Commission and presently Director of State Institute of Rural Development has cemented my conviction that this unorganized sector has not received due attention because of lack of holistic appreciation by all shareholders.

Though this book has not been revised substantially, there are some additions to clarify important areas. The demystification issue has been further updated since my knowledge of 1995-99 has also been upgraded based upon time test.

Lobbying for Unorganized Sector

As time passes, one realizes how policies are framed and from time to time amended and implemented. The case study method and codification and research help in identifying over a period of time how many policies have badly harmed the non-vocals .

It is a pity that the unorganized sector does not possess any organised lobby to assess and monitor their overall cost from time to time. If somebody asked what is the real strength of India, one would like to answer without *hesitation that it is the unorganized, decentralized sector. This sector calls for all the attention*. There are issues of multi-dimensional nature which will have to be tackled if we want to solve the problem of unemployment and on the whole accelerate sustainable human development. We have to collectively think of convergence in the right sense of the word.

These are some of the areas for consideration.

26 January, 2002

Dr. KAMAL TAORI
(Vidyarthi), *I.A.S*

CONTENTS

CONTENTS

1

THE CONTEXT

With the march of time, the importance of "the small is beautiful' has become an established reality the world over in the sphere of industries and their contribution in the overall economy is fast becoming a factor to reckon with even in developed economies. A massive change seemed in the offing not only in the last decade of the 20th century but symbolically in the last millennium when the change in outlook approached and even consciousness of the humanity was at a crossroads where intimate desire to be or not to be was at stake. Changes are taking place, at a speed no one could imagine some years ago, in every aspect of our existence, i.e. social, political, cultural, economic, approaches, outlook, habits, behaviour, climatic conditions, religious understanding and so on and so forth.

A trend towards 'small'—be it scale of industry, plan, project, family, society—is emerging in the consciousness of those who have hitherto been votaries of the 'big'. And there has emerged an urgent need too for heading towards conditions in which everyone could be provided some outlet for his creative urge. The very urge in a human being to create has to be met with whether it fits into the economic behaviour of the day's advancement or not and more well-to-do people of the developed world would be taking up traditional occupation as a hobby. Necessity is the mother of invention and people have to invent skills whieh keep their minds and fingers creative. This reverse process has already started in most economically advanced countries. May be it is because of the global feeling that the greed of technological growth has reached to the point where it has become suicidal for the humanity as a whole. We are standing at the very threshold of a great transitional period and a momentous one with far-reaching changes in the economy too. Faced with gigantic populations. Japan, China and India, though with obvious different strategies, have nursed village and small industries. While Japan has a policy of adopting and developing highly sophisticated technology through the large sector even in a free market system, China with its closed economic system has laid down norms to be fulfilled by each such unit through Central Planning Agencies.

India, pursuing a 'mixed economic policy' up-till-now, has followed a protectionist policy in developing these industries with a certain success but not without fears. A similar movement has been running like an under-current even in the economies of the U.S.A., U.K., Canada, Korea, etc.

But in the total scenario and with all the efforts put in, in India, these industries could not be spread as envisaged because of the non-existence of an institutional infrastructure and other factors like change in the developmental strategy, technological gap or backwardness, strange and unpredictable behaviour of the markets with the advent of industrialisation on a gigantic scale and so on and so forth.

However, there is a silver lining too in that rural unemployment and destitution have had their own pressures on the planners to accord this sector a befitting status, i.e,. making it a priority sector, at least in the Approach Paper, to make it a thing that cannot be ignored or be left unattended. Though much is left which is desired, today evolving a strategy for marketing of rural artisans' products has emerged as a must for the sector.

According to Peter Drucker, 'Marketing' is so basic that it cannot be considered as a separate function. It is the whole business seen from the point of view of the customer. In a business organisation, in order to discuss and understand the role of marketing, it is necessary to consider all the aspects of production, finance, personnel and lastly the most important customer. This book is an effort to consider all these aspects in reference to the marketing of the products of the Rural Sector in India and particularly the products of village artisans and not to be confused with the theoretical books for developing marketing strategies for the Rural Sector. This book deals with a tactical plan of action for practical marketing of the rural artisans' products where theory is required only so long as the practical remains secluded. What ultimately remains is the practical approach, in other words actions. An effort has been made here to combine an ideal blend of experience, innovations, thinking and creativity of those people who have been working in the Rural Sector for years.

In the case of 'Rural Industries', marketing plays a comparatively more important role than other aspects, viz. production, finance and personnel, as these industries are in the second-most labour-intensive sector after agriculture in the Indian economy, providing maximum employment to the countryside class called artisans whose only assets are their hands. Utilisation of these hands productively can be thought of as a solution for solving the rising unemployment problem. In the Indian context, agriculture has now a very limited absorption capacity, particularly in the case of educated manpower because of a variety of factors such as declining land-man ratio, low level of skill requirement, meagre earning, etc. The only alternative, therefore, remains to resort to creation of employment opportunities outside the agriculture, i.e. in the rural non-farm sector.

The rural non-farm sector provides a variety of options as shown in the table below:

Areas		
1. Production of agricultural inputs 2. Processing of agricultural produce 3. Processing of mineral and natural resources 4. Production and processing of forest-based materials 5. Production of building materials 6. Production of consumer goods and basic needs 7. Traditional handicrafts	Rural Industrial Sector	Rural Non-farm Sector
8. Repairs and maintenance service 9. Provision of inputs and services to various rural economic activities		Rural Tertiary Sector

Options 1 to 7 in the table constitute the Rural Industrial Sector while 8 and 9 form the Rural Tertiary Sector.

DURING PLANS

Since the beginning of the planning era, increased emphasis has been laid on the development of Khadi and Village Industries in rural areas. The First Five Year Plan explicitly recognised the need for closely integrating the Rural Industries Programme of agricultural development. In the Second Five Year Plan, serious attention was given to rural industrialisation and a committee was set up to examine the problems and prospects of Rural Industries. The committee's recommendations were promptly implemented with the setting up of specialised boards, entrusted with the responsibility of initiating and monitoring development in their respective spheres. The Third Five Year Plan intensified industrial development efforts in the rural areas through a systematic Rural Industrialisation Programme (RIP).

Rural industrialisation was also the main focus of developmental efforts in the rural areas during the Fourth and Fifth Five Year Plans. The Fifth Plan, in particular, added a new dimension by recognising the need for developing appropriate technology and technology transfer to rural areas. Recognising the importance, the Sixth Five Year Plan stressed on rural development, particularly rural industries, through an Integrated Rural Developmental (IRD) approach wherein all the sectors to rural economy, viz. agriculture, livestock, forestry, industries, irrigation, communication services and all special purpose state development schemes were taken up for development in an integrated manner. Rural industrial development has thus become an integral part of the massive IRD programme initiated from the Sixth Five Year Plan.

Further emphasising the need of rural industrialisation, the Seventh Five Year Plan stated that rural industrialisation had to be given adequate emphasis so as to check the exodus of rural artisans to urban concentrations. Accordingly, the need for a separate commission for rural industries and handicrafts was to be examined. The policy to be pursued during the Seventh Five Year Plan period aimed at rationalization of the fiscal regime to ensure rapid growth of rural industries. Infrastructural facilities were to be strengthened at various levels. Adoption of modern management techniques was to be encouraged. Development and dissemination of appropriate technology to reduce drudgery, productivity and quality improvement and to lessen the dependence on subsidies received due emphasis. It was proposed to further upgrade skills in line with the degree of sophistication of production processes. Care was to be taken to ensure that introduction of technological improvements did not damage the distinctive character of products such as handicrafts and handloom.

Measures were to be taken to adopt coherent marketing strategies for both domestic and export markets. Linkages were to be forged with marketing organisations so that products of the sector were competitive in the domestic and international markets.

All these measures led to considerable success and KVI activities registered an increase of 103.5 per cent at the terminal year of the Seventh Plan, i.e. 1989-90.

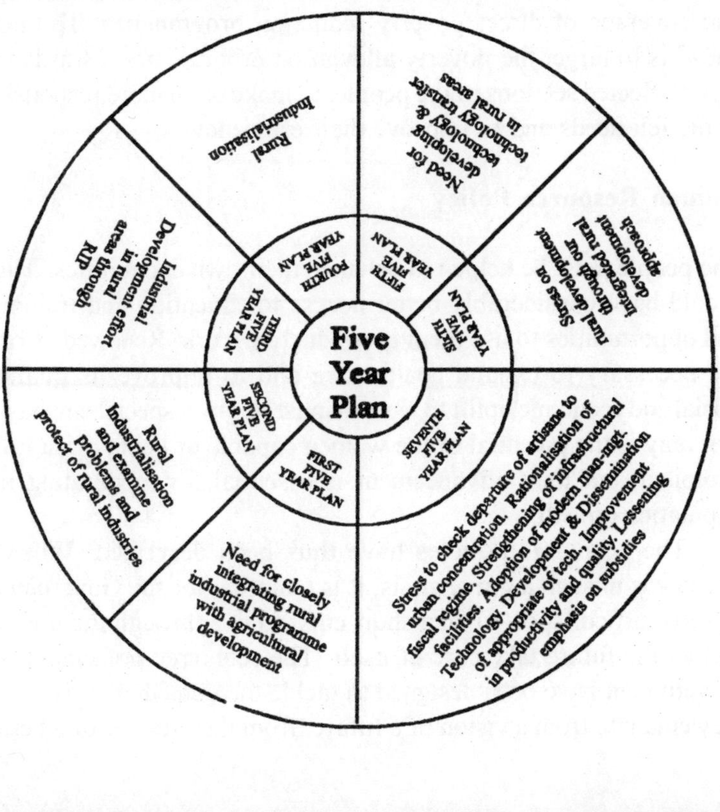

On the threshold of a new economic approach with its trends towards liberalisation, privatisation and market friendly inclination the Government of India had in early 1990s declared a separate industrial policy for Small Scale and Cottage Industries. The Village and Small Industries (VSI) sector has fast emerged as a dynamic and vibrant one registering its contribution of nearly 35 per cent of the gross value of the output in the manufacturing sector accounting for 40 per cent of the total exports from the country by the end of the Seventh Plan. The total employment reached around 12 million.

Poverty Alleviation Policy

It is the task of the Government to ensure that the people's basic needs are met and distress prevented. This task becomes more important at times of economic stress and change, that is, when there is the greatest need for extending a safety net to the weak and the poor. The Government is committed to expanding the scope and coverage of direct poverty reduction programmes. The task ahead is to target the poverty alleviation programmes towards the worst affected sections of the people, to make them more responsive to the felt needs and to improve their efficiency.

Human Resource Policy

The people must be helped to enhance their own capabilities. They should have considerably better access to education and training, and opportunities to use them in productive work. Renewed efforts are necessary to expand health care and to improve its quality. Social and economic uplift to women must be given special emphasis. Not only is the potential of the women capable of being more fully exploited, but their advancement is essential for moderating the population growth.

The economic policies have thus been described: When a country is in such a grave crisis, it is tempting for the Government to stave off collapse, to take short cuts, to live through the present and let the future take care of itself. The economic policies of the Government have been designed to tackle the immediate crisis, but they emanate from a vision of a future, from the promise of a better life for our people. The crisis has involved hardship for the people. The Government has tried to ameliorate it, but not enough. The resources of the Government are limited, and more needs to be done to ensure that they are used efficiently and for the most deserving. But the immediate options are limited. It is important to broaden them and that is where the vision comes in.

The basis of this vision is self-reliance. It has been the foundation of our economic policy for over four decades. Even if anyone wishes to abandon self-reliance, India is too large a country for the rest of the world to look after. There is thus no alternative to self-reliance.

This means that our achievements depend on our own efforts. Our standards of living depend on our productivity; the only fruits we can enjoy are the fruits of our labour. Our hard work, creativity, enterprise and intelligence — they will decide how well our children live. We must build a society that cares for the people today and builds for their tomorrows.

But self-reliance does not mean isolation. We live in a world of great variety — of people, resources, of knowledge and behaviour. It is there for us to cooperate with, trade with, learn from and contribute to. It is there for us to measure ourselves against. From it we must derive our standards of excellence — standards to equal and surpass. To it we must contribute to care — care for the weak and the unfortunate.

The Government has tried to expand the economic space in which the people can exercise their initiative and ingenuity. It hopes to do more to expand their opportunities, to enhance their potential. But what shape the economy takes ultimately depends on what the people make of it. In that sense, the future is in their hands.

One need not be surprised to find that the KVI sector forming a small part of the VSI sector has the highest potential in providing whatever little earning is possible to an artisan at his/her very doorsteps and has the larger contribution on the employment front. Thus falling in the category of industries it also has a peculiar characteristic of its own, being a fore-runner in contributing to the efforts of the nation in its various poverty alleviation programmes even in remote, inaccessible and difficult areas where none dares to go.

Some Relevant Aspects

Labour Intensive Sectors of the Indian Economy

Agriculture with Limited Absorption Capacity

Factors :

- Decline of land-man ratio
- Low level of skill requirement
- Meagre earnings

Rural Non-Farm Sectors Including Rural Industries

Areas :

Rural Industries Sector

1. Production of agriculture inputs
2. Processing of agricultural produce
3. Processing of mineral and natural resources
4. Production and processing of forest-based materials
5. Production of building materials
6. Production of consumer goods and basic needs
7. Traditional handicrafts

Tertiary Sector

8. Repairs and maintenance of service
9. Provision of inputs and services to various rural economic activities

Hindrances in the growth of Rural Industries

1. Technological obsolescence
2. Inadequate and irregular supply of raw materials
3. Lack of organised marketing channels
4. Imperfect knowledge of market conditions
5. Lack of effective coordination
6. Absence of quality products

2

VILLAGE AND SMALL INDUSTRIES SECTOR
Prospects and Retrospect

Today it is openly acknowledged that 50 per cent of the employment and 35 per cent of the exports are from Village and Small Industries (VSI) particularly the Small Scale Sector. High employment potentials and quality products coming out of this sector have even become popular in the lands abroad. And the share of Village Industries, i.e. Handloom, Handicrafts and Khadi and Village Industries (KVIs) is not negligible. The weakest among these village industries are Khadi and other village industries whose share in employment generation is big, however, exports are not that big to boast of but a beginning is there.

In our times, trends, life-styles, philosophies, systems, etc., all change fast and one has to keep abreast with the wherewithal to the passing days and our times. That is how Philip Costler in the preface to his 7th Edition of *Marketing Management* writes:

> The decade of 1990's is one of great promise and great uncertainty…. Western Europe is moving rapidly towards the world's largest common market with 324 million customers. Eastern Europe is emerging as a promising market for Western goods. Asian economies continue to expand their internal market and their global market share. Add to this general promising new technologies of the 1990's, high definition,

> television, new wonder drugs, super conductivity, genetic engineering and other miracles of science.
>
> On the other hand, the problems are also great. Hunger, disease and illiteracy continue to plague most of the world population. Environmental quality continues to deteriorate because of unabated pollution. Many nations are paralysed by internal strife and corrupt leadership and saddled with enormous internal and external debts. The gap between the wealthier and poorer nations keeps widening.
>
> The supreme irony is that the underdeveloped world has a crying need for food, clothing, shelter and other basic goods but lacks purchasing power. The developed world has enormous industrial capacity to satisfy these needs but will sell only to those with purchasing power… fights fiercely for market share in the fiscal markets—Western Europe, North America and the Far East—while rest of the world languishes.

Here, we in India particularly, working for the VSI sector, can see where we stand. After 50 years of our independence we are retracing our footsteps towards market-oriented economy in spite of the enshrined goal of our socialistic pattern of society with a huge population living in the countryside depending only on agriculture and allied activities. We are consciously leading our economy to commensurate with the world today seeing very well the failure of the State-managed economy of the erstwhile USSR. Tracing back our footsteps we see that the dream of the Father of the Nation as a Nation of Village Republics never got a start at first in spite of the theoretical and philosophical pressures and Vinoba's Gramdan and other movements. The new vistas that the industrial march supported by the technological breakthrough and advancement of science opened, the systems of village settlements of the yore have gone into a tremendous metamorphosis supported by many social movements like democracy, removal of untouchability, education, All India Radio, TV, new methods of farming, electricity, communication and other infrastructure and a self-sufficient and food-surplus nation.

The KVI sector plan after plan has been attaining a steady growth and now is considered a 'priority' sector component in the Plans because of its inherent qualities such as generation of large-scale employment in the areas where nothing else can be done. It can put whatever meagre earning is possible in the hands of those who have nothing to fall back on. Their potential is tremendous provided requisite infrastructure including organisational support is available for them for which something needs to be done.

Whether the country adopts totally market-oriented economy or some protected economy for the less fortunate among its citizens, one thing seems sure and that is once again 'production by masses' will hold good for the country in spite of the country's efforts to resort to 'mass production' systems. The world of tomorrow holds good news for products used by masses — a trend visible transparently in so far as the basic needs are concerned. And it is here the KVI sector has a prominent role to play — whether it changes its organisational strategy to spread its coverage to every nook and corner of the country or replicates existing systems to work it.

It will be worthwhile to look back at how marketing efforts in the past were made to reach customers for the coarse and crude products of the KVI sector since Gandhiji gave them a helping hand to restore village economy of India for self-sufficient villages which remained a dream and will continue to remain so.

Academically speaking, the economy of the country stands at different stages of marketing concepts taking different areas and regions of the country so wide and varied that all can be found in our country in more than one way or for different products.

There are areas where the stage of economic self-sufficiency indicating absence of exchange and concept of marketing is still functioning where small family units are producing all their requirements like food, clothing and shelter. In certain tribal and remote areas, it is still valid and functioning.

The second stage of exchange orientation, rather the first stage in the evolution of the marketing concept, when producers used to trade for each of their products (barter), can be traced in remote and inaccessible areas in the country at least in respect of local products and produces.

With the industrial revolution the concept of production-oriented stage of marketing comes into play in establishment of large-scale industries and mass production. In this stage production has been the sole object of business and place of selling and consumer satisfaction is relegated to the back. In this century even after independence Indian industrial scene has been an open example of this trend and it is still prevalent in the case of many products.

Then the stage of sales orientation arises where importance of sales and not mere production is in the play and selling of goods produced becomes the sole end of production and place of consumer is recognised.

Thereafter in the market-oriented stage customers' importance is further recognised as they are the ultimate aim for goods produced. This stage experiences competition and needs an efficient sales force for distribution.

Lastly visible in the stage of customer orientation being referred to as modern concept of marketing, recognising the place of the customer, his satisfaction and welfare. Peter Drucker rightly describes 'the purpose of a business is to create a customer'. This concept incorporates in it customer-orientation, integrated management and profitable sales through customers' satisfaction.

Apart from the above there are a few alternative concepts of marketing such as distribution of goods and services, standard of living, utility, revenue earning and social systems.

Now what all do these mean and what they indicate ? Coming to the core of marketing concepts one has to embark upon how to define marketing for which various definitions are offered by different authors. Philip Costler likes the definition, 'Marketing is a social and managerial process by which individuals and groups obtain what they want through creating, offering and exchanging products of value with others. Upon this rests the core concepts of needs; wants and demands; products; value; cost and satisfaction; exchange; transactions and relationships; markets and marketing; and marketers.'

Elaborating them, Costler underlines human needs and wants to be the starting points. While need is a state of felt privation of some basic satisfaction, wants are desires for specific satisfiers of these deeper needs and demands are wants for specific products that are backed up by an ability and willingness to buy them. Thus products broadly are anything that can be offered to someone to satisfy a need or want. Though physical products (objects) are really vehicles that deliver services and persons, places, activities, organisations and ideas too supply services. The term 'products' covers physical products, service products and other vehicles that are capable of delivering satisfaction of a want or need and these are also indicated by offers, satisfiers or resources.

All these lead them to value, cost and satisfaction which further involve exchange, transaction and relationships. And the concept of exchange leads to the concept of market — which consists of all the potential customers sharing a particular need or want who might be willing and able to engage in exchange to satisfy that need and want.

To understand the critical role of marketing in organisations and societies, the concept of a market arises consisting of all the potential customers sharing a particular need or want who might be willing and able to engage in exchange to satisfy that need or want. Thus originally the term 'market' stood for a place where buyers and sellers gather to exchange their goods. Economists use it to refer to a collection of buyers and sellers who transact over a particular product and product class like housing market, grain market. Marketers see sellers as constituting the industry and buyers as constituting the market. Business people use it to cover various groupings of customers, i.e. need market, product (as shoes) market, demographic (as youth) markets and geographic (as French) market extending to non-customer groupings such as voter market, labour market and dough market. Even the government is another market that plays several roles in buying goods from resources, manufacturers and middlemen markets, paying them, taxing these markets and returning needed public services. Thus each nation's economy and the whole world's economy consists of complex interacting sets of markets that are limited through an exchange process.

And this brings us to a circular concept of marketing, meaning human activity taking place in relation to markets, and working with them to actualise potential exchanges for the purpose of satisfying human needs and wants.

Marketing (management) is the process of planning and executing the conception, pricing, promotion and distribution of ideas, goods and services to create exchanges that satisfy individuals and organisational objectives.

This recognises marketing management as a process involving analysis, planning, implementation and control covering ideas, goods and services, resting on the notion of exchange, making its goal to produce satisfaction for the parties involved.

Our journey through the academic understanding of modern marketing concepts brings us face to face with realities in India as to how meanings change. Our country is so big and varied that self-sufficient stages to internationally developed stages of markets stand as if the country, like its mixed economy, endures bullock-cart age and jet age simultaneously. The interaction of inland and international behaviours of economies has been a part and parcel of the growth process of the feeble KVI sector and it has its own peculiar market orientation.

Stepping into the 1990s (last decade) with whatever small products, the KVI sector is faced with the problem of marketing its products as these goods, produced in far-off interior places, have their own quality and consumer satisfaction. Modern marketing management is very badly needed to help this sector to make it a potential contender in the market for its own growth, providing the needed, support to the valid and viable idea of 'production by masses' in a country plagued by unemployment and under-employment particularly in the countryside.

Up-till-now the KVI sector has been protected by government policies and preference in funding. Production and purchase preference for their products have been forthcoming but their growth has not been that spectacular in our 'mixed economy'. But there have been many products which can be marketed adopting modern marketing techniques helping to stand this even in a market friendly economy which is just going to be experimented in our country to expose it to international standards in the country of developed economies.

This is a challenging task as this sector is composed of the KVIC at the helm and State KVI Boards in each State and a vast number of voluntary organisations, autonomous by nature and also cooperatives. The role and responsibilities of the KVIC and industries under its purview are given elsewhere in the book. However, these are not sufficient keeping in view the large size of the country and the felt need of their spread to reach every village to put something in the hands of those who have nothing to support them and to cope with a challenging new world of open market oriented economy in the offing. This sector too needs structural and organisational overhauling to enable it to match the occasion and opportunity lying before it in the fresh context.

Marketing as a tool for its healthy growth must be made handy by the responsible quarter and the KVIC with its cooperative has the key as selling of the village products to the present-day expanding consumers in urban and even in rural areas is certainly going to strengthen the roots of these activities in the very fabric of our centre and society in a different but very meaningful way which was not even visualised by Gandhiji.

In the KVI sector, marketing strategies and planning have to be different altogether in the sense that unlike organised sectors, it has to collect goods from far-off villages, settlements and channel them to the potential markets existing mostly in urban concentrations where 30 per cent of the country's population lives, earns and consumes. And this is challenging, imaginative and innovative in the sense that the KVI sector has to tread the pathway it will make for itself, away from the open market.

During the course of time, the KVI sector has developed products which have consumer preference and a product of a certain area has a nationwide market (i.e. muslin khadi, honey, etc.) Market channels through Vastragars are available for Khadi cloth. However, in the case of Village Industry products such facility is needed. A wide range of products will require different infrastructure and channels. Handmade paper can be a best bet for the international market. Fibre too has that potential. Machine and tools for traditional industries like pottery have a good market in the underdeveloped countries. Even technology export to such countries is some example to refer.

But the whole burden is on the shoulders of communication, product identification, quality control and feedback information and a well-knit service organisation to provide these facilities. As consumer is the sovereign in modern society, the KVI sector with its name for priority supported by fresh movements of environmentalists and other groups has to rise to the occasion fulfilling Gandhiji's dream in changing the market scenario in a singularly different way as challenges are opportunities and fear of market uncertainty has little impact on KVI products. All the conceptual stages are available with the modern market too.

We need not recapitulate here the need for product planning, pricing, physical distribution, promotion and advertisement and feedback delivery system, etc. The stereo type, unimaginative, poor quality, lustless goods cannot be sold in the highly competitive world of today. Quality and simplicity along with fierce marketing capacity only would help this sector.

When it comes to techniques for marketing, it is necessary to develop team-spirit, learn lessons from past mistakes, adopt non-conventional approach, cash in on the strengths of our products, scientifically and rationally.

The western civilisation is urban-based. Small countries like England or Italy may afford to urbanise their systems, a big country like America with a very sparse population, perhaps cannot do otherwise. But one would think that a big country with a teeming population with an ancient rural tradition which hitherto answered its purpose need not and must not copy the Western model. What is good for one nation situated in one condition is not necessarily good enough for another differently situated. One man's food is often another man's poison. Physical geography of a country has a predominant share in determining its culture. A fur coat may be a necessity for the dweller in the polar regions, it will smother those living in the equatorial regions.

Some critics assume that Gandhiji was against the machine as such. There could not be a greater mistake than assuming so. Gandhiji wanted the machine to minister to the needs of man, to serve man, not to be the master of man. Let man improve the machine in his control so as to save his labour and increase production, but let him not be the automation that the power-driven machinery had made of him. The factory civilisation of the day has made machine the master of man not only because it is based on exploitation, but because of the inherent limitations of the factory itself.

In the same way, strategy will have to be devised for various other products which are either in this sector or are likely to come due to the new definition of village industries added to the amended Act of the KVIC.

One invariable conclusion emerges that in the competitive world of today, production, funding, storage, transportation, etc., all have important roles. But the most important role can be attributed to marketing entrepreneurship. Even though the products are best, i.e. handmade paper, honey, herbal medicine, ghani oil, handspun hand-woven khadi, cottage match and Agarbattis, pickles, condiments, etc., unless it is backed with aggressive marketing efforts nothing can sustain these industries. Marketing assumes a very important role because of the induction of the organised sector into the field of activities falling so far within the category of decentralised rural industries. Unless this aspect is imbibed right from the training stage, subsequently it will be impossible to inculcate the value of marketing. Another related issue which emerged during discussion is connected to the pattern of development and expansion of the Government sector in the last few decades. As Governmental activities have been expanding both vertically and horizontally through government or semi-government organisations, those who were trained found jobs easily. While perception of the problem has become more realistic however resistance of those in permanent job make it impossible to accept the harsh realities.

3

CONCEPTUALISING ON EFFECTIVE MARKETING OUTFIT

Traditionally in the field of governmental activities, most government shops are departmental, and government-aided shops are mostly cooperatives. In the sphere of government launched schemes, organisations were taken as *sine qua non* for all problems as if when such an organisation is set up all is going to happen like a miracle. But today these organisations have become mostly high-cost low-impact bodies. If government budgetary allocations or institutional funds are stopped, they will collapse like a pack of cards. There is no internal resource generation and cost effectiveness and the authorities of such organisations have no options but to think of winding up, whereas the organised workers will always ensure that their salaries and other perks continued unabated. A host of information is available on how to organise these types of marketing organisations, but time has come to either accept Joint Marketing Culture (JMC) as a theme involving the existing marketing channels to take up marketing activities on a low-cost high-impact basis or remain in the state of strife and gloom. The advantage of joint marketing will benefit from the available infrastructure and financial resources at concessional rates while the organisational and labour inputs will be on a turnover basis. Payment Per Performance (PPP) will have to be accepted as the essential theme under the JMC strategy.

The job specifications and task assignments for these areas

will have to be so planned as to focus themselves on the necessity for reducing overheads on the product turnover. High turnover with minimum cost must be the essence of the marketing organisation and cost structure of the product. The cost of production of these rural industries' products will have to be reduced over a period of time. Hence, whatever other advantages for overall cost reduction can be made available to these organisations must be continued but in the long run the overall cost must be brought to the minimum and the marketing organisations have to be so devised. In this regard the Tamil Nadu pattern of institutional marketing deserves kudos. There is a lot to be learnt from rural sector marketing through institutions which have been aggressive during the past few years. They were found to be innovative, objective and result-oriented.

While competition has kept them alive to the marketing needs like consumer preferences, provision of subsidised institutional finance, consumer surveys, cost reduction exercises, raw materials supply at reasonable prices can go a long way in developing a healthy organisation for successful marketing.

In case these organisations can provide the desired linkages in the overall economy with reference to governmental rural development departments to rural unemployed and people below the poverty line, the disabled, environment and ecology experts, planners and fund distributors and also to social responsibility groups, etc., all these would go a long way in expanding the marketing network. These bodies should attach special importance to the aspect of improving their management capabilities apart from providing service to their members and organising them properly in order to market all that they have produced in the highly competitive 'Pressure Group Pressurised' . This is called (PGP) administrative system, the word of our time.

The marketing organisations should be able to provide leadership and motivational aspect to those involved in the overall development of this sector. This indirectly means product strategies, cost reduction, integrated publicity and maximising the overall essential development through the organisation which can be of much effective use. Instead of getting concerned by future vested interest groups, it will have to have tactical and organisational superiority not to become the stooge of any select vested group. Social and trusteeship aspect of its role will invariably require openness in its operation and linkages with consumer organisations and producers will be essential. Hence, to meet these needs, this sector will be low-cost high-impact, replicable, open and committed to overall social development based on sustainable self-supporting development.

MARKETING CONVICTIONS

Convictions are essential for success of any programme. Conviction attitudes are shaped by exposure, training, education, and observation. It is a pity that majority of people and organisations working for the development of rural industries are not convinced about their cost effectiveness, acceptability to masses, relevance to national needs and priorities and there is certainly an apparent lack in effective communication. Without getting into the specialized and practical aspect of an efficient communication, we would like to mention here a few points for consideration.

Communication has various aspects. There is performance, target group and objective. A time has come when the communicator has to play a very important role. For marketing of the products of the rural sector, its concepts, its equipment, its products, its viability and relevance, and the various target groups have to be communicated and convinced properly. Particularly in this sector, communication can be understood in terms of the following:

Communication with Buyer

Buyer is the person who has to be convinced and communicated with most properly. He is the ultimate authority to accept or reject.

The buyer desires sustainability and replicability. Gandhiji understood him to be doing great service to the institutions. Everybody in today's world has to depend on the buyer. It is also a fact that the buyer is not born. He can be convinced, educated and made to buy or not to buy these products. In this highly competitive world, he has various choices. Then, he is also not bound by the ideology of tradition and cannot be ignored for long. Since he pays and sacrifices something, it is essential to keep in mind that he should get the maximum for his value. Hence, communication and its convictions through publicity of products, sense of satisfaction and ego boosting have to be the main factors which the communicator has to keep in his mind while doing his job. Communication with buyer can be direct, indirect, through institutions, reminding him of the great service he is doing in patronising the KVI sector but this should not be mistaken for charity, which causes a great harm to the entire system. The buyer is likely to be easily attracted by the merits and quality of products and on their own infrastructural merit and not on charity. What is required is a broad attitude and enough professional capacity to tackle communication directly and in a forceful manner.

Communication with Producer

The second group for whom the conviction and communication will be required comprise the producers, artisans and workers who while staying in rural areas are not only keeping alive the age-old skills but are still doing greater service to the country and to those living in cities. Their convictions will help only if enough income is generated to sustain them. This means their skill upgradation and drudgery reductions and enough timely and adequate income generation for them. Their working hours have to keep some relationship with those who are engaged in the organised sector. They should be convinced with the assurance regarding the future of their children and their quality of life. This will help them to appreciate the need and utility of their continuing with these activities required by the society. The communicator has to convince them only through an assured economic proposition.

Responsibility of Communication Managers

The responsibility of communication managers and administrators of federations, good institutions and the apex organisations is to involve themselves in making these producers or artisans of workers capable to understand the implications of their future *vis-à-vis* improvement in the quality of life. The entrepreneurship, confidence and urge not to migrate to cities have to be brought home especially among the risk takers and they should be brought under a proper group.

Importance of Marketing

With the traditional societies vanishing and systems being replaced all around the world, competitive marketing has occupied the pivotal position in the day-to-day life of the society and its individual members. Again with the industrial revolution, mass production has replaced the concept of production by masses. Aggressive marketing has changed the entire scenario which is especially detrimental to the unorganised decentralised sector. Those who cannot survive in such a fierce competition have to either vanish or learn better/different skills. Many of them become very skilled artisans and craftsmen and others have no option except being simple labourers.

In fact, emphasis may be laid on the other difficult aspects of marketing. If marketing is accepted as a very wide concept and not confined to products alone, it encompasses consumer orientation, his satisfaction, and also what is good for the society. This includes concept of skills, ideas, products, advantages, technology and even problems. There has been an apparent shift in the marketing outlook—from product towards the consumer and concern about the consumer being well informed and conscious of the sacrifice he makes in terms of paying money. His ultimate satisfaction has become the focus for marketing managers following the changes in the crazy world of marketing. Hence, marketing has to be taken in a very broad sense and the problem of marketing must be understood correctly. If the unorganised cannot even codify their problems properly, they must pass on to those who are in a position to solve them, namely, organisers and those who manage the system.

One of the reasons why entrepreneurship in this field could not help the unorganised sector is the non-availability of cheap funds and better avenues leading to migration and merger of artisans totally with the city culture. Those who have risk-taking capacity and are intelligent, hard-working and influential find it much more profitable to shift from rural areas to urban areas and thus become part of it. Those behind could not be expected to market whatever they had effectively and efficiently.

In the area of marketing under the KVI field empirical evidences can be cited to prove the point that problems of marketing exist to appreciate the holistic replicable capacity relating to the problems apparent as well as latent in the sphere of widely scattered village industries encompassing product formulation to delivery to the end user with all its stages, and involvement of human and material relationships is a must. Many people confronted with the sales development, actual sales and marketing as a whole oriented towards consumers feel that the best course to avoid the problem is to disown and brand it as a figment of imagination. Others who are wiser and practical say, 'let the problem come we will examine it'. Still more intelligent say that the problem has not yet arisen. But very few sensitive people are those who probably perceive and accept that the problem of marketing has been staring into their very faces and there is an urgent need to attend to it. It is only when one gets into the business of decentralised, unorganised sector, its programmes, its strengths, weaknesses and threats, that one realises the immense potential and sad factor of improper marketing. It is not only the question of finance, as it is seen that on various occasions finances have been in surplus, but of actually marketing. The major problem in marketing relates to effective conviction on the part of the concerned buyers, communicators and managers directly related to communication, which in turn is a product of weak attitudinal development and response to the multifarious affairs of the programme rather than an isolated practical segment.

INFORMATION SYSTEM FOR MARKETING

In today's competitive, highly changing and cost-effective world, unless the information system is up-to-date and properly utilised at the most opportune time, any programme is bound to fail. Depending upon various aspects, tailormade information systems will have to be devised to suit the requirements of decentralised sector of KVIs. The ultimate purpose of the marketing information is for marketing the best for longer time and keeping excellence. The margin system, product packaging, stocking, survey, product development, etc., all will be codified by the simple objective of excellence. Marketing, planning and control will all necessarily need information.

According to Shri V.S. Ramaswamy (Indian Environment, p. 235), the following are the major benefits that flow from a well-organised marketing information system:

- It helps marketing planning by gathering reliable information on external business environment as well as internal company realities.
- It helps effective tapping of marketing opportunities and effective defence against marketing threats faced by the firm.
- It helps in spotting trends and facilities in formulation of basis of assumptions on economic and business conditions.
- It facilitates the development of action programmes for achieving set goals.
- It helps the firm adjust its products and services to the needs and tastes of consumers.
- It provides market intelligence to the firm.
- It helps controlling marketing activities.

The quality of marketing decisions is decided to a great extent by the quality of marketing information.

While the above benefits have been confined with special reference to organised industries, we must remember the added advantages which will flow for decentralised industries. Since decentralised industries essentially need a computerised and directly controlled information system, Marketing Information System (MIS) through computer will help in solving one of the biggest problems of decentralised industrial sector. Because of the time lag and delay in its processing, it is important that the information flow takes place directly from field units to control units. While going down, the processed information should be made available to those who matter. This will reduce the time lag and ensure the maximum dissemination of information to all those who matter.

As far as Rural Industries are concerned, with the help of the State Khadi and Village Industries Boards and the Khadi and Village Industries Commission, as also their federations and major institutions, the MIS should be developed through no-work-no-payment (NWNP) system. Obviously, the NWNP concept can work only when payments are related to performance. The Payment Related to Performance (PRTP) concept has to be ruthlessly implemented in an inefficient system like the KVI sector where linkages between payment and performance are missing in most of the cases. For marketing of the decentralised sector, the major information required will have to be based on product-wise studies. Since buyer groups, stocking period, price margin, shelf life, area of availability, etc. will differ from product to product, there is a need to undertake an exercise specially in relation to the paying capacity of the buyer. Hence, while devising MIS the following points must be kept in mind:

(i) Identifying special characteristics of concerned rural industries' products;

(ii) Major producing institutions, their federations, their capacities, expertise and maximum supply capacity along with fund and time required;

(iii) Present and potential buyers, their location, mode of communication and paying capacity of the buyers;

(iv) Distribution network, its cost, margin required–month-wise, area-wise and product-wise.

(v) Evaluating the cost of raw materials, value addition, transportation, storage, distribution—wholesale and retail, including insurance, miscellaneous risk etc.; and

(vi) Periodicity of information and what will be made available by the computer group and how those informations will be used to achieve the objective of ultimate marketing.

Since MIS will be a costly affair, it is essential that it is developed in packages. Producers and federations have to be more cost conscious and certain disadvantages hitherto inherent in rural industries have to be transformed into wanted advantages. The

Government should consider sharing these costs to make the rural industries an attractive proposition to solve multifarious problems of rural development and also benefit in that flow the unemployed urbanites, etc. This will be helping the output parameter of performance rather than inputs for which traditionally this sector has been resorting to computer centres and various other institutions who have no problem in marketing of their own. These facilities may be made available to federations, good institutions, Rural Industries Board, etc., if not fee, then on a differential payment system. Ultimately a good MIS system will be able to meet the objectives of information, that would be self supporting, replicable and useful over a longer period. To fulfil the needs, MIS must be under continuous examination by professionals. Today, we have various professional organisations which can also be cost effective in developing not only an information system but also marketing research. We have enough studies on how scarce resource funds were frittered away and those studies on marketing have been under serious doubt because there is hardly any practical relevant information available from them. There exists all-round scarcity of resources, the high-cost-low-impact research and information system can favourably be replaced by a low cost high-impact system.

Work Culture of Boards and Bhandars

The entire work culture of the State KVI Boards and their hierarchy, as it is, is different. There exists an utter lack of professionalism to bring change in the attitude and inculcate perception of the task even today. The defiance to the needs, time demands from them is natural when the personnel are asked to associate and identify themselves with marketing activities and objective assessment of the things.

Creation of Cadre and New Set-up of Marketing

The organisations have no marketing cadre. The scheme incharges of the different village industries are responsible only to look after the production and sale aspects of their industry financed by the

KVIC and State Boards and that too limited to the compilation of figures once in a year. Hence, a separate marketing cadre headed by an officer of the rank of Deputy Chief Executive Officer is to be created by drawing other personnel from the existing strength without making any fresh recruitment. Eminent specialists and experts from the respective fields can be brought on deputation from other organisations for the purpose.

Government Agencies and Marketing

While the government and its various organisations are experts in their fields as of activities, their intervention in the field of development and commercial activities virtually worsens the situation for institutions carrying out KVI work including marketing. The difficult area of social development needs competitive atmosphere to learn from mistakes and to fully utilise the buyers psychology. While the regulatory machinery created involves the role of umpire and judgement giver, the player role changes their attitude from umpire to an actual competing party. Without getting into these complexities one can only draw an attention to the changed scenario of the marketing world not only in India but in most of the third world countries where open resources, both internal and external like creation of buildings and godowns, etc., are allowed to fritter away.

Lack of marketing as a concept and over obsession with budget utilisation result in general degradation of all that makes the society agile. With the efficient use of the existing level of knowledge, skills, goodness should have been competitively utilised and skilfully upgraded both in respect of technology and otherwise as well. The weakness of learning lessons from world history has to be so in today's shambles. Those who run, must run faster but those who are limping must be trained to walk. Some of the KVI programmes which were capable of walking have been rather made to limp. The output incentives should have been a major criterion rather than input incentives. Ultimately, what matters is the output. The role of umpiring is much more superior to the role of an active player.

SOME REPORTS ON MARKETING

The Ramkrishnayya Committee has very rightly advocated that while local raw material and local markets should be utilised to the maximum, there is a need for a flexible attitude towards wider markets. The committee has appropriately given the example of village potters who have found the traditional market for ordinary pots and because of inroads made by aluminium utensils and plastic products available in the village environ their diversified products are there for distant markets. These numbers can be multiplied. Rural industries have also brought out products for the local or distant markets implying that the products offered for sale are in accordance with the taste of the buyer, to their expectation in quality, price presentation, etc. There is also an emerging class of buyers who are attracted by price and the fashion of the day, convenience and other such factors. The KVIC has recommended the market approach or better arrangement for marketing. As per new market approach, the entire attitude towards the programme funding, monitoring, linkages, etc., have to undergo massive changes. Much more than the programme of production of the KVI sector, it has to be a marketing programme. While suggesting the formation of a marketing team, the KVIC has also suggested integration of various activities relating to this sector. The IIMA reports on marketing of rural products has suggested the following points in this regard:

(i) There is a need to study the consumer preference and for this purpose the KVIC should ask Bhandars/Bhavans to watch the changing patterns of the demand. There should be an in-built system to study consumer preferences;

(ii) Any unsold produce remaining, say, for three months or more, should be noted and reasons for the same be ascertained;

(iii) Guidelines to remove the causes for slow movement of certain varieties may be published in *Jagriti*;

(iv) Attention may be drawn to the fast-moving articles either due to lower prices or better quality *vis-a-vis* the products of the large sector;

(v) A proforma laying down some guidelines may be issued to the Bhandars/Bhavans and after collecting information, it should be passed on to the producing institutions;

(vi) Institutions may be requested to consider changes in the pattern of production. The information may also be published in the form of a regular newsletter;

(vii) A study on the organisation of dyeing, printing, processing and tailoring for khadi may be entrusted to some specialised institutions so as to induce improved processing of khadi (bleaching, dyeing, mercerising, wash 'n' wear, anti-shrink, printing, permanent press-wear, tailoring, embroidery, etc.;

(viii) Prices should be based on the principles of what the consumer traffic can bear. The Committee felt that there is nothing wrong in having different sales pricing. Though Rural Industries do not have a purely profit motive, there need be no reluctance to change a higher price than the cost price which compares favourably with that of similar products of the large-scale sector;

(ix) A summary of Rural Marketing report may be circulated amongst all the institutions; and

(x) The report may be placed before the Rural Industries Committee immediately for seeking orders for various recommendations.

A CASE STUDY ON PRACTICAL MARKETING

A case study of bakery trainees in the general training institute of Processing of Cereals and Pulses Industry, Wardha, is presented here for on-hand information as an example.

Introduction

The marketing of village industries products seems to be the bottleneck in the development of the village industries programme. Efforts are being made in various directions for effective marketing of rural products by the KVI organisation, VI associations, federations, etc., to build thereby the link between village industries artisans/entrepreneurs and consumers, co-ordination with existing marketing organisations in the public sector like DGSD, NAFED, etc., participation of eminent personalities in marketing areas, effective marketing training for entrepreneurs, etc. The Central Training Institute for PCPI, Wardha, is conducting managerial and bakery artisans courses. This has proved to be a successful approach for building confidence of marketing in trainees and the participation of these trainees will be much helpful for marketing of KVI products.

Description

The trainees are given the responsibility of manufacturing bread and other bakery products such as biscuits, cakes, buns, etc., under the guidance of trainers. The marketing of products is exclusively done by the trainees. The nearby Professors Colony and the locality of middle class society are major target areas for marketing. The production is increasing according to the marketing ability of trainees. The wheat flour consumption of 5 kg initially rose to 30 kg. The average net earning per day of each trainee amounts to Rs. 15. Data of earnings of 9 trainees as bakery artisans are attached. The trainees have also narrated their experience which is presented below:

1. Fear of Self-Respect

Most of the trainees are S.S.C. pass and a few are graduates. Some of the trainees hesitated initially and showed their reluctance for door-to-door marketing. The concept of the present education system is getting a job and the work they are offered is termed as hawker's job. Some students avoided to do the job and some ran away. This shows that the concept of happiness in the present system is leisure and, therefore, white-collar job. This restricts the youth from hardships. On the contrary, hard work is useful for shouldering responsibility. The trainees very joyfully mentioned that they had dispelled such fear and realised that one should be ashamed of only begging. Any work for survival with self-respect is really appreciable.

2. Ability to Convince

Initially the trainees were doubtful that they might not be able to convince the customers fully. Of course, this is an important factor since the concepts of the products should be accepted by the customers and this depends upon how the seller is presenting the products. In the initial stage, some were disappointed by the refusal of customers to purchase the offered products but later on being convincingly explained by narrating various advantages, assurance of purity of Rural Industries Product, freshness, reasonable prices, the sales picked up. Although the wrapper is simple, the convincing ability of the trainees plays an important role. Almost all trainees have realised this ability and their convincing power has improved.

3. Awareness of Quality

As the trainees are experiencing the trend of daily demand of products, they are aware of improvement in the quality of the product and awareness to taking precautionary measures for maintaining the quality and thus the product is improved. This improves the work culture.

4. Confidence of Earning

Although the trainees earn a small amount, they feel the pleasure of earning which builds confidence and removes the fear of unemployment. This is a great achievement in the present situation of unbridled unemployment in the country's workforce.

5. Ability of Shouldering Responsibility

Most of the trainees are prepared to shoulder responsibility of marketing the Rural Industries' products, apart from the bakery products and show a positive attitude for running the marketing sales depot as per the pattern of the KVIC. This is also a great achievement. As an illustration, the success story of Johnson should be useful to note. Johnson was a leather artisan in a shoe-making company. At one time the owner had thought of closing the factory due to heavy losses. Johnson then requested the owner to give him the charge for running the factory under his control. He shouldered the responsibility and revived the factory and earned the profit. The owner was prepared to offer him a reward. Johnson refused and resigned the job and started his own factory. Very soon he became the owner of Johnson Shoe Company which is a leading and reputed company in the world. The secret of success of Johnson lies in his confidence of shouldering responsibility and regaining confidence through hard work. Thereby improved ability enabled him to shoulder the responsibility of challenging work.

CONCLUSION

The approach of practical marketing removes the fear and negative misleading thought and creates self-respect, releases the brakes which restrict the improvement in practical ability, improves personality with convincing ability, improves work culture which makes the trainees aware of quality, removes fear of unemployment and gives confidence of earning as also makes them positive for shouldering responsibility. These trainees can actively participate in the marketing of the Rural Industries' products.

RECOMMENDATIONS

Practical marketing, i.e. marketing of the products produced by trainees, can be introduced through Rural Industries Entrepreneurship Training.

The earning opportunity can be given to the unemployed youth desirous of undergoing training in Rural Industries by opening sales booths at the right places, i.e. bakery products booths near milk booths, food products at railway stations, etc. Thus the area of sales can be increased.

The active participation of the trained entrepreneurs is possible for marketing Rural Industries' products by motivating them to have Rural Industries' clusters, viz. formation of association/institute for bakery, Rural Industries' sales depots and other Rural Industries at block level.

The quality control programme involves evolution of specifications of standards, sampling, analysis, providing packing and quality mark, which being an important factor for marketing should be introduced in training programmes.

Rural Marketing : Conceptual Analysis

As emphasis shifts from agriculture to rural development, more and more emphasis will have to be laid on rural industrialisation. Based on the availability of abundant raw materials, unemployment, skilled and educated manpower with adequacy of entrepreneurship suited for rural areas coupled with greater thrust of the government, rural industrialisation is bound to pick up. But it will need appropriate technology, easy availability of funds and most important of all, the attitude for replicable self-supporting low-cost high-impact programmes for employment generation. Rural industrialisation involves certain amount of structural, financial and attitudinal changes. Unless this is properly understood, the concept of rural industrialisation is bound to remain unchanged.

Another most important point relates to generation of employment especially for educated unemployed in rural areas. This is also related to the problems of urbanisation. A developmental effort must ensure holistic development and the marketing as a concept to spearhead all these activities. It is a pity that our philosophy has so far been production-oriented. The marketing orientation in all phases of life is coming gradually but very slowly in various other activities. This is attributed to the slow moving nature of the society. It also leaves those unorganised in a very bad situation while the organised ones make the best use of the facilities available.

Marketing has been described as the process by which the demand structure for economic goods and service in a society is accepted or enlarged or specified through conception of promises, exchanges of physical distribution of goods and services. The comprehensive coverage includes monetary needs, while education, servicing, satisfaction, follow-up, etc., are the vital parts of marketing.

Till now only buying and selling of products has been the

concept. This means overall potential of marketing, i.e. products-concept, skills, technology, consultancies have to be tapped and marketing environment has to be suitably created and sustained by-products. Value Affordable Price Concept (VAPC) holds an important place in the overall modern field of activity while various studies bring out this aspect of totality in the sphere of modern marketing management. The communication is also essential for decentralised production, hence marketing assumes greater importance. The inaccessible villages have the least access to communication and those doing this work do charge a premium.

As the systems become sophisticated, rural industries are bound to suffer and are suffering badly and the time has come to learn to compete and accept harsh realities. This means developing not only products but also marketing skills. This also means rural entrepreneurship as the essential input for an overall development of rural areas which is a silver lining in an atmosphere of darkness and gloom.

Market, as Shri L.K. Johnson says, is People + Buying Power + Buying Habits. We have people and buying power. What is required is making buying habits our faith. The modern communication systems have to be utilised for our products and industry-wise strategy has to be developed to stand in competition. It is possible and is also the need of the hour.

SUMMARY

Present Status of Government Organisations

- High-cost Low-impact
- Restricting governmental budgetary allocation or institutional funds to an organisation results in its collapse because there are no internal resources and absence of cost effectiveness
- Lack of marketing as a concept
- Overobsession with budget utilisation resulting in general degradation of all that make the society alive

Options Available for Organising Marketing Channels

↓

Joint Marketing Culture (JMS) to be evolved with the object of:

Ensuring payment per performance (PPP) with job specification and taste assignment for reducing over-heads on product turnover

Involving existing Marketing Channels on the basis of Low-Cost High-Impact

Thus JMC will include:

↓

Available infrastructure and financial resources at concessional rates

Organisational and labour inputs on turnover basis i.e. on PPP

↓

Such marketing organisation will have linkages with:

- Rural Development Department
- Rural unemployed and people below poverty line, disabled
- Environment and ecology experts
- Planners and funds distributors
- Social responsibility group

↓

And attend to market competition bringing:

- Awareness towards marketing needs
- Consciousness about consumers
- Performance
- Provision of subsidised institutional finance
- Consumer surveys
- Cost reduction exercises
- Raw material supply
- To develop healthy organisation for successful marketing

Services of Marketing Organisation

- Leadership and motivational aspect to those involved in overall development of rural sector

Resulting in:

Effectiveness in:

- Product strategy
- Cost reduction
- Integrated publicity on various costs
- Maximising overall development

Marketing Convictions Attitude

It is a result of:

- Exposure
- Training
- Education
- Observation

And results in finding

- Cost effectiveness
- Acceptability to masses
- Relevance to national needs and priorities
- Ways and means of effective communication with

(a) Producer and

(b) Buyer

Marketing concept as a very wide one encompasses:

- Consumer orientation and satisfaction
- Study in what is good for the society
- Concept of skill
- Ideas
- Advantages of a product
- Technology
- Even problems related to a product

Benefits of well-organised Marketing Information System (MIS)

- Marketing planning through reliable information on external business environment and internal company realities as well
- Effective tapping of marketing opportunities and effective defence against marketing threats
- Spotting trends and facilities for formulating assumptions concerning basis of economic and business conditions
- Facilitating evolvement of action programmes for achieving set goals
- Helping adjustment of products and services to the needs and taste of consumers
- Provision of market intelligence
- Control of marketing activities
- Improving quality of marketing decisions

Evolving Market Information System (MIS) for Rural Industries

Points to adhere to:

- Identifying special characteristics of concerned rural industries and products
- Major producing institutions, their capabilities, expertise and maximum supply capacity and also assessment of funds and time required
- Present and potential surveys, mode of communication and paying capacity of payers
- Distribution network, area-wise and product-wise
- Evaluation of cost, raw material, value addition, transport, storage, distribution, wholesale and retail including insurance charges

- Periodicity of information, which will be computer group and how the same is used to achieve and objective of ultimate marketing

Economics of Cost Affair and MIS

- Government should share the cost–then only rural industries would play a major role in solving multifarious problems of rural development and unemployed urbanites

↓

Objectives of Market Information

- Being itself self-supporting
- Replicable
- Useful over longer period

↓

Leading to Social Development for:

- Competitive atmosphere to learn from mistakes
- And to advantageously utilise the buyer's psychology

↓

Products: (Requirements that they should fulfil)

- Should be in accordance to the taste of the buyers
- Should meet the expectations of the buyers in terms of quality, price and presentation.

4

PROBING THE WHEREWITHAL

The Khadi and Village Industries Commission (KVIC) is dedicated to the cause of rural development. Basically the objective of the KVIC is to harness local materials and skills for production of fancy and other articles and to generate employment in the rural areas. The simple technology adopted in this tiny sector ensures prevention of pollution and maintaining of ecological balance. The products are mainly grouped into 'Textiles viz. Khadi' and 'Utility Articles' required for day-to-day use by the community. Rapid mechanisation in many parts of the world has displaced the labour and created unemployment leading to near anarchy. To alleviate this sort of situation, Mahatma Gandhi advocated the maximum use of local materials and manpower instead of sending the raw materials to mills for processing, although it increases productivity but deprives work to the artisans living in rural areas. He was all for production by masses instead of mass production by machines.

To achieve the objectives spelt out by the Father of the Nation, the KVIC was established and it has been working for more than three decades by providing technical know-how, raw materials, management, inputs and forward and backward linkages to rural poor through State Khadi and Village Industries Boards, Charitable Institutions, Cooperatives and Voluntary Agencies.

There is a strong need to diversify industries in rural areas, and to encourage rural and tiny industries, much has already been done and is still being done to that end but no systematic, coordinated efforts have ever been made to understand the various problems connected with the marketing of rural varied products being manufactured by artisans in these industries. It is a felt need to understand the very characteristics of these products and their manufacturing process so as to solve their problems of marketing on a long-term basis. It has been generally presumed that whatever a rural entrepreneur produces would be sold. But in times to come, the rural industries' products have to stand on their own corresponding to the needs, tastes and expectations of their customers and in many cases to surpass these basics with sheer artistic, aesthetic or use value added to them to attract consumers for their quality and presentation, that is within their reach with innovative artisans.

Despite an enormous employment potential, the rural industries sector marketing efforts have been most disappointing, as no serious thought by responsible quarters has been lent to the fact that the products of rural artisans need an intelligent planning taking a wide view of the present day, when really in the era of a consumers' world these products have a place of their own in the life of a gentry residing in metropolises, cities, newly sprung up townships and old ones as well, where the population explosion has been causing concern for the planners. When a product is to be sold in a totally new environment where it is not produced, marketing comes in and caters to the needs to both consumers and producers.

There has been a wrong presumption that there is no marketing problem for rural entrepreneurs.

The following are some of the factors due to which organised marketing could not develop in the KVI sector:

(i) Too much emphasis on marketing of Khadi;

(ii) Lack of design, packaging, and lack of cost reduction efforts for the products and also lack of commercial culture;

(iii) Lack of co-ordination between Khadi and Village Industries Boards and other organisations working in the same field;

(iv) Lack of marketing organisation/structure based on modern concepts and techniques which have so far been very conservative; and

(v) Lack of desired and imaginative publicity and propaganda based on changing market needs and trends.

MARKETING ISSUES

Reservation

Because of social factors and low level of technology, non-competitiveness of the products, face-to-face organised sector and their desirability in the wake of their rural employment potential, reservation of certain products by Government and its Public Sector Corporations has been suggested as one of the spheres of marketing channels, which is of the nature of captive market. However, its desirability in the long-run is a big question mark as it would pose a big threat in the longer run as the captive market tends to buy from outside and the producer tends to supply low quality goods.

The following are the main observations in such citations:

1. The reservation can help only for a very limited period and therefore efforts are to be made to make the products competitive, qualitatively attractive and easily available.
2. The tendency to compromise with the quality increases as the marketing system gets established. Vested interests also tend to develop. One answer could be to expose the product to open competition and develop a marketing system based on open market.
3. Diversification of products with maximum value addition in the rural areas itself is a must (in view of the absorption of rural workforce there itself on the one hand and helping creation of the skilled in native products in the long run with certain specialisation on the other).
4. Low-cost delivery system based on competition and performance incentive is a must. Obviously, to widen the market base, captive purchases must be made gradually non-captive. Government machinery and permit distribution attitude can never be entrusted with most difficult, onerous and risky job of marketing even to the captive market.

5. Organisations of ex-Army men, ladies, disabled, below-poverty-line people can be developed to cater to both captive and non-captive markets. Regular contacts must be developed with these agents to share experience and sort out the difficulties. Suitable guidelines, incentive schemes and monthly stock reporting system should be developed.

VOLUNTARY AFFORDABLE PRICE CONCEPT (VAPC)

VAPC concept visualises that despite various strengths which these products possess, the buying organisation would buy these products only if they come within VAPC. It is common knowledge that despite 15 per cent price preference available to the small-scale sector for many years, those units which depend on this price preference have all gone sick. It is only the competitive, result-oriented and prompt institutions and those ready to change that have survived in this competitive market. Hence, one may conclude that even if 5 per cent extra preference is given to rural and tiny industries' products, it will still not solve the problem.

The strengths of these products lie basically in the following:

1. The product does not pollute the environment.
2. It helps to solve the problem of over-crowdedness in cities in terms of housing, transport, water supply and other congestion problems.
3. It provides employment in the rural areas on a decentralised basis. This sector is ideally suited for unemployed, disabled, ladies, etc.
4. If designing, packaging, costing facilities could be provided on a cluster basis, it may provide value-added remuneration to entrepreneurs at their places of residence.
5. Many products involve use of raw materials which are not imported or may be termed as 'rags'.

With all the strength of these products, it must be made very clear that unless VAPC is fully tapped, on marketing programme would succeed. The entire concept would have to be explained to marketing people and depending upon the type of buyers the VAPC of the product would have to be suitably revised. This also means that the same product may not be sold at the same place. Here, the role of the marketing agent would be really paramount and no fixed price concept may work.

Once the concept of VAPC is clear, we must understand very clearly that the profit margin in various products at various places at various times would vary.

Innovative measures can be adopted to overcome this difficulty. For example, good manufacturing units which are financed be allowed to obtain orders on behalf of the KVIC/State KVIBs and supply their products at their own cost directly to the buyers. They have to pay only one per cent or even less for utilising the umbrella of the name of the KVIC/State KVIBs and thus they can be brought in the organised structure at absolutely minimum cost. Depending on the products, discretion can be given to officers to reduce this margin to make the product competitive and to sustain the interest of the agent to market these products under such an umbrella. The concept of utilisation of the brand name can be introduced to standardise some of the products. The responsibility for the quality, etc., has to be left with the financing unit but the quality symbol be made available. For use the common brand name be developed for marketing of the products of rural industries sector without causing disadvantages to this sector.

The workforce of the KVI sector itself can be encouraged to enroll their relations, friends, other unemployed disabled people to work as agents of the KVIC/SKVIBs to develop a low-cost influential, self-sustained marketing structure. Knowing the very difficult area of marketing, it is essential to tap the potential of people connected with the sector. Similarly, special discount sales are often held to encourage new buyers to off-load old stocks.

Incentives to the workers of the KVIC/SKVIBs for promoting sales can also go a long way in solving the problem in an effective way.

SUGGESTIONS TO IMPROVE MARKETING

Black-listing the units and publicising the black-listed units can ensure the strength which goes with the KVI sector's name unblemished. Same way, total encouragement must be given to all those who come out with new ideas, to reduce cost, to improve the quality and design.

Maximum value addition should take place in the rural areas. Wherever it is impossible to do so there should not be any inhibition to tap the scientific and technological inputs available in the city. To market these products and prepare this sector for the 21st century, it is essential that profits of high-tech that are available in any field are properly blended with the products of this sector making them attractive, competitive and commensurate with VAP (Voluntary Affordable Price). There is a *strong need to pull resources* available with Government Corporations, KVIC, other State KVIBs and organisations like ex-army people, Nehru Yuva Kendras, Divisional Development Corporations. To improve resources and keep distribution cost to the minimum, even the services of existing distributors may be availed of. Good units working in this sector must be persuaded to diversify in the marketing activities and funds at a concessional rate of interest of 4 per cent made available for the KVIC should also be made available to these institutions. Efforts may be made to involve the big houses of Bajajs, Birlas and Ambanis to market these products though they may feel quite apprehensive about the regular supplies. The question of high marketing cost and lack of initiative at the apex level are some of the reservations but this has to be pursued relentlessly because there is no option if this sector wishes to make the products available to consumers with a low distribution cost.

The *role of institutions like ISI, Agmark Authorities, PFA Departments* would need close co-ordination. Even research institutions and universities would have to be involved to carry further value addition efforts. A classic case of value addition is honey products which can be examined separately. It needs no emphasis that every village industry must be ruthlessly forced ro diversify its products so that more consumer acceptance is possible. This can be done only by involving professional bodies and autonomous institutions along with voluntary organisations. It presupposes getting over tendencies to work in a closed protected cell.

The role of modern 'management information system' and development of officer-oriented work culture needs to be given emphasis. Marketing is too difficult a field to be left to clerks. Those who avoid responsibility can never be entrusted with this onerous, demanding and difficult task.

ROLE OF TRAINING IN MARKETING

A scheme can be developed by the KVIC/State KVI Boards (with IDBI) with the following salient features:

1. Advertisements inviting ladies, etc., to take up agencies to be put up in selected metropolitan towns.
2. A very short-term training be imparted with special reference to SWOT of the sector, marketing problems, buyers scheme and backward/forward linkages.
3 Stockists be appointed by the KVIC/State KVIBs in selected major towns to supply goods on the orders of the agents. Agents may help in getting the bills cleared and payment of the commission may be made to the agents on a weekly basis.
4. A meeting with the agents and stockists every fortnight by IDBI, KVIC/ KVIBs, training institutions to monitor the programme for a period of 3 months is needed.
5. IDBI is to give only a small amount for training purposes as backward/forward linkages can be provided by the KVIC/KVIBs. It is a pity that such a scheme was given to this national organisation by one Board in a State and they are still sitting over it. The lesson to learn is that those who can run should not be told to walk. But the importance of right type of training to the agents calls for much greater attention. Though the basic principles of marketing would remain the same, *the characteristics of this sector make it imperative that special personalised skill is imparted to make the same agents successful for these products.*

There is a prevalent view in this sector that marketing cannot be forced. To develop marketing system for a long term, a specialised organisation has to be developed but if unutilised capacities are available, they must first of all be fully utilised. The KVIC/KVIBs are engaged in the multifarious task of rural industrialisation. Their strength does not lie only in the training centres, funds at the rate of 4 per cent interest and network of shops but also in their capacity to make entrepreneurs really successful. The test of success lies in expansion and diversification of these activities in rural areas. The organisations like the KVIC/KVIBs which distribute funds worth hundreds of crores of rupees at 4 per cent rate of interest must have managers who know the ins and outs of the difficult areas known as marketing. No wonder, the KVIC/State KVIBs have to develop their capacities, ingenuity, expertise to shoulder this onerous responsibility to make the rural entrepreneurs and the programmes of rural industrialisation a success for future.

Efforts to market rural industries' products, especially tiny industries' products have not succeeded as desired but they must succeed. But success can never come without hard work, clarity of objectives and team spirit. This will call for leadership of professionals, high commitment and capability to co-ordinate with both official and non-official organisations at regular intervals.

Given the opportunity, the experiences of this sector in the field of marketing of these products can be an eye-opener. There have been complaints, various suggestions, financial difficulties, letting down by national institutions, but still the most difficult activity in entrepreneurs' success stories is that marketing must be taken up in right earnest.

SUGGESTED STRATEGY FOR VALUE ADDITION

Honey

Various by-products can be made from honey in terms of honey shampoo, honey lemon drink, honey soap, honey *chatni*, honey jam, etc. Research quality, packing, firm orders, guaranteed supply, advertisements and common brand name would ensure the success of the strategy. Research should be undertaken on a systematic basis.

Handmade Paper

Only file covers will not do. In Kalpi, utilisation of quality test instruments has been introduced by U.P. KVI Board. Offset printing has its own problems as machines breakdown due to lack of standardisation, quality and foreign material in the paper. Sustained effort and constant evaluation along with quality consciousness can help considerably to bring out the best quality products. The recognition, the will to do something, the earnest desire to work for non-conventional task can help in making any experiment a success in respect of printing on handmade paper on offset. One can speak with authority that handmade paper has a very bright future if VAP is suitably publicised. Cost reduction studies can also be done with the help of NPC with successful results. Common raw material storage facility can be provided. Interior decoration with HMP designing can be taken up as a new line of activity.

The days are gone when Khadi-Kurta could be sold without getting it stitched as per consumer taste and well packaged. For value addition in Khadi garments through designing, tailoring and salesmanship will have to be introduced on a very sustained basis. Quality designers, packagers have to be professionals. The facility of home delivery may also have to be thought of. The strong tendency to market these products during a rebate period may have to be considered *de novo* and the other strength of Khadi would have to be tapped to make its VAP competitive. Silk and Muslin Khadi have their own problems but their marketing has no problems and export orientation is to be exploited fully with market studies abroad and evolving a product-mix to market.

Agarbatti

The highest problem has been the sickness of this industry because of various reasons including policy support absence with regard to its marketing. Lack of monitoring, lack of marketing tie-ups, funding to wrong entrepreneurs have been some of the major weaknesses. To get over this difficulty, some efforts can be made by the KVIC/KVIBs but due to lack of sustained will, success cannot be had to the desired extent.

Our policies regarding extraction of oil-seeds in villages are faulty. Hence, the unsuccessful units take shelter under the excuse of non-availability of funds for stocking raw material. The question of economic viability, competitive market quality tests, packing, etc., assumes much more important role. The KVIC/KVIBs can try to make entrepreneurs in clusters successful as drive for oil-seed production as one of the technological omissions is going to enhance oil-seed production on the national front. It will need a detailed study to find out the results of these efforts but an effort has to be made. Ghani oil can again gain its lost ground if the challenge is converted into opportunities.

Efforts can be made by the KVIC/KVIBs to link up production of herbal plants like *tulasi*, *methi* and other items of medicinal value by linking it up with IRD beneficiaries. Areas can be identified in the first place. Simultaneous efforts in the hill areas are to continue. Selected products have to be manufactured by the organisations of *Vaidyas* and their marketing tie-up is to be organised with KVIC/KVIBs and other institutions. Help of other voluntary organisations can also be taken in this field. The expertise of *Vaidyas* can be pooled with that of prominent allopathic doctors, and an organisation, for instance, a society for the Propagation of Herbal Medicines, can be encouraged as these herbs are getting popularity abroad too which can open up new vistas of an export market in times to come.

Efforts can be made by the KVIC/KVIBs to pool the resources available with the Leather Corporation, Directorate of Industries, DRDAs,etc. The objective is to develop a co-ordinated low-cost marketing linked system under the cover of a suitable umbrella to develop a self-sustaining system. It is well known that the vast potential existing in the leather industry has remained grossly underutilised. Modest efforts have been made by the KVIC and some KVI Boards in this direction by pooling resources of Government organisations and by soliciting the help of exporters, mostly located at Kanpur and Agra and other centres. These agencies can offer backward and forward linkages to the societies in the rural areas to be formed by KVIC/KVI Boards. Leather garments and sports goods have a potential export market and need constant management of world standard.

Export Potentials

Apart from production of Khadi and using local materials like cotton, silk, woollen and blended fibre, the production of polyvastra has also been taken up by the Commission to provide more employment and also improve the quality of the hand-made cloth to suit the consumer taste of the day.

The trend in the world today is rapidly changing due to the health consciousness and also non-dependence on the artificial fibres made out of the synthetic products and allied materials. The demand for pure cotton fabrics is increasing rapidly throughout the world. The handspun and handwoven textile (Khadi) is very comfortable to wear since air can pass through it easily and prevents any skin rash, etc., and is more comfortable when compared to the man-made synthetic fabrics like Nylon, Rayon, Terylene etc.

KVI institutions produce very fine varieties to coarse varieties out of various handspun and handwoven materials in cotton, woollen, silk and mixture of both, i.e. cotton and silk cotton polyester, woollen and polyester. The Khadi production is worth around Rs. 300 crores per annum and it is planned to increase the production to almost twice of the present capacity.

To cater to the needs of the customers all over the world and also keeping in view the change in consumer world and preference, the KVIC has taken up the responsibility to bring out latest designs in readymade garments, printed materials, dress materials in cotton, wool, silk and polyvastra. The Khadi material can be exported directly by the KVIC or through recognised merchant exporters registered with its Directorate of Marketing. The trade discount and incentives available for the textile exports can also be arranged by the KVIC as per prevailing rules approved by the appropriate authority.

Khadi produced in the decentralised sector required some time for collection from various producing centres, processing and supplying to the buyers. However, the materials as ordered can be supplied as per the specifications at a predetermined price fixed traditionally through a pricing system evolved by Gandhiji himself which is on 'no-profit-no-loss basis' and is followed by the producer agencies under the KVIC. Around Rs. 30.00 lakhs worth of Khadi is exported per annum to the countries like Japan, Middle East and Europe.

VILLAGE INDUSTRIES PRODUCTS

In the case of village industries products, though we have many products which are produced by our aided institutions in the rural areas, an attempt has been made to supply a few products for exports. The details of the products are furnished below:

Agarbatti

Incense sticks with a variety of fragrance, depending upon the perfume used in the production, are manufactured by the KVI units. These sticks are popularly called *Agarbattis* in India which are used in temples, religious places, homes, and also as room-freshners. These are made by women workers completely by a hand-process. It is a very highly labour-intensive industry. The KVIC can organise huge supplies with specific orders from buyers. The KVI institutions are already exporting *Agarbattis* to Malaysia, Singapore and Middle East countries. On an average, Rs. 80 lakhs worth of *Agarbattis* are exported per year.

Cane and Bamboo Products

Fancy utility articles made by using cane and bamboo as raw material, i.e. items like furniture, sofa sets, partition screens, etc., can be supplied in bulk quantity for exports. On an average, a few lakh rupees of cane and bamboo articles are exported every year.

Fruit Processing

Processing of fresh vegetables and fruits is one of the activities taken up by individual entrepreneurs, and institutions and cooperatives financed by the KVIC. This industry provides large-scale employment to women. The products like mango pulp, tomato ketchup, jam, syrup, juices, pickles, chutney, canning of fruits and vegetables, tutti-frutti, squashes, preserves, etc., are supplied in large quantities.

Handmade Paper

The usual process of paper making uses conventional raw materials, viz., bamboo, wood, etc., for making pulp. The consumption of bamboo wood by paper mills has destroyed areas of forest around the world leading to ecological imbalances and rapid deforestation. Keeping this in view a simple technology has been developed for producing paper in the decentralised sector by using cotton rags, agro-waste and re-cycling of waste paper. The paper produced in sheet-form is popularly known as handmade paper.

Handmade paper apart from having strength and durability is famous for its elegant and exquisite surface for writing, indestructibility and superb strength for performance, unmatched texture for drawing by artists and engineers, countless personalised stationery/greeting/invitations, industrial paper like insulation papers, filter papers, leather board, jacquard board and scores of fancy varieties for decorative wraps, lamp shades, partition panels, wall paper, etc. Value-added articles like drawing blocks for art work, letterheads with matching envelopes, greeting cards in attractive shades and designs, paper bags and such other items can also be prepared out of handmade paper.

Footwear and Garments

India as a country is lucky for having highly skilled craftsmen/artisans in the field of tanning, footwear and leather goods making as well as fabricating leather garments and sports goods. These crafts are practised by a particular group of people for ages. They are following these vocations from generation to generation and thus attain their high degree of proficiency in their craftsmanship.

Fortunately, India is also lucky in having the second largest population of bovine animals in the world. All over the world, Intelligent people have understood the importance of going towards nature. This change in consumer preference towards natural products has created attraction for Indian leather products, whether it is sea-beach chappals, bedroom slippers, bathroom slippers, sports shoes, office shoes, fashionable footwear, sports goods, leather garments and sports goods like volleyball, football, cricket ball, hockey ball, etc., and also industrial gloves for civilian use, industrial boots, etc.

It is estimated that about 14 lakhs of leather artisans are engaged in this vocation, i.e. in the Leather Industry as a whole. This shows the great potentiality of the country as a whole to manufacture sophisticated quality leather products for domestic users as well as for the users abroad.

By using simple tools, these artisans can produce any type of article according to design, specification provided to them. These products are so exotic in sophistication that buyers will be thrilled, to use these leather products hand-made by highly skilled Indian artisans which carry personal affection and care of the artisans. Agra, Kanpur and Faizabad in Uttar Pradesh are famous for leather products.

Pulses and Cereals Processing Industry

Processed raw materials required for food preparation and also ready-to-serve items like Papad, Dry Chutney Powder, Masala Powder, etc., are produced in the rural sector mostly by using manual labour. In addition, paddy and pulses are processed and various items from rice and pulses are made for daily use. These are finding a market abroad among Indians settled on foreign soils because of their food habits and also among other communities there as tourism has made the earth a global village where demand for such products persists.

Palm Leaves and Palm Products

Sugar-yielding palm trees are the gift of mother nature. Palm jaggery, palm sugar, candy syrup, etc., are nutritious and have medicinal value. Conventional and non-conventional palm fibre brushes are manufactured from fibre obtained from Palmyrah trees. Fancy utility articles are produced from palm leaves. Annually, on an average Rs. 6 crores worth of palm fibre and leaf articles are exported to eighteen foreign countries. Orders to supply can be taken up on specific indents from buyers.

Under village industries incentives are available for various products which are given by the different export promotion councils set up for the purpose. The Khadi and Village Industries Commission can liaison and arrange incentives for suppliers to enable them to make products available at a competitive price to the buyers.

EXPORT OF TECHNOLOGY

Khadi

Under Khadi, the technology can be exported from raw material selection to pre-processing, spinning, weaving, dyeing, etc. The KVIC can arrange training through recognised training centres wherein adequate facilities are available. Spinning and weaving can provide large-scale employment in the developing/under-developed countries.

Studies for project formulation, types of machinery required, raw material, etc., can be undertaken by the KVIC experts on the usual terms and conditions prescribed by the U.N. agencies or any other agencies which are interested in helping the developing countries.

Village Industry

The KVIC can undertake the transfer of technology to the developing countries in the areas of project formulation, potentiality survey, etc. The KVIC has already arranged setting up of handmade paper units, oil ghanis, lime kilns, bio-gas pottery, leather, palmgur, etc., in Tanzania, Sri Lanka, Bhutan, Bangladesh, etc. The laundry soap manufacturing and toilet soap manufacturing by using non-edible oils can be taken up by many of the developing countries since the oilseeds like neem (Margosa) are available abundantly in these countries. Project preparations, training of personnel, setting up of the project from concept to commissioning can be undertaken. The training in soap making can be arranged at the departmental training centres at Nasik. The training in fancy fibre articles made out of vegetable fibres like sisal, banana, pineapple including project formulations for setting up of production units, etc., can be undertaken by the KVIC. This industry can provide large-scale employment to the women in the developing countries. The training can be conducted in the departmental training centre at Bombay.

Bio-gas

In the field of renewable energy, Khadi and Village Industries Commission has done a tremendous job which has been recognised all over the world. The KVIC has arranged three training courses for the personnel from the developing countries and also taken up turnkey projects in Sri Lanka, Tanzania, etc. The KVIC can provide technical guidance for project promotion, training, etc., to the developing countries at the KVIC's departmental centres.

The KVIC also undertakes the production of fancy fibre articles, palm sugar, palm candy brushes, etc.

Apart from providing on-the-job training in different village industries, the KVIC undertakes specific project preparation, evaluation, installation of machinery, establishing production routines of various products. This is undertaken with the usual terms and conditions approved by the United Nations agencies like UNIDO, UNDP, etc. The training can be provided to persons from the developing countries sponsored by the different agencies like UNDP, Commonwealth Science Council, etc., which may consider to meet the cost of travelling, boarding and lodging and other contingency expenses and the training fees which may be determined depending upon the duration of training, type of personnel to be trained, i.e., managerial, artisan, etc.

The KVIC has, for over three decades, developed the machinery ideal for the rural areas which can be operated easily with training and these machineries are designed keeping in view the local raw materials available and the skill of the artisans. The KVIC can arrange the following machineries and also take up installation on a turnkey basis:

1. Setting up of spinning units by exporting charkhas and preprocessing equipment.

2. Setting up of semi-automatic looms for weaving different designs in cotton, silk, woollen, polyvastra, etc.

3. To obtain oil from oil-seeds, the KVIC has designed a power-operated oil-seed extracting equipment named Power Ghani. This Ghani can be supplied for crushing groundnut, til, sunflower, etc. Ghanis can be arranged on a turnkey basis including installation, training, etc.

4. A simple loom has been developed by the KVIC for preparing table mats out of grass, etc. These looms can also be supplied and training can also be imparted locally.

5. The KVIC has designed Standard Bio-Gas appliances like industrial burners, lamps, etc. These have supplied either directly by the KVIC or through its various agencies which are producing as per the specification laid down by the KVIC.

6. The KVIC can also take up production and supply of bee-boxes made out of teak-wood for producing apiary honey. The training can also be imparted for managing bee colonies and the project on a turnkey basis can be taken up by deputing experts.

7. The cups and plates made out of leaves available in various parts can be produced with polyurethene layers and will be

very useful for domestic consumption as well as for trade. The machinery required for making leaf cups and plates can be supplied on a turnkey basis which include installation, training, etc.

8. Handmade paper machinery, like beater, paper lifting vat, hydraulic press, cylinder mould machine, calender machine can be arranged for producing many varieties of paper out of locally available raw materials. The projects are taken up right from site selection, feasibility study, preparation of project economics, procurement and installation of machinery and trial production.

Though in this chapter emphasis is laid on understanding of the khadi and village industries sector, the same analysis applies to other rural sectors as well. Whether it is sericulture, jute, coir, leather or handicrafts, the principles have to be properly understood to enable very clear focussing of multi-dimensional issues.

5

MARKETING RESEARCH FOR PRODUCTS OF RURAL SECTOR INDUSTRIES

Marketing research is an important tool of marketing management. Managements need an information system which is identified in marketing research.

Marketing research includes investigation of market segments, product differentiation, channel relationships, effectiveness of sales representatives, advertisements, pricing practices, etc. The point is that marketing research applies to any phase of marketing and is not restricted to any given type of marketing problems.

The essential purpose of marketing research is to provide information which will facilitate the identification of an opportunity or problem situation and to assist managers in arriving at the best possible decisions when such situations are encountered.

The importance of marketing research cannot be over-emphasised. This will reveal the trends of consumer behaviour, their preferences for certain products, possibility of introducing new products or new designs in old products and other essential facts that have to be fed into the production system.

AREAS OF MARKETING RESEARCH (M.R.)

The types of marketing research done by an organisation depends on the type of activity in which it is engaged. The following are five major areas of marketing research:

1. Sales and Marketing Research
2. Product Research
3. Organisational Responsibility
4. Organisational Economies
5. Advertising

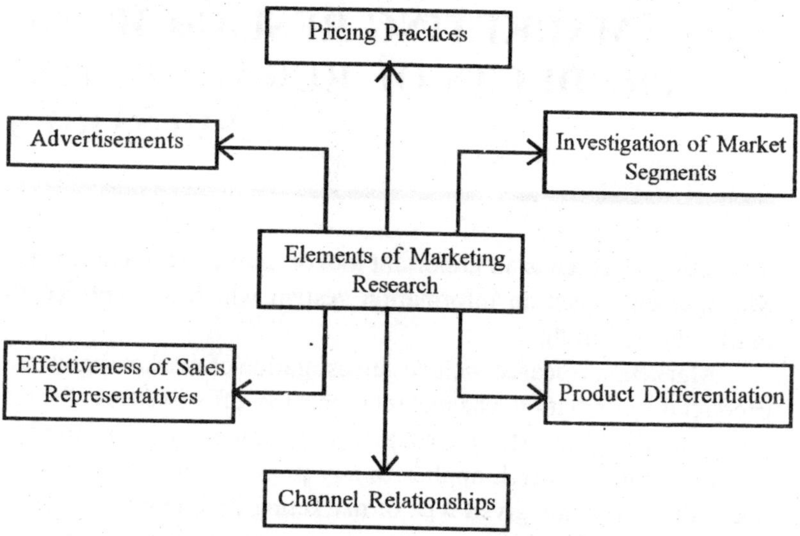

CHART 5.1

RESPONSIBILITY AND INVOLVEMENT IN MARKETING RESEARCH

There are five occasions when an organisation's top management has to contribute inputs to the marketing research process or participate in decisions relating to marketing research. They are:

(i) Indian Research Projects,
(ii) Specifications of Information needed for Decision Making,

(iii) Evaluation of Proposed Research Projects,
(iv) Evaluation of Commercial Research Services, and
(v) Acceptance or Rejection of Research Findings.

These five points are elaborated below:

Indian Research Projects

Managers generally expect more than what marketing research can deliver. On the other hand, marketing researchers have a tendency to re-interpret or modify a management problem in order to make it researchable. That is why discussions between managers and researchers help managers avoid over-confidence on how much actually marketing managers can deliver. It would also help researchers to focus on the management problems. Thus, the managers should attempt to avoid ineffective communications by clearly identifying in the problem statement the specific alternative courses of action which are to be considered (see chart 5.2).

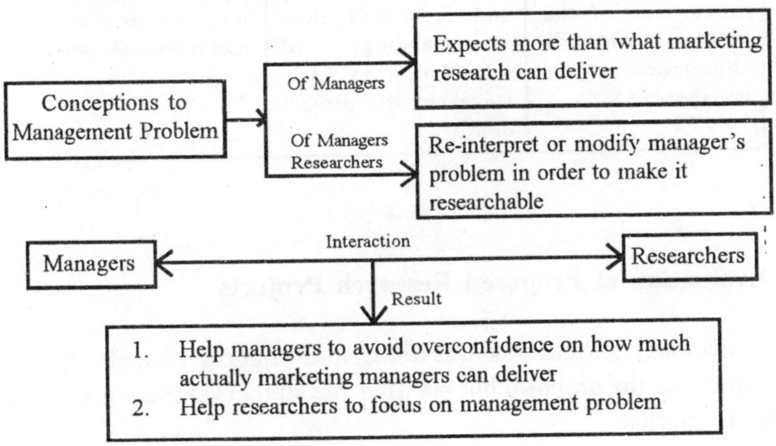

CHART 5.2

Specifications of Information Needed for Decision Making

In designing a project, managers can assist researchers by providing information on the background of the problem and its importance to managers, if in the early stages of the projects design, the managers and researchers get together and develop a clear understanding of the information. Managers are to provide inputs which researchers need in order to design a useful research project.

The final version of the research project will be much more useful to managers if, in the early stages of the project design, the managers and researchers get together and develop a clear understanding of the information, which the managers expect from research and also how it can lead to a decision (see Chart 5.3).

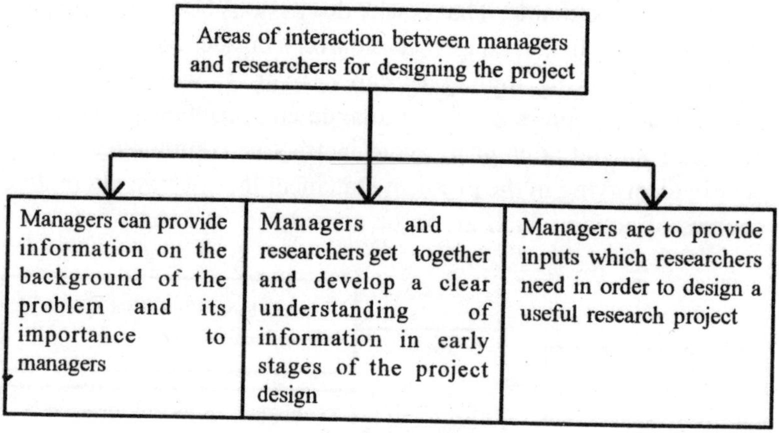

CHART 5.3

Evaluation of Proposed Research Projects

A manager should ask questions and suggest changes before approving the proposal but not after the study is started or finished and reported.

Evaluation of Commercial Research Services

Regarding commercial research services, a wide variety of types is available in the market, although the personnel have to select. Managers will also be involved in specifying information needs and then compare these with the information which can be obtained from the commercial research services.

Acceptance or Rejection of Research Findings

Acceptance or rejection of research findings is a management responsibility. It is, therefore, the manager's responsibility to avoid a decision based on invalid research findings, since decision making is not a researcher's responsibility. Therefore, an inquiry can be made to check the validity of the findings of a completed research. The managers have to review the research project to assure that it has been carefully carried out (see Chart 5.4).

A marketing research activity which provides the management the maximum possible support will be the one which reflects management's responsibility and involvement.

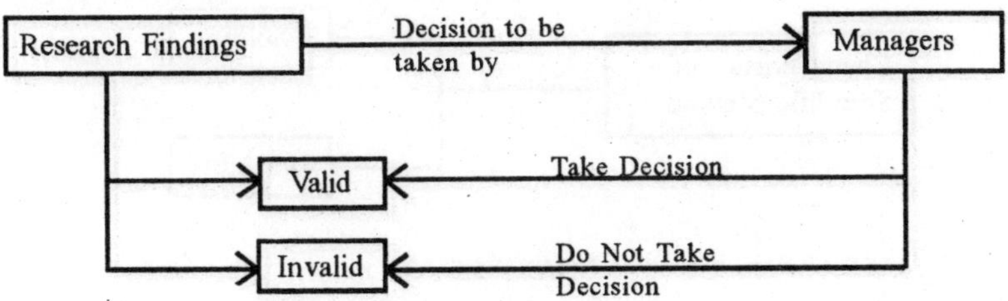

CHART 5.4

It is to be remembered that not all the information a manager might want is obtainable through market research. It is better that the user managers spend some time reflecting the types of valid information that can be obtained through marketing research.

Although, market research cannot predict the future, it can help to reduce some of the uncertainty that the managers may be facing regarding the result of a decision. Thus, it is necessary to gather information on current and recent events and also on consumer attitude and behaviour, to understand a phenomenon better.

Thus, market research is most applicable to those situations where additional information about the present and recent past can help to reduce the uncertainty about the future. Also, those managers who make effective use of market research should learn to identify the kinds of situations where market research can reduce uncertainty.

MARKET RESEARCH AS A BODY OF SCIENTIFIC METHODS

It needs to be appreciated that whenever managers use research, they are indeed applying the method of science to the art of marketing. It is the function of market research to reduce the degree of uncertainty in a decision.

The term research might be substituted for scientific method. The scientific method is characterised by two traits: validity and reliability. Validity is the characteristic used to describe research, which measures what it claims to measure (see Chart 5.5).

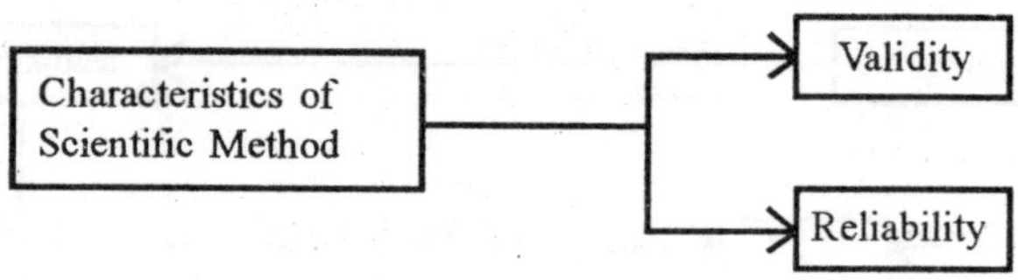

CHART 5.5

The likely Interaction between Marketing Researchers and Top Management

The researchers generally complain the following:

- (i) The management does not include research in discussions of fundamental problems and ask for only specific information about the parts of problems.
- (ii) They do not really understand research.
- (iii) They have a propensity of not allowing enough time for research.
- (iv) Mere reliance on institutions and judgement than on research, and that research is used as such but not as an essential tool.

Regarding these complaints and interactions between market researchers and top management are likely to occur.

Need of M.R. for Administration of Organisation

The problems and opportunities faced at the different levels of administration lead the managers to use market research in different ways.

The Senior Administrators of an organisation are generally concerned with the allocation of resources between a number of product groups. This requires estimation of the sale and profit which will be derived from different types and amount of investments as applied to individual products.

The Marketing Managers are mostly concerned with specific product needs. They always think how their products fit the need of the target audiences, change in the growth rate of demand for the products and the marketing programme of competing brands. They also need information about the probable response of target audience to advertising, promotion, price and packaging.

The Advertising Managers are likely to be concerned with effectiveness of a new copy format and with the frequency with which the target audience will be exposed to a new media schedule.

Thus, at each level of management, different types of problems are faced and decisions are taken. In most of the cases, unique types of information are required which can be obtained only from especially designed Market Research Projects (see Chart 5.6).

Problems of Market Research in India

The major problems of M.R. are the lack of secondary data and as a consequence of not having an adequate sampling frame.

(a) Neither the census nor the National Sample Survey gives monthly incomewise breakup of population or households.
(b) Lack of separate data on industrial products.
(c) Heterogeneity of different States. In conducting all- India

studies, it is often necessary to translate the questionnaire in five or six main languages.

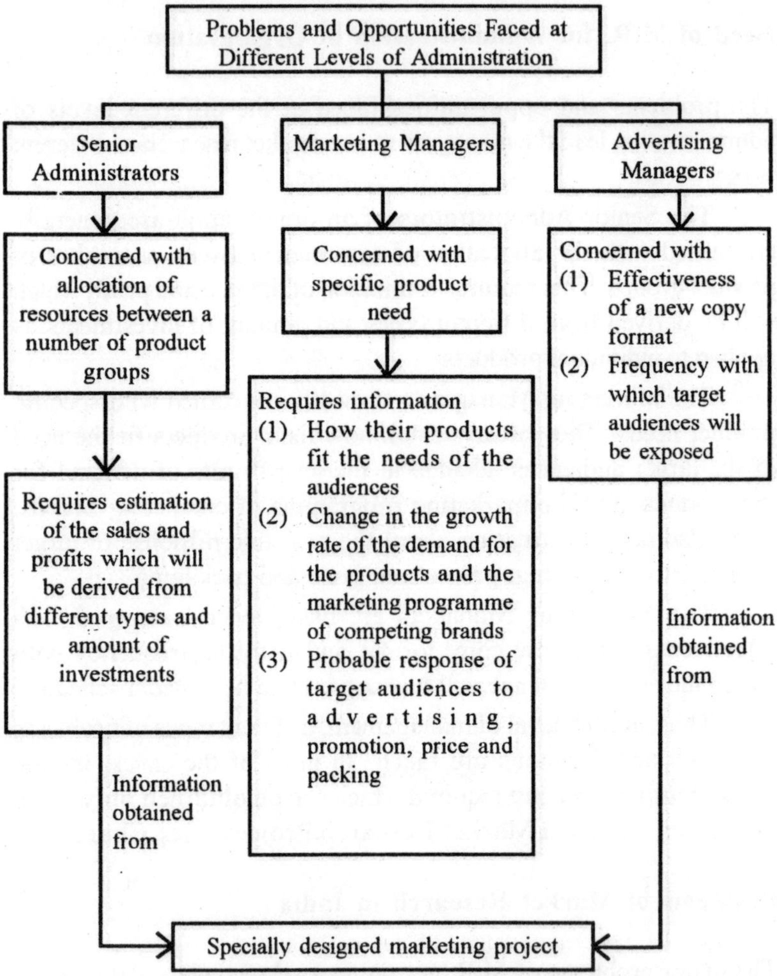

CHART 5.6

In quantitative surveys, where sealing techniques are used, it becomes very complicated, when they are to be translated into regional languages (see Chart 5.7).

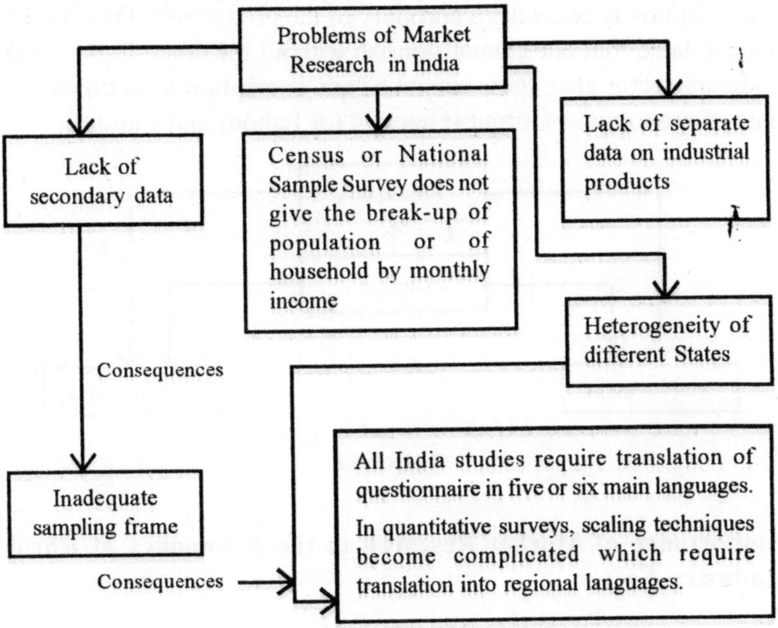

CHART 5.7

Rural Marketing: Economists' View

Although ours is a mixed economy and we aim at a full employment economy, it is no longer possible to ignore the sovereignty of the consumers. In the rural sector also, we have to pursue the golden means of full employment and full satisfaction to the consumers. Consumers are also part of the people, just as employees are, and thus the great cycle of employment, production, consumption continues. Capital is intervened with these.

Cycle of Employment: Production: Consumption

Thus, whenever we speak of the production function, the main parameters of output, Labour (L) and Capital (C), i.e., Q + f(L,C) type, wherein production, employment and finance are shown, consumption is generally a corollary of the production. They are so inter-related that one cannot flourish without the other. In the rural industry sector also, there cannot be any exemption from this basic law of economics– Output=Function (of Labour and Capital)

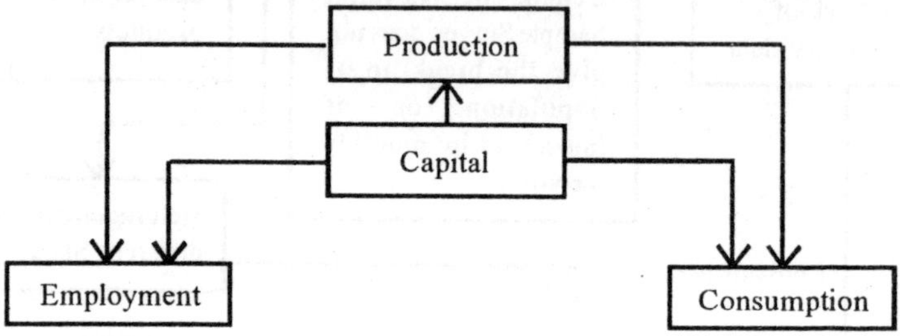

CHART 5.8

Importance of Market Research in the Economics of Rural Industry Sector

For any successful endeavour on the path towards the marketing of rural industries products, the importance of market research cannot be overemphasised. The marketing information system of the rural sector has to be designed to aid planning, control, feedback and evaluation tasks:

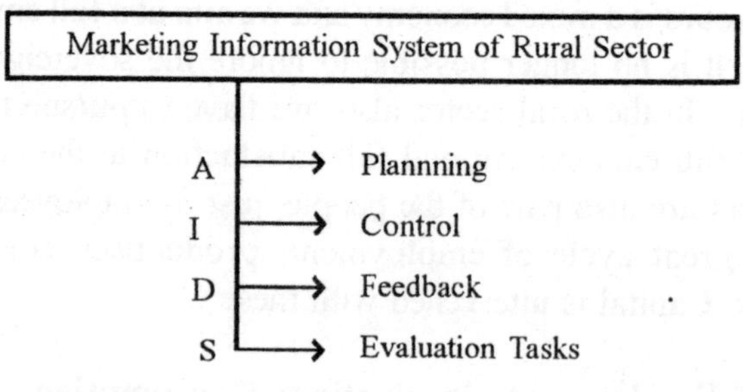

CHART 5.9

Gandhiji's Remark

In this regard, it may be worthwhile to remember Gandhiji's message to the rural industry sector— "A customer is the most important visitor in our premises. He is not dependant on us. He is not an interruption in our work. He is the purpose of it. He is not an outsider in our business. He is a part of it. We are not doing him a favour by serving him. He is doing us favour by giving us an opportunity to do so.

This advice is not only applicable to the marketing outlets for KVI products, but it is equally applicable for any type of marketing outlet anywhere.

The ASCI Report on Marketing of Rural Industries Products

The ASCI (Administrative Staff College of India, Hyderabad) report on Rural Industries (1974-75) says that the marketing of rural industries is rather complex as the problems differ from product to product, unit to unit and also according to the consumer of the product whether local, regional or international (see Chart 5.10). There cannot be a general marketing strategy for the rural industries products in view of the varied nature of the products, ranging from products of mass consumption, intermediate goods, goods for industrial use and also due to major differences between rural consumers, private and government consumers and national and international consumers. The marketing strategy has to be different depending on the nature of the commodity and the type of consumer.

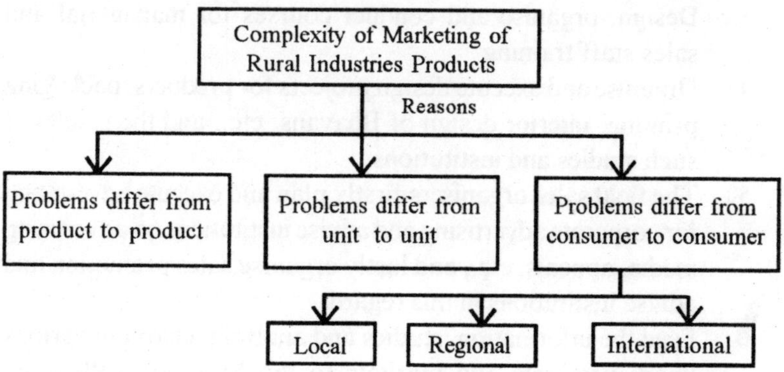

CHART 5.10

The success of the product of rural industries in the market depends on how effectively the various marketing skill are used in the number of complex activities, beginning with the assessment of the need of the consumer, advertisement and publicity, and the sale of the products of rural industries.

This ASCI Report (1974-75) recommended that a Market Research cell to be set up at the State level to keep estimating the quantity of demand according to the product, type of consumer and territory, identification of changing demand pattern and analysis and the impact of the Government policies and the demand for the various products.

Recommendations of the IIMA Report

In the IIMA (Indian Institute of Management, Ahmedabad) Report 1976, three separate functions of rural marketing were identified as Commercial Operations, Marketing Services, and Marketing Planning.

The duties to be performed under marketing services are as follows :

1. Collect and analyse the information related to broad economic outlook and textile industry.
2. Periodically conduct market studies to delineate the consumer profiles, fast-moving Khadi items, etc.
3. Design, organise and conduct courses for managerial and sales staff training.
4. Organise and execute design projects for products, packaging printing, interior design of Bhavans, etc., and the results of such studies and institutions.
5. The field sales organisers firstly plan and execute advertising for corporate advertising and advise institutions on advertising media, appeals, etc., and lastly organise sales promotion and advise institutions in this regard.
6. Feed the information, studies and analysis regarding various khadi products and markets to the Marketing Planning Section.

7. Conduct studies to analyse the reasons for good and bad performance of institutions and feed this information to managements of institutions.
8. Advise institutions on the number and proper location of distribution outlets.

The duties to be performed under marketing planning functions, as recommended by the IIMA Report (1976) are:

(a) Engage in environmental scanning to find out the trends in the economy and textile industry.

(b) Make long-range plans for khadi products and markets.

(c) Identify new growth areas, products and market segments.

(d) Do annual/quarterly planning for different product lines and regional markets, monitor the performance of khadi enterprise with respect to annually/quarterly plans.

(e) Develop and monitor sales targets (product-wise, region-wise, etc.)

(f) Prepare and monitor performance budget for Rural Marketing Organisations.

The IIMA report visualised an important role for the marketing information system and marketing research. It also emphasised that there should be a nodal point for execution of all the marketing tasks.

The IIMA team conducted an All India study on urban Bhandars, which brought out that one of the most stoutly felt needs of Khadi Bhandars and institutions was a central clearing house agency which could be used for the purpose of exchanging information about the availability of stocks in various parts of the country. Such a clearing house, it was felt, could also become the nerve-centre in the exchange of information regarding new designs and trends in khadi readymade garments and the innovating marketing practices successfully tried out by some of the Bhandars and Khadi Bhavans.

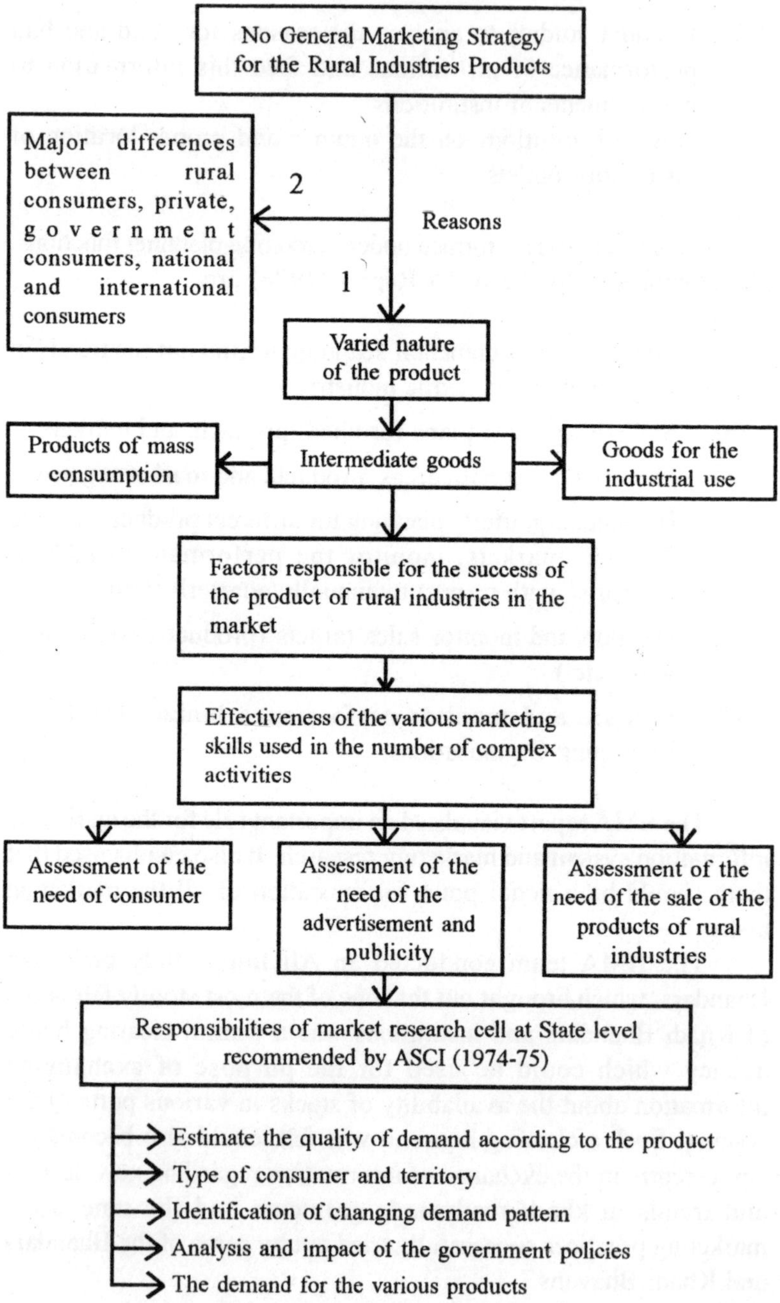
No General Marketing Strategy for the Rural Industries Products
Reasons
1
2
Major differences between rural consumers, private, government consumers, national and international consumers
Varied nature of the product
Products of mass consumption
Intermediate goods
Goods for the industrial use
Factors responsible for the success of the product of rural industries in the market
Effectiveness of the various marketing skills used in the number of complex activities
Assessment of the need of consumer
Assessment of the need of the advertisement and publicity
Assessment of the need of the sale of the products of rural industries
Responsibilities of market research cell at State level recommended by ASCI (1974-75)
Estimate the quality of demand according to the product
Type of consumer and territory
Identification of changing demand pattern
Analysis and impact of the government policies
The demand for the various products

CHART 5.11

The IIMA report recommended that the marketing information system should be designed to aid planning, central feedback and evaluation tasks. A detailed information outlining data sources, processor of data, user categories, frequency of reports, etc., has also been proposed.

6

NEED FOR COMMON BRANDING OF RURAL SECTOR PRODUCTS

The advantages and disadvantages of Common Branding are as follows:

Advantages

1. It helps in product identification.
2. It helps in identifying the manufacturer.
3. It helps to propagate the prestige of the manufacturer.
4. It assures the customer of the quality being offered against the brand name.
5. It helps in the display of shelf product identification.
6. It helps in warehouse identification.
7. It helps in creating an identity for the product itself.
8. It helps in product differentiation.
9. Publicity for a particular brand automatically brings publicity to all the products covered under the particular brand.
10. A popular brand calls for greater demand from dealers, distributors and stockists.

Disadvantages

1. Common branding can be very risky in the sense that if a product covered by a particular brand becomes unpopular in the market the general feelings of the customer will be that all

the other products covered under the same brand may be equally bad.

2. If the logo, colour, design, copy of a brand is not appealing to the market then not only one product but all the products covered under the brand suffer.
3. A common brand may lose its charm of appeal in the long run while different brands of attractive dimensions may attract, different customers in different shapes and moods.

The rural sector is predominantly using the resources available in different geographical locations. The ingredients which are generally being used in the products produced by the sector have a unique attribute. The use of natural ingredient in the products is used by our innumerable institutions which are playing the role to maintain the health of the citizens. The question that always arises is: why should we buy the product? It is the need of the large consumer segment which a producer has to satisfy. The consumer preference for individual items and the industries engaged in producing such products is a gigantic task to satisfy the market segment. Since the rural sector is enjoying natural resources, we can at once claim that the KVIC is marching ahead in building the image and rendering such services. We, therefore, must have a profile of the product which includes the attributes which prevent health hazards, environmental pollution, and such other adverse effects on mankind. It is, therefore, necessary to have a common brand for the rural sector.

NEED FOR COMMON BRANDING IN RURAL SECTOR

To increase marketability of the products produced by the rural sector's units, it is very necessary that a common brand name must be used. There are innumerable products produced in a rural sector and are marketed in different names. As there are many advantages of the common brand name, there are also some disadvantages. A common brand name helps in product identification and identifies the manufacturer and assures the customer of the quality, which is offered under this brand name. Publicity is done for all the products covered under the particular brand, and thus a popular brand calls for greater demand from dealers, distributors and stockists.

On the other hand, the main disadvantage of common branding is that it can be very risky in the sense that if a product covered by a particular brand name becomes unpopular in the market, the customers will have some adverse feelings and other products of the same brand will be adversely treated by the customers. If the logo, colour, design, copy of a brand are not appealing to the market, then the whole range of the products covered under the same name would suffer. There is also a possibility that a common brand may lose its charm of appeal in the long run while different brands of attractive dimensions may attract different customers in different shapes and moods.

Introducing common brand name and its adoption by the entire sector needs to be examined from the view point of violation of its use from (a) the standard of the product and (b) quality control.

This is because the producing institutions have decentralised arrangements and different infrastructure having its impact on production.

The following brand names can be suggested which may be used as common brand names for marketing of the KVI products– Cottage, Gramshilpa, Kutir, Kutir Shilpa, Gram Shilpa, Gramya, Gramin, Gopuram, Khadi ka Shilpa, Gram Udyog, Gram Bandhu, Maur Shilpa, Gram Mitra, Swatha Rojgar, etc.

It may be necessary to search whether these names are patented or not. It is also worthwhile to consider whether the logo of the brand name can be embossed or super-imposed on the map of India to denote the products handled by the KVIC. Its departmental units and its directly aided units can use the same brand name and logo by the respective KVI Boards. At the State level, the State Boards may also use the map of their own State and compass their brand name and logo inside it.

SUMMARY

Suggested Common Brand Name for Marketing of the KVI Products:

1. Cottage

2. Gramshilpa
3. Kutir
4. Kutir Shilpa
5. Gram Shilpa
6. Gramya
7. Gramin
8. Gopuram
9. Khadi ka Shilpa
10. Gram Udyog
11. Gram Bandhu
12. Maur Shilpa
13. Gram Mitra
14. Swatha Rojgar

In such a big country as India with different States, cultures, languages, contomers and habits among the consumers and giving due consideration to different cultural traditions, it is quite probable that one common brand name may not be sufficient to cater to the needs of such a big country and, therefore, we may have to think of some different names which are given in the beginning of the chapter.

SUMMARY

However, that list is not exhaustive and some more additions can definitely be made, keeping in view the regional languages, and regional demands.

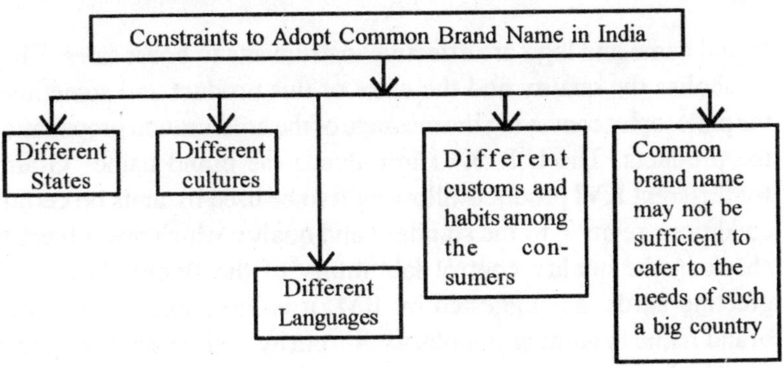

On the other hand, if only one brand name, i.e. *Kutir* is introduced and made mandatory to all the Khadi Boards, Khadi and Village Industries Commission has to coordinate the matter and keep a strict vigilance whether there is any misuse of the common brand name or not. Since some of the State Boards are already having a common brand name, their comments on this are also interesting.

In case it is accepted that Kutir will be the sole common brand name, the KVIC may go for registration of different products being produced and marketed. The KVIC is well within its rights to use the name Kutir being the first applicant and also has the right to sue anyone found copying it. Suggestions from trademark agents for its use by various State Boards, institutions and departmental units should be invited to work out the *modus operandi*. In the licensing agreement, it is necessary to provide the trade mark used in relation to licensed goods. It may be indicated on the label that it is under licence from the KVIC. It would be mandatory that the registered user abides by the procedures. The KVIC can charge any royalty or other remuneration for use of its brand name which is to be decided by it. Proper follow-up of action on the part of the KVIC would be necessary to ensure that the licences are using the word in the proper spirit. A routine inspection would be necessary on the part of the KVIC. There will be a thorough cost benefits analysis of introducing a common brand name.

BRAND NAME AND LOGO (GRAM)

Brand name and logo are effective instruments to boost sales. They symbolise the quality and the class of this product and sometimes the philosophy conveying the message of the organisation propagating the products. The U.P. KVI introduced the brand name "Gram" for different KVI products allowing it to be used by units on certain conditions relating to the standard and quality which are subject to check in the quality control laboratory of the Board. In case of greeting cards, as suggested by IIM, it is Parampara. The Gram brand name is gaining popularity for purity and something special for which craze is growing day by day. This is found to consolidate the market performance and create goodwill. Efforts are also there to register this brand name for exclusive use by the Board.

The philosophical base of the Khadi Movement in the preindependence era was the creation of village-based production economy to be self-reliant, self-initiated and self-directed. Therefore, as a product, it could not go through the national channel to the national market satisfying the taste and the requirements of the customers. Now the liability of Khadi as an industry would have to depend increasingly on the generation of market, shifting emphasis from rural self-reliance to cater the needs of different age groups without depending on outside assistance.

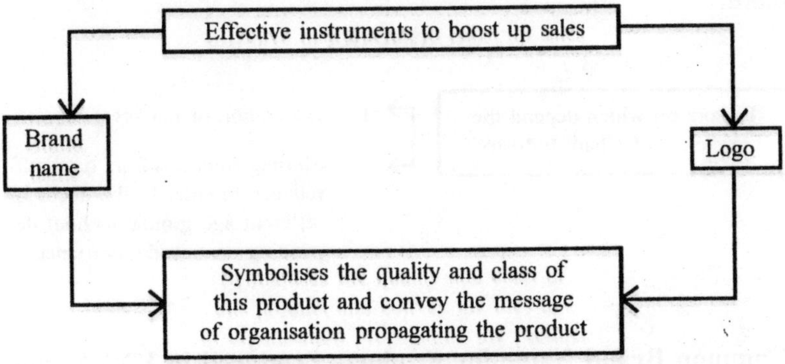

SUMMARY

In view of its potential to generate subsidiary occupations in rural area, especially for women, serious thought was given to convert it into such garments which could generate demand not only in the domestic market but also in the international market without elements of charity.

Rural industries make laudable efforts in this direction by taking help of designers to give an ethnic appeal to their products. A voluntary organisation was associated with these experiments. The Board also tried a tie up with the Indian Institute of Fashion Technology as a part of the strategy which however could not succeed. The exhibition-cum-sales were organised in schools and colleges to attract new classes of dominating buyers like students, newly rich and fashion conscious people with improved packaging and delivery system. The result was amazing. An exhibition of three days organised in the Hotel Clarks Awadh during the off season, i.e. non-rebate period, had a grand success recording a sale of Rs. 3 lakhs. This amply proved that if goods are made according to the need of the modern society, Khadi will be saleable throughout the year. However, again, the problem of marketing through the regulatory system, the Government organisations comes in the way and so the role of voluntary organisations will have to be appreciated without option. Had the Board not associated a voluntary organisation, the result what we see today would not have been there.

SUMMARY

Factors on which depend the existence of Khadi Industry →

1. Generation of market
2. Shifting emphasis from rural self-reliance to cater to the needs of different age groups without depending on outside assistance

Common Brand Name for Products Produced in KVI Sector

To increase marketability of the products produced by the KVI institutions, it is necessary that the common brand name must be provided. There are innumerable products produced in this sector which need to be covered by a common brand name. The Kutir word is being used by the KVIC for marketing its products throughout the country.

In this connection, it is necessary to remember that there are over 3,000 registered institutions, 30,000 cooperatives and over 5 lakh individuals assisted by the KVIC which are engaged in the production of KVI products. In addition to this, there are departmental units run by 26 State Khadi and Village Industries Boards as well as a few by the KVIC. These producing institutions are assisted directly either by the KVIC or by the Khadi and Village Industries Boards.

Introducing the brand name and its adoption by the entire sector is a right decision which needs the administrative support for implementing the same while practising in the market. This needs to be examined from the viewpoint of violation of its use from– (1) the standard of the product, and (2) quality control. Since the producing institutions are having a decentralised set of arrangements and different infrastructures, its impact on production is bound to remain. It is interesting to have adequate measures for introducing its brand name by the KVIC for such variable products.

The KVIC being a statutory body, the implementation of the existing brand name as '*Kutir*' if at all being used by any other similar organisation may be identified to assist merit and demerit of the adoption of the brand name.

The KVIC has already registered one emblem and the brand name *Gramodyog* for 16 industries' products and they are covered under the said emblem with the registered name. We should have a clarity about what will happen to the brand name already registered under the products already covered, in case the KVIC is introducing this brand name '*Kutir*' for the innumerable products produced by the institutions.

The Rural Sector under the KVIC will have its own departmental units. Similarly, the State Khadi and Village Industries Board will also have their own production units. In addition, other agencies and individuals will also have to be assisted by KVIC engaged in the production. Introducing a common brand name and its purposeful implementation can be possible only if the KVIC introduce the registration and licensing system by which the user (the institutions which want to adopt the brand name) shall be permitted to use the said name and the related logo under certain terms and conditions. Moreover, this licensing shall be renewable periodically on payment of a renewal fee with the provision for penal measures of deterrent measures against the unauthorised users of the common brand name. The role of patent registering authority and other parties involved in this regard need to be spelt out.

It is worthwhile to consider the introduction system of the brand name. The logo can be embossed or superimposed on the map of India to denote the products recognised by the Khadi and

Village Industries Boards. This also may be explored.

In different market environs one product may face, in due course, violation or misuse of the word *Kutir*; the likelihood of its consequences on the other products covered under the same brand name will also be considered or taken into account. Hence, provision to keep a record of such misuses to sue/to be sued in such cases also be examined.

The use of word Kutir be introduced and should be made mandatory on the Boards, is also a point for consideration. Since some of the State Boards are already having their own brand name, in such cases Boards may offer their comments for consideration to the KVIC.

For enforcement of the proper use of the proposed brand name, it would be necessary to have a very efficient and fool-proof inspecting mechanism which will bring a desirable change in the entire KVI sector.

It should be provided in the licensing agreement that the trade-mark used in relation to the licensed goods which should be indicated on the label with the mark that it is being used under licence from the KVIC. By this the goods produced by the KVI sector production units and the goods produced by the licensees can be distinguished. It is mandatory that a registered trade mark is used by the user in relation to his goods, other than the goods for export. The mark shall also be described clearly to indicate that it is being used by the permitted users.

The KVIC should charge any royalty or other remuneration for the use of its brand name which is to be decided by the Commission. In that case the rate of royalty is to be determined. Also the KVIC have to permit others in respect of their application for use of this brand name under a licensing system. Licences may be granted for a particular period of time and may be renewed from time to time. There should be an inspecting mechanism to ensure proper use of the word '*Kutir*'. The KVIC should have trained staff to monitor and inspect the products produced as per the standards laid down by the respective Industry Directors. In order to ensure that the licensees are using the word in proper spirit, there should be a follow-up action from the concerned

Directorate. The KVIC will have to build a record of inspection maintained for the licence user levying inspection charges on the licensees.

It is not easy to assess the cost benefit of the brand name but for the purpose of introducing a brand name *Kutir*, it is easy to identify the goods of rural industries and other licensing user. Without brand name it is not possible to make the public know that the goods concerned are the products of the rural industries or their licensees. If any improvement in using the brand name can be made, such improvement can be a part of benefit resulting from the use of the brand name.

Necessary introduction may be incorporated in certification norms so that adequate measures are ensured to produce the goods under the common brand name and to make it possible to market them from one point to another point.

Brand Position, Brand Loyalty and Marketing Strategies

The brand name and the position of the product help analyse the consumer level. By knowing the consumption level of a product by the number of families or sales by retailers and wholesalers the image of the product in the market can be obtained, and merchandising of products and turnover rates give the necessary feedback to adopt certain measures to improve upon the stock position of a product.

SUMMARY

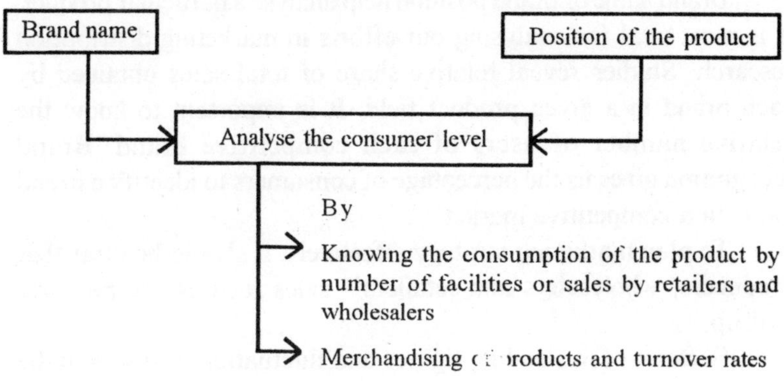

The business houses which have accurate measures for competitive sales for their consumable products have a genuine advantage for many of their competitors. The value of analysing sales performance of an industry by various marketing units helps the producer to plan production and ultimately the risk of investing funds may be decided. By means of competitive sales information, importance of specific market segment is known.

Brand positioning of the product will analyse the image of the product in the market. The organisation may collect the relevant information about the brand image of the product from various sources such as retail stores, consumers and wholesalers by conducting periodic surveys. Management can develop the strategy for developing the image of a product by adopting various measures. This periodic survey may be conducted for consumer preference and brand recognition. This may be made by the individual organisation also.

It is to be known as to who are the buyers of the product, why do they buy, how the product is used and the percentage of the consumption rate ? Once we know the answers to the above questions, it is easy to develop marketing strategy.

Many companies or organisations are enjoying brand loyalty because of their long-standing practical existence in the market. The researcher studies the in-depth loyalty of the customer to a product over a length of time for a particular brand. This also gives a brief idea of the rate of consumer loss and also causes of consumer disloyalty to a brand name.

Brand name or brand position help analyse a particular product. It is most vital for analysing our efforts in marketing distribution research. Studies reveal relative share of total sales obtained by each brand in a given product field. It is important to know the relative number of users of each competitive brand. Brand recognition gives us the percentage of consumers to identify a brand name in a competitive market.

To plan marketing strategy effectively, it should be clear that producers, wholesalers and retailers' sales records are properly built up.

Because of misleading figures and fluctuation of stocks in the hands of retailer and due to cross-distribution of products by various Vastragars and Bhandars, the records are not properly furnished. Such practices result in irregularity in furnishing the information, ultimately resulting in an unclear picture of consumer position for a particular brand.

The brand name of the product strengthens the organisation's base in the competitive market and the image of the organisation is also raised in the minds of the consumer.

7

APPROPRIATE TECHNOLOGY

Let us define what is 'appropriate technology'. The appropriate technology is a technology which contributes the most to economic, social and environment objectives of development. It should be utilised for development purposes in the name of social justice and should be capable of satisfying the felt need of the people. Appropriate technology should also be economically viable, technically feasible and should fit in the socio-economic fabric of local communities. It should be able to produce some surplus, so as to encourage capital formulation and stimulate further growth. It should be labour-intensive and capital saving also. It should ensure dispersal of wealth among the largest number of persons and create a sense of participation and decision-making at the local level. Thus appropriate technologies will vary over a period of time in response to the area and changing conditions. During the development of these appropriate technologies, emphasis should be given to make them labour-intensive as well as simple technologies which can be used by the ruralites. The development of the technology may have to be on the following norms:

1. Technology should help in reducing human drudgery;
2. Technology should enable the users to earn living wages comparable to the rural agricultural wages in that area;
3. Technology should improve the scale, production and quality;
4. Technology should utilize local resources;

5. Technology should utilize more and more non-conventional sources of energy; and
6. Technology should not only improve the tools and instruments but should also diversify the products.

As we are aware, our country is facing serious economic problems. It is high time that our planners define its social and economic objectives in the context of the prevailing situation so that unemployment may be contained. It is better to give even less wages to a worker than to keep him without job or to keep him on the dole, as is being practised in some countries. India cannot afford to go in for full-scale unemployment insurance either. It can, however, try to implement employment guarantee schemes, as is being practised in some States like Maharashtra in our country. But all these things are of a temporary nature and solid solutions of permanent nature have therefore to be found to improve the overall socio-economic conditions of the masses.

Appropriate technology, which is an improvement over traditional technologies, and in many cases involves miniaturization of the sophisticated or innovative processes recently developed, offers some hope for solving the unemployment problem. A number of misconceptions have crept in regarding the application of appropriate technology. Sometimes the impression is created that appropriate technology aims at the complete rejection of modern technology and is exclusively based on traditional technologies. Both the impressions are incorrect. Appropriate technology can be developed either by upgrading traditional technology or by scaling down technology through miniaturizing its different components, thereby reducing the investment costs and thus capital investment while increasing labour input.

WHAT SHOULD BE THE CRITERIA FOR SELECTION OF APPROPRIATE TECHNOLOGY

In order to find out whether the model of technology falls within the category of appropriate technology, it has to be tested on the following parameters:

1. Satisfaction of Basic Felt Needs of the Concerned Communities

The satisfaction has to be decided on the basis of availability of resources. For example, a community made up predominantly of agriculturists, problems pertaining to growing of certain crops may include supply of seeds, fertilizers, irrigation facilities and other technical services may relate to storage and marketing of the produce. For the artisans, there may be problems of supply of raw materials or introduction of new techniques and skills or creating suitable organisational and managerial structures for marketing the furnished goods. For landless labourers, there may be the problem of employment throughout the year.

2. Economic Viability and Technical Feasibility

Any model introduced purely on sentimental grounds or due to some other consideration, if not economically viable and technically feasible, is not going to last long. It may therefore have to be ensured that the technology adopted is economically viable and technologically feasible.

3. Reduction in Human Drudgery

In the operation of traditional equipments and tools, there is a lot of drudgery involved which often creates boredom. Moreover, the production is not sufficient and results in little scope of expansion and further growth. As such technology should be such as to reduce the drudgery and boredom to which they are usually exposed.

4. Labour-Intensive and Capital-Saving

India is blessed with abundant human power. It should therefore be ensured that while introducing modern technology it does not unduly replace the human power and at the same time it helps in capital-saving. This mix has to be holistic.

5. Marketability of Product

As we know, there is stiff competition in the market. Our technology should therefore be such as to improve the quality of the product, finish, packaging and cater to the taste and preference of the consumer.

6. Utilisation of Non-Conventional Resources of Energy

The conventional types of sources of energy like petrol, diesel, coal, etc., may not last long. However, India is having the vast resources of water, sun, wind, biogas for the production of consumer goods. It would therefore be proper that the technology introduced in the rural areas concentrate on the utilisation of local energy sources which would ultimately reduce the production cost as well as the cost of financial products.

OPPORTUNITIES FOR APPROPRIATE TECHNOLOGY

To wipe the tears from every eye should be our aim, said Mahatma Gandhi, who often reminded that India lived in her villages. Poverty is a socio-economic phenomenon which defies any precise definition; its concept varies from country to country depending upon what a particular society accepts as a reasonably good living standard for its people. In USA it would not be surprising if a family owning less than two cars may be dubbed as poor. But in India, poverty means something like semi-starvation, ill health and lack of basic amenities.

India is predominantly an agricultural country. About 75 per cent of its population lives in rural areas. More or less about 69 per cent people depend upon agricultural activities. As such the agriculture sector is already overburdened. In the circumstances, there is vast scope for creation of employment opportunities for the growing number of unemployed people through non-agricultural activities, viz. village and cottage industries. But because of the stiff competition from the organised sector, these industries have been destroyed. Through the introduction of improved craft, tools and simple machines, these activities can be revived and they can be instrumental in providing employment to a vast number of people in the rural areas.

VILLAGE AND SMALL INDUSTRIES

The spectrum of industries in our country extends from the organised large-scale and medium industries to the modern small-scale industries and the traditional industries such as Khadi, handlooms, handicrafts, sericulture etc. The modern small-scale industries and the traditional industries collectively called "Village and Small Industries" constitute an important segment of our economy providing largest employment to the people next only to agriculture and accounts for over one-fourth of the country's export trade. This sector has a crucial role to play in assisting the growth and wide-spread dispersal of our industries, increasing the levels of earnings of artisans, sustaining and creating avenues of self-employment, ensuring regular supplies of goods and services through use of local skills and services and resources. Developing entrepreneurship through appropriate training and package of incentives, in preserving craftsmanship and heritage of the country are other areas for attention.

TECHNOLOGY DEVELOPMENT AND APPLICATION

It is a fact that mechanisms for technology transfer and technology choice are in need of considerable improvement in most developing countries. However, this improvement alone may not be sufficient to ensure achievement of the overall development objectives. What are needed are comprehensive national technology policies corresponding to the overall socio-economic development strategy of the countries concerned to guide the decision-makers in their choice of technology.

POLICY CONSIDERATIONS AND PRIORITIES

While introducing appropriate technology for rural industrialisation, we should concentrate on priority areas. Some of the areas are as follows:

1. National technology, policies and plans.
2. Support to National Appropriate Technology Centres.
3. Liaison/communication between national and other centres.
4. Training for appropriate technology choice:
   (a) at professional level
   (b) at artisan level
   (c) at supervisory and managerial level.

ADVANTAGES OF APPROPRIATE TECHNOLOGY

1. Solution of Rural Employment Problems

Unemployment is one of the biggest problems of our country. In the face of available employment exchange data and unofficial available estimates about 100 million people are unemployed of which about two-thirds live in the rural area. Appropriate technology offers means for tackling this problem in an effective manner. Most of the consumer goods can be manufactured in the cottage and small-scale sector for meeting the internal needs of the country and such a step can ensure greater employment opportunities to the people. In fact if this policy is pursued rigidly and effectively, it would provide a great boost to cottage industries in the rural areas.

2. Decentralisation and Dispersal of Industries in the Rural Areas

Appropriate technology is less capital intensive and is usually operated with local resources which enables the decentralisation of production. Appropriate technology therefore is an instrument for providing social justice to the people at local levels.

3. Ecological Balance Maintained

With the appropriate technology suitable ecological balance is maintained and people find work in their own settings and surroundings and find living more congenial to their traditional tastes and habits.

4. Job Satisfaction and Emotional Attachment with Tools

Since rural people are encouraged to work in their own setting with their own tools and implements, they develop an emotional attachment to them and thereby are able to get more job satisfaction, which they are unable to find when they have to work in big factories and mills, miles and miles away from their native places.

NATIONAL RESOURCES FOR RESEARCH AND DEVELOPMENT

Scientific research in India is organised under four broad headings: (i) research organised under various institutions in different ministries of Central Government, (ii) research carried out by State Governments, (iii) research undertaken by universities and institutes of technology, and (iv) industrial research programmes of the private sector.

A lot of models have been developed by different organisations, which are being used in the rural areas. These developments have come through individuals, organisations, government institutions, universities, and private firms which have been engaged in the development of appropriate technology suitable for acceptance in the rural areas.

Some of the organisations/institutions which are engaged in the development of appropriate technology are given below:

1. Indian Council for Agricultural Research (ICAR)

The contributions in scientific and technological research have induced a phenomenal transformation in Indian agriculture. The role of the Indian Council for Agricultural Research in this regard has been pioneering. In fact, the modern techniques in the farm sector through the use of modern tools and implements, improved variety of seeds, and the use of fertilizers had helped in bringing about the green revolution. Not only this, ICAR, through its lab-to-land programme, brings the farmers, researchers, and extension scientists in close contact and introduces simple low-cost, relevant farm technologies, which could help in the diversification of labour use and the creation of supplementary sources of income. The programme is being implemented through 102 lab-to-land centres comprising 24 agricultural universities, 32 ICAR institutes and 46 voluntary and government organisations.

2. Council of Scientific and Industrial Research (CSIR)

The Council of Scientific and Industrial Research is a major organisation promoting research and development in the areas of science and technology in the sphere of industry as well as other sectors of the economy such as agriculture, irrigation, transport, etc. It has under it, a network of 42 research laboratories and institutions with 100 regional centres spread all over the country. It also supports research in universities and other centres of learning. While opening the new areas of research, CSIR has developed a lot of technologies through its laboratories spread through the length and breadth of the country, which are equally important for the rural sector.

3. Indian Institute of Technology and Polytechnic Institutes

The role of Indian Institute of Technology and Polytechnic Institutes has been very important in developing appropriate technological models particularly in the industrial field. In fact, each of the five Indian Institutes of Technology has one exclusive department devoted to development of appropriate technology for the rural sector.

4. Cooperatives and Voluntary Agencies

A number of cooperatives and voluntary agencies are devoted to the cause of development of appropriate technology meant for rural development. Amul, National Cooperative Federations have done a wonderful job in their respective areas in the field of rural industrialisation.

5. Khadi and Village Industries Commission

From the very inception, the approach of the Khadi and Village Industries Commission has been to improve the level of technology in Khadi and Village Industries Sector. KVIC has established various research organisations such as J.B. Central Research Institute, Wardha (Maharashtra), Central Village Pottery Institute, Khanapur (Karnataka) etc. These organisations are not only contributing to the development of technology but are also helping in transfer of technology to the level of field. Training is also given to the artisans by these institutions.

FILLING THE TECHNOLOGICAL GAP AND MOBILISING KNOWLEDGE

There is no doubt that the technological attainments so far have been numerous. However, the results have not been percolated to the level of the actual gap which need attention. Now our aim should be to provide at least two or three levels of technology to cater not only for people who are already within a market system, but specially for those who are partly outside the conventional market economy.

As such, while making efforts to fill the "technology gap" we should also attempt to spread the technological knowledge to those who need it most.

MARKETING OF AGRICULTURAL INDUSTRIALIST

When we talk of the transition from agriculture to industrial economy, it follows that agriculturists would be switching over to becoming entrepreneurs and subsequently to industrialists. It is true that Indian economy has definitely achieved a measure of growth but it cannot be called as substantive progress in the direction of attaining self-sufficiency with respect to key performance indicators. As long as the problem of unemployment, rural backwardness and poverty remains, development and planning policy will need a dual approach. This has to encompass the efficient use of resources on the one hand and steps for structural improvements on the other. The role of appropriate technology in this transition needs to be fully understood. States like Punjab, Haryana, Western U.P. and some pockets in country have, on the one hand, made good progress, on the other, the attitudinal problems, entrepreneurial weaknesses, slow change system and excessive reliance on politics have made things difficult. The low prices of agricultural produce have also perpetuated the mind-boggling problem. The green revolution has not genuinely benefited majority of small and medium farmers. In this scenario people do want to get away from agriculture because it does not offer an attractive way of life. The 'glamour' which cities offer has to be countered by appropriate drudgery reduction, income generating strategies. Take the case of need for dry land farming and technological innovations in that field. While empirical evidence clearly drives home the point that without a breakthrough in dry land farming, no worthwhile progress is possible, trend analysis reveals that agricultural production has recorded only a limited growth during this decade. While granting that agriculture itself is a big science, there are suitable technological inputs, not necessarily dependent on imported technology, are very important. The change in terms of seeds, water fertilizers, irrigation, machinery and crop rotation need upgradation from the existing level of knowledge. While efforts have been to implant imported know-how in other fields, the local resource base has hardly been used. The dry-land farming and the problems related to it do need employment generation, strategies to be understood in proper perspective. While producing farm products is only one part of that strategy, the more related are storage system, pricing system, value addition of that product, marketing and appropriate technologies related to it. These aspects have hardly been attended to in a coherent, organised manner. While the financial sector has gone out of hand due to multiplicity of agencies, the output has hardly been activised based on scientific and technological information available. There is also the question of sustaining the level of output. While development of irrigation during the plan period has progressively gone up the product yield and utilisation of capacity do not justify the correctness of figures. In the case of important crops like oilseeds, there is negligible gain. In the case of pulses there is no cause for much jubilation though there is a slight increase. The fertilizer units have their own problems in meeting the cost and recovering the subsidies from government account. These are various issues requiring an integrated approach through marketing based use of science and technology. The slip-shod method would not help. Even programmes like integrated area development, command area development, dry area development and selected other integrated development, special programmes, etc., have hardly served the purpose. Probably they may also not be blamed for the failure. The successes have been judged through money spending capacity. To sustain, maintain and give push to the developmental scenario, it is essential that science and technology gears itself to accept the following challenges:

1. Differential strategies for dry-land farming area and wet and irrigated areas;
2. To have a comparative study through technology of cost effectiveness and crop rotations;
3. Value addition to various raw materials available in the rural areas not only generate better income for rural people but also glamorise rural areas through better incomes and productivity.
4. Studying entrepreneurial developmental pattern for rural development and identifying contributions of various institutions working in industries, rural development, specialised groups, State Governments and autonomous organisations.
5. Identifying energy needs and comparative estimates of solar energy, biogas energy, wind-mill energy and power driven

along with their long-term and short-term cost and productivity.
6. Selecting limited areas for studies from beginning to end and spreading them to every likely affected area.

All that has been said above also needs a 'market attitude'. Marketing of even the concept of converting 'agriculturist into adventurist' or 'industrialist' presupposes certain transformation. It has to be followed by some basic value changes. These have to be marketed to people who plan and execute. These changes cannot come overnight. But as conditions develop a smooth transition can be ushered in. 'Resistance to change' has to be substituted by induction of gradual reform. It cannot be forced. But by realising the need for gradual and sustainable marketing values its ushering in becomes easier and tolerable.

MARKETING OF HOME-MADE SOLUTION

Many VIPs have recently been talking of home-made solutions in solving our problems. Whether they relate to health care, pollution control, employment generation, road construction or even bullock-cart design, there is a feeling that the more the simple requirement for change the more it has been neglected. The sophisticated and organised could definitely take all the advantages, it is the most needy who have been neglected. The chemical fertilizer has definitely done great harm to the productivity and overall quality of agricultural soil. While for the increasing mouths, there may be a certain amount of justification in the shorter run, but in the longer run, things have to be examined properly. Naturally home or hand-made or own model based on our cultural values will have to be the theme for which the following may be the action plan:

Identify in each area traditional technologies. Since the caste system has been the historical repository of various kinds of knowledge in various fields, in principle, need to involve caste-based expertise has to be accepted. The following may be the areas of expertise in the rural area:

1. Animal husbandry–traditional caste which has been dealing with various types of animal such as cow, buffalo, sheep, goats, hens will have to be involved.
2. Fisheries–fishing communities
3. Horticulture
4. Pottery
5. Ayurved
6. Teaching
7. Health
8. Oil-crushing
9. Cloth-making
10. Carpentry
11. Blacksmithy
12. Tailoring
13. Agriculture related
14. Irrigation related
15. Tourism related
16. Stone-crushing related

Areawise/languagewise various skilled–expert community knowledge is available. They may be called and known by various names and may belong to communities.

The above are only some examples where a concerned community may be able to give appropriate technology and the need for upgradation.

There are no short-cuts to attitudinal changes. Obviously if scientists try to look at the things from their angle, additional better results will come in a short time and at short expenses. What is required is will power and how it is developed will be clear from Chart 7.1.

This follows ecology must blend with economy. The environmental degradation and economic deterioration cannot be swept under the carpet for all time to come. There is a deep interaction. Hence sustainable economic growth cannot flourish in a sick, degraded, polluted and unsustainable environment and energy base. Therefore, there is a need to understand the following for a replicable sustainable model development (Chart 7.2).

It is only by broadening of vision, adopting a friendly approach to technologies and environment, systematic planning with better technological inputs that progress is possible. For this what is required is the attitude for accepting change as a way of life.

This also again highlights the importance of adopting 'marketing' approach to solve gigantic problems. Conviction is not a substitute for marketing. Certain amount of surplus resource

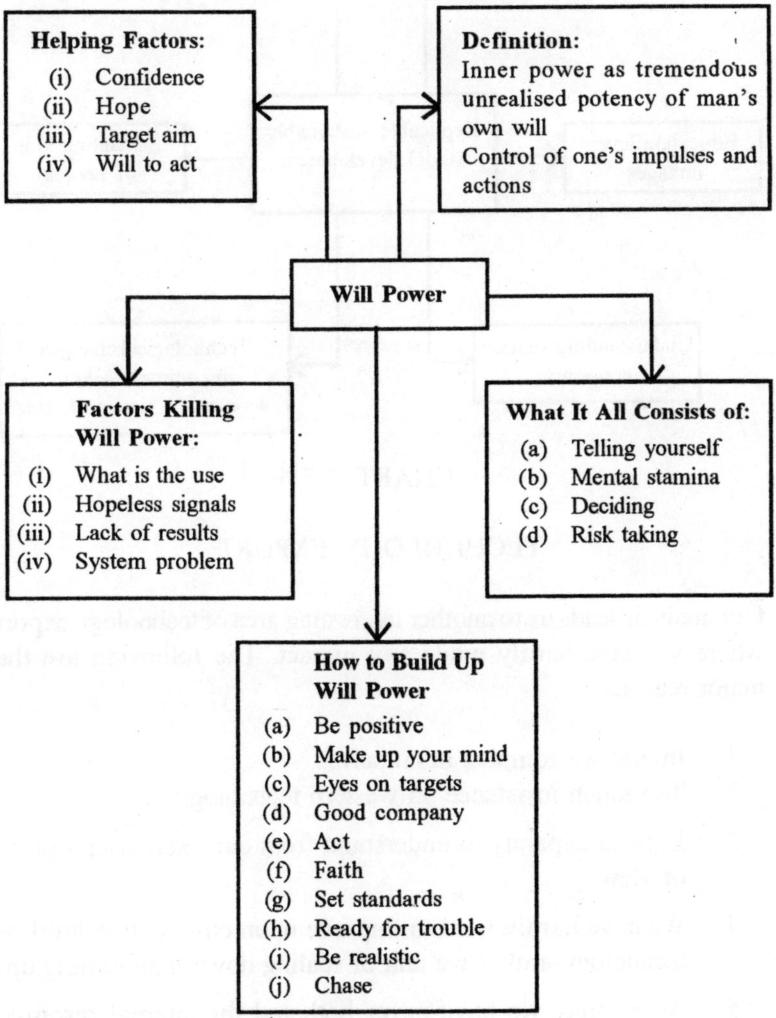

CHART 7.1

generation follows marketing. This is possible in the materialistic world by developing conditions of an effective marketing approach.

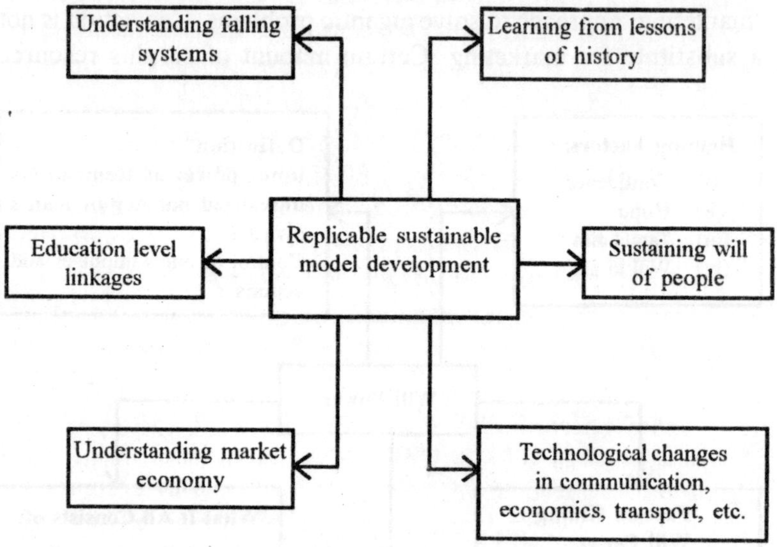

CHART 7.2

TECHNOLOGY EXPORT

Our analysis leads us to another interesting area of technology export where we have hardly made any impact. The following are the major reasons:

1. Inferiority complex in ourselves.
2. Too much insistence on western technology.
3. Lack of capacity to understand from our likely user's point of view.
4. We have hardly tried to improve upon our existing level of technology–rather we talk of scaling down than scaling up.
5. As a state we have never bothered for internal resource generation or marketing of our technology, products, or even concepts.

6. Sporadic successful efforts have not been codified in the right direction.
7. Emphasis in export has been traditionally through government organisations which have hardly bothered to examine the programmes from internal resource generation capacity.

Needless to say that our scientists, technologists and bureaucrats have been more interested in borrowing western models of technology. Whether it was technology development or technology substitute, it will mostly be western. Needless to say that our technologies remain totally neglected. Wherever development took place, even that was not propagated and marketed. This has also led to duplication. In selected areas, many organisations managed to get grants and fully utilised them without any development. Science, pollution, technology and development are the issues requiring our constant high level attention. But effects have remained only on paper and success was confined to budget utilisation. The following are suggested areas for export of technology:

1. All departments which have spent crores of rupees on technology development must be made to market their technology inside and outside the country.
2. To achieve the above objective a liberal output-oriented incentive scheme should be started for all organisations which will help them in internal resource generation.
3. Technology or equipment manufacturers, writers, foreign embassies should be brought together to see, feel and market these technologies.
4. Existing trade channels and infrastructural strength should be fully utilised to make best use of the potentials.
5. Technology export houses should be recognised to take up turnkey projects abroad.
6. IITs and other institutions of repute should have compulsory motivation to worl. in rural areas.

7. Those who prefer to work in difficult areas must always be given incentives. It is only through coordinated effort that replicable models of development will be possible. While some technology may be more useful for African countries, others may be asked to satisfy the requirement specially in the unorganised sector where the need may vary.

In the competitive field, the SWOT analysis of every programme is a must. We as a nation must develop capacity to stand in competition and take up programmes for betterment. Our betterment will not depend on our exploitative capacity but our capacity to develop an integrated view of humanity in all those who live in this cosmos. There are no short-cuts and no limitation of vision. There is need to rise above parochialism and have a broad outlook. The technology should not be an instrument of exploitation, but of an all-round sustainable development which is the need of tomorrow.

8

MARKETING OF ECONOMIC ISSUES IN PANCHAYAT RAJ PROGRAMME

With the Constitution Seventy Third Amendment 1992 on the Panchayats, the areas of operation of Panchayat Raj institutions have considerably widened. As a matter of fact, Panchayat Raj institutions are the grassroot local organisations which mingle with the people freely and are aware of their needs and aspirations. They can give a fillip to all activities in rural areas with the sole aim of bringing about rural industrialisation in rural sense of the term.

As defined in the Constitution,"Panchayat" means an institution (by whatever name called) of self-government constituted for the rural areas. Panchayat area means territorial area of a Panchayat.

Here it is pertinent to point out that the Panchayat Raj system is not totally new to India. However, with the amendment of the Panchayat Act, Panchayats have been accorded the recognition as harbingers of change in the rural scene. What is to be noted is that all the 28 items added to the Eleventh Schedule of the Constitution were directed towards economic upliftment and with their true implementation, economic status of villagers will be elevated. Following are the 28 items of activities as enunciated in the Constitution.

1. Agriculture including agricultural extension
2. Land improvement, implementation of land reforms, land consolidation and soil conservation

3. Minor irrigation, water management and watershed development
4. Animal husbandry, dairying and poultry
5. Fisheries
6. Social forestry and farm forestry
7. Minor forest product
8. Small-scale industries, including food processing industries
9. Khadi, village and cottage industries
10. Rural housing
11. Drinking water
12. Fuel and fodder
13. Roads, culverts, bridges, ferries, waterways and other means of communication
14. Rural electrification, including distribution of electricity
15. Non-conventional energy sources
16. Poverty alleviation programme
17. Education, including primary and secondary schools
18. Technical training and vocational education
19. Adult and non-formal education
20. Libraries
21. Cultural activities
22. Markets and fairs
23. Health and sanitation, including hospitals, primary health centres and dispensaries
24. Family welfare
25. Social welfare including welfare of the handicapped and mentally retarded
26. Welfare of the weaker sections, and in particular of the Scheduled Castes and Scheduled Tribes
27. Public distribution system
28. Maintenance of community assets

Rural Enterprise Development is a must to achieve the desired result as expected of Panchayat Raj institutions. Pooling of resources is a *sine qua non* for success of any venture, particularly those related to rural areas. But it has been seen that pooling of existing available resources of manpower, infrastructure and expertise have been lacking in the past. Hence it calls for new orientation in the entire gamut of economic activities so that the rural sector is endowed with plentiful resources to feed myriads of activities, including 28 aforesaid items.

To concretise Rural Enterprise Development, there is a need for working together. For this purpose, we have to bid good-bye to the callous attitude now gripping our minds. At the same time, Planning, Action, Research, Codification, Extension and Loaning (PARCEL) concept must be practised. It is so because it presupposes policy changes at various levels. This concept also ensures fuller utilisation of investment through organiser-entrepreneur with a view to facilitating sustainable self-employment enterprises.

PANCHAYAT RAJ AND ACTION PLAN

Poverty is directly an offspring of exploitative policy. Hence it is essential that a participative system is developed. This participative system has to encompass all aspects of life. It has a bearing on various issues influencing the policy planning. The removal of poverty visualises certain amount of co-ordination, linkages, monitoring, funding and internal resource generation through marketing. As far as the monitoring aspect is concerned, it is not only social consciousness but also the self-management. This will lead to attitudinal changes in the long run. The diversity of these problems can be understood better with reference to the local approach, i.e., with active involvement of Panchayat Raj institutions. Which are capable of taking up a holistically designed plan of action for sustainable employment generation. It calls for a well-conceived tied-up programme also. In this connection, the case study of Bass (Rajasthan) would be of great interest. This brings forth the following aspects:

1. Linkages with Panchayat Raj for income generating programmes
2. Diversification of income generating activities with greater

thrust on women programme
3. Long-term region-wise plan of action
4. Development of replicable model.

It is essential that for evolving cooperative, integrated, well-monitored and co-ordinated plan of action, attention ought to be paid to planning, action, research codification and implementation aspects with bank finance. To derive best result, simultaneously there must be a well-developed approach too.

PANCHAYAT RAJ ACTIVITIES

The Panchayat Raj institutions will have to mobilise resources not only by taxes, fees and licences, but also by borrowing from banks, cooperatives and even from private money-lenders. Their funds will be required not only for direct activities to be run by the Panchayat Raj institutions themselves but also for the unemployed youths, cooperatives and the institutions wanting to generate activities in this sphere. It means the question of privatising some of the activities within the villages need not be ruled out. Though, it may seem a difficult proposition today. But if we look into the cost effective aspect and need to mobilise and galvanise the activities, we will find no other option. Hence, some consideration of proper pricing would be essential if resources have to be mobilised, generated, and properly utilised.

The experience of rural bank or cooperatives had not been very encouraging. Even the Integrated Rural Development Programme's funding by commercial banks had not been satisfactory. In this situation, we have to learn from the past experiences. Why has this failed? Why the tendency not to repay loans? Why social pressure could not be built up?

We have to remember that ours has been a starved society. Whether it was consumption, way of life, material resources accumulation, traditionally we have been told to sacrifice and be satisfied with the limited resources. Still in the last few decades, there has been clamour for materialisation. Hence, now a situation has developed where the tendency of consuming the root of programme is discernible. As a result, we find the poor utilisation of resources and investment. Hence, the first lesson to remember is that in a starved society, human behaviour will need very close, open and interlocked monitoring. This means two things. First, the principles governing bank finance must be so articulated as to provide incentive for outputs. Secondly the strategy and tactical efforts must help the society to develop empathy and broader vision so that the investment, generated surplus and resources themselves are not consumed.

Principles to Guide Mobilisation of Resources

(i) Project must be from small to big;
(ii) Emphasis of social measures for sustaining the project and ensuring recoveries;
(iii) Costing of linkages must be inbuilt without depending on state interventions;
(iv) Activities must be replicable and self-employment oriented;
(v) Emphasis should be on human resources rather than capital resources;
(vi) Existing raw material both of skills and material must be processed with effective technology and stored to gain maximum economic advantages for the rural area; and
(vii) Transparency and openness should be the hallmark.

Once the principles for formulating the projects, implementing them, monitoring them, as also evolving an integrated and holistically developed model is clear, efforts can be made to mobilise resources with proper strategy and tactics which will include:

1. Maximum use of existing infrastructure. It may belong to any banks, the policies must be tailored to the requirements of the Panchayat Raj enterprise.
2. Regular studies on replicable and failure models should be ensured with the active involvement of schools or academic institutions in that area so that a vocational type of linkages could be built up.

3. The parameters of judging and grading the good work should be transparently disseminated.
4. Role of women and weaker sections should always be highlighted.
5. Self-employment oriented self-supporting model should be developed, training should be linked with it and teachers should be involved in all activities.
6. All the compatible competitiveness and strengths, weaknesses, opportunities and threats of rural areas always to be kept in mind.
7. The social accountability and social pressure should invariably be resorted to.
8. To achieve this, intermediatory interaction with successful managers as well as unsuccessful managers should take place.
9. Emphasis should be laid on self-financing or borrowing from within the village or indirectly minimum dependence on funding agencies. This will indirectly mean building up of self-confidence in enterprise developers who will indirectly call for various policy changes.

LOCALLY BASED ECONOMY

In the above perspective, we must view the local economy. Local basically refers to lowest entity, analysis and intervention. Local has to be understood with reference to political, economic and social interests. Overall commonality of interest becomes its spareable part. It is a qualitative criterion and significant area approach. Panchayat in India has been formed based on population and it has something in common. Hence local enterprise would definitely encompass indigenous commonalities. The enterprise concept with reference to income generating activities in a given area visualises capacity to develop income generating and risk taking entrepreneurial capabilities.

Local approach is opposed to regional or state approach,

signifies certain differences. The reason for this emphasis can be explained in the following ways:

S. No.	Point of Difference	Local Approach	State Approach
1.	Accountability	Much more	Much less
2.	Distance	Very near	Very far off
3.	Social aspect	Very relevant	Remote
4.	Sensitivity	Much more	Much less
5.	Nearness	Very much	Remote
6.	Trust aspect	Has to be there	Remote
7.	Language	Local language	Different languages
8.	Accessibility	Very much	May be

If we understand the point of difference properly, it should not be very difficult to fathom the need to give an economic thrust to Panchayat Raj institutions for developing successful models.

ROLE OF CASTE

Caste has played a very important role in sustaining villages both as social and economic homogeneous self-supporting and self-governing institutions. Traditional caste structure, which has undergone a sea change in the last 6-7 decades has to be understood with reference to latest happenings in some of the backward states. The fact remains that life in India is still governed by caste factors. From birth to death, many activities are governed by this factor. Can it be neglected? The political survival of many parties and personalities solely depends on the way castes can be manipulated. If that is the reality then why not use state as a source of income generating activities? Various traditional activities are still surviving in villages. Despite efforts to totally do away with them, they are still present. In the stage of liberalisation, they may get impetus because of their competitive capacity and lack of other avenues. With better income generating policy prescription and dignified way of self-employment, it should be possible to give a new thrust to employment generation by properly analysing the strengths, weaknesses, opportunities and thrusts (SWOT) of the caste structure. For this purpose, a new vision is essential for sustainable self-employment generation with active involvement of Panchayat Raj institutions as detailed below:

When tickets are distributed by political parties, the caste structure is invariably considered. Even Panchayat Raj operates on dominant communities and the caste structure. Can this leadership be motivated to pay attention to dominant industry, services and business activities of the area? Can policy issues with reference to that activity/enterprise be considered like:

(a) Policies with reference to payments;
(b) Policies with reference to thrust on jobs;
(c) Policies with reference to working hours and local tradition;
(d) Policies with reference to involving local skills and expertise;
(e) Policies with reference to local ownership of resource;
(f) Policies with reference to life-style, aspiration and communication possibilities;
(g) Policies with reference to involving of traditional structure for offering important facilities; and
(h) Policies with reference to appropriate tools and machinery for reducing drudgery and maximising output without compromising quality.

The economic dimension in Panchayat Raj has to understand these aspects to make it sustainable or alive.

SUCCESS PARAMETERS

Before we proceed ahead, it would be in the fitness of things to examine in detail the success parameters. It is a fact that a successful individual may not be successful for the society and the state. Success parameters codify evaluation, replication and need of holistic approach.

By generating internal resources, a successful programme has to become self-supporting. A parasite whether economically, physically and socially, cannot be termed as successful. Cost effectiveness is yet another point which vouches for the success of any programme. A programme which is not cost effective cannot survive the test of success. It is bound to be unsustainable. Cost can vary. But the total package of costing has to be done to ensure cost effectiveness in the longer run.

There is a general consensus that the traditional quality of products from rural areas is considered to be below standard. This is a very important element which can partly be got over by utilising the quality infrastructure and experience of various institutions successfully working in the area. Also by involving existing marketing oriented institutions at low cost, the problem can be solved.

ESSENCE CENTRE FOR INDUCING ENTERPRISE IN RURAL AREAS

Panchayat Raj institutions will definitely succeed in the longer run in this regard. This is not a new concept in a country like India. There are many evidences in history to show how the village communes are run. They had their own culture, rules and regulations, practices, habits and ways of life. Various groups in the villages are supposed to contribute to village activities. They had their own systems to resolve conflicts and ensure harmonious environment for sustainability of life and society.

All the 28 items are to be looked after, managed and funded by Panchayat Raj institutions. But can we adopt "Enterprise" concept, so that full justice could be done. Can there be different ways of locking many of these activities to spare the society from paucity of resources. There is definitely a need for rethinking.

Answers to the following may indicate some of the areas to be considered:

1. Can there be cost effective basis?
2. Can there be bank finance?
3. Can there be backward, forward linkages?
4. Can there be value addition?

5. Can there be appropriate technology provision with ready availability of spares and services?
6. Can there be sharing of cost?
7. Can there be regular openness and interaction?

Some of these issues have to be understood with reference to the policy issues for sustainable Employment Generation.

In an unorganised society, the importance of pressure lobby needs no over-emphasis. The Centre for Inducing Enterprise in Rural Areas would precisely attend to these aspects. There is a need to look into the following aspects:

1. The advantages of inducing enterprise concept in rural areas.
2. Linkages with self-employment and internal resource generation.
3. Linkages with communication, information sharing and effective technology development and dissemination.
4. Value addition and skill upgradation.

The enterprise development concept in rural areas needs change as also massive coordination and understanding of the transitional problems. It is essential particularly when an agriculturist or an artist is to be converted into an entrepreneur.

A marketing of shift from agriculture to industry invariably calls for the following requirements:

1. Public policies, planning and tax systems.
2. Regular flow of information.
3. Infrastructure—roads, godowns, communication, transport, security, electricity/generators.
4. Raw material stocking.
5. Entrepreneurship and development and training facilities.
6. Development of value addition item and ideal industrial climate and appropriate technologies.
7. Packaging and further value addition.

8. Finished or semi-finished stocking and marketing facilities.
9. Banking systems.

The above points have to be considered in totality and Panchayat Raj institutions have to take additional responsibilities in this regard. They can also provide the following facilities:

1. Arrange land, water and training facilities to the enterprise.
2. Take up the policy issues with the Government and Zila Parishads.
3. Ensure backward and forward linkages.
4. Develop suitable local enterprises through self-supporting institutions.
5. Take up promotional and regulatory mechanism for sustainable growth of enterprises.

The Panchayat Raj institutions have to play a very important role with increasing emphasis on decentralised areas planning approach. There is a need for clarity, commitment, willingness to learn from other's experiences and evolve an implementable plan of action with local initiatives. The solution lies in area plans with better linkages and marketing approach. All activities have to become self-supporting and self-sustaining. Hence any amount to time spent on better plan formulation should be welcome.

TRAINING

Training has become so important and ever changing. Many government departments have opened training centres, but they face the problem of grant, stipend, subsidy, etc. How this has affacted, is a moot point. There are many issues to be considered in this. They include past experience, effectiveness of linkages, success of vocationalisation, utilisation of infrastructure, privatisation possibility and so on and so forth. The following extract from *Rural Industrialisation – A Plan for the Future* (Kamal Taori and S. Singh) may be of interest:

"The privatisation of education taking place all over the world also calls for change in system. But there are some prerequisites before the vocational education could be a successful endeavour in creating jobs in the industries, services and business sector. This prerequisite would improve the following:

1. Make relevant infrastructural available either through state or private investments.
2. Have policy framework both of State Government and local Governments to involve organised institutions, philanthropic groups and their association to mobilise students towards vocational education.
3. Develop inbuilt economics and suitable internal resource generation in each programme.
4. Imbibe entrepreneurship and risk-taking capacity in the youth.
5. Lay greater stress on development of marketing skill and to learn from mistakes.
6. Develop multipurpose skills with special emphasis on women and the disabled.
7. Based on strengths, weaknesses, opportunities and threats of each activity, create conditions for economic linkage building and publicise success stories.

The role of a teacher in successful implementation of the vocational educational programmes for employment generation needs no emphasis. In this connection, one may also look at the success parameters from the point of view of a government organisation, the self-employed entrepreneur and the society at large and why as a concept it has failed?

Vital Points for Consideration

Various programmes relating to agriculture, rural development, forestry, employment and overall sustainable development including education, etc., would be under their purview. Their success depends on the following:

1. Capacity to give impartial, dedicated, widening, political,

economic, social leadership to the members to create conducive condition and pooling resources where self-employed could become the coveted member.

2. Integration of various theoretical and practical concepts for replicable model development with simple laws and minimum of reports and returns.
3. Creation of conditions where all should react to their maximum level of efficiency.

Besides, we all know how the power structure ensures continuation of the vested interest–whether it is political, religious, social, bureaucratic or academic. Its basic issue of exploitation of the unorganised remains the same. Patternised approach, *mai bap* concept would work so long as leaders are not sensitised and adopt humanistic approach.

PANCHAYAT RAJ AND LOCAL EXPERTISE

The society does not live or die with generations. It is a historical process and with proper creation of conditions, enterprise development is possible. Hence the local expertise of arts, crafts, enterprise service, manufacturing, processing, selling and reserving should always be incorporated. It means the local bio-diversity, not only on biological factors but also on instructions and the individuals need appreciation and propagation.

Shri Madhu Gadgil of Centre of Economical Sciences, Bangalore, has brought out beautifully the bio-diversities prevailing in rural India and efforts are to be made to conserve and protect them. This presupposes acceptance of certain facts which have a bearing on the economic aspects of Panchayat Raj institutions. There is a plethora of activities in rural land which would improve the quality of life provided suitable policy incentives are given and checks and balances are ensured. While talking about the bio-diversity, we may also mention various types of employment generating possibilities which are available in the rural area. In *Rural Development and Privatisation*, the author Kamal Taori has suggested measures for identifying rural employment generation on a self-supporting basis.

Constructive Programmes

Constructive Programmes as propounded by Gandhiji in early twenties have a close relation with Panchayat Raj institutions. By construction we ordinarily understand engineering work. But the Father of the Nation used this term for rebuilding India according to his vision of non-violence, non-exploitative social order. The constructive work is a unique concept. It is a positive contribution in our time to win both socialist and capitalist models of development which are under dispute. However, we should not forget that the principles of constructive programme invariably follow decentralisation, building from below scratch self-reliance and willing cooperation. The edifice of constructive programme of man is to stand on five pillars. They aim at decentralised development.

Decentralisation needs availability of trained, willing, competent managers, appropriate trainer of supervisors, servicing facilities at affordable cost and binding factors accruing from income. The Sarvodaya social order is in fact based on these principles. But can it be selfless? In this connection articles by Gandhiji published in *Young India* in 1924 make an interesting reading. The Father of the Nation wrote: 'I am a humble seeker of truth. I am impatient to realize myself, to attain *Moksha* in this very existence. My national service is part of my training for freeing my soul from the bondage of flesh. Thus considered, my service may be regarded as purely selfish. For me the road to salvation lies through incessant toil in the service of my country and through that of the humanity. I want to identify myself with everything that lives. So my patriotism is for me a stage in my journey to the Land of Eternal Freedom and Peace.'

Thus we see that the framework of the constructive programmes is truth and non-violence coupled with determination and dedication. Truth is the end. Non-violence is the means.

In fact, constructive programmes aim at holistic growth. They are a rigid codification, implementation in the stage at which we are today. It is interesting to look at these problems holistically. The Father of the Nation in 1941 listed 13 items under his constructive programmes. They are:

1. Communal unity,
2. Removal of untouchability,
3. Prohibition,
4. Khadi,
5. Other village industries,
6. Village sanitation,
7. Neo of basic education,
8. Adult education,
9. Uplift of women,
10. Education in health and hygiene,
11. Provincial languages,
12. Propagation of *rashtra bhasha* (National Language), and
13. Promotion of economic equality.

Revising this list thoroughly, in 1945, he added the following five items:

1. Kisans, 2. Labourers, 3. Adivasis,
4. Lepers, and 5. Students.

As a matter of fact, after the sad demise of Gandhiji additional 5 items such as (1) cow protection, (2) nature cure, (3) *bhoodan*, (4) *gramdan*, and (5) *shanti sena* were added to it to strengthen the constructive movement and march towards the realisation of Sarvodaya's social order. But at least a few will not accept '*Cow Protection*' as a separate item. *Bhoodan* and *Gramdan* may be as a single item and other items such as *shramdan* and *sampattidan* also may be added to this 'Nature Cure' is yet to become a movement. Some would like to include peace and disarmament as a separate item.

It is very interesting, enlightening and self-satisfying to go into the details of the various aspects as enshrined in the goal of constructive work to know why today the youth do not believe constructively in this concept.

In a nutshell, we may sum up that the constructive programmes comprise self reliever, self-help, voluntarily sharing of what one has with other's cooperation, mutual aid, sacrifice, fellow-feelings and giving due respect to other's feelings. Let us all march towards this goal with proper understanding and firm conviction.

Constructive programmes had their framework, principles, concepts and also the organisational structure to ensure sustainability of life and society. It also ensures the changes required. Self-unification has become the essential part of constructive programmes. Over a period of time, constructive programmes have become part and parcel of national life.

CONCLUSION: A MARKETING APPROACH

From all the above discussion, it will be clear that a good number of schemes on training, monitoring, funding, marketing, etc., will not help the sustainability of Panchayat Raj institutions unless economic aspects, policies, principles are suitably analysed. This calls for a holistic vision and deep commitment and conviction of the inherent quality of the masses. The commonsense approach will have to be blended with scientific approach to ensure the growth of self-supporting systems of the village's self-sufficiency. This will be an essential part of marketing approach.

9

DEMYSTIFICATION ISSUES AT A GLANCE

I. The Unorganised Suffers from

1. Casual employment
2. Ignorance
3. Illiteracy
4. Small establishment
5. Scattered work place
6. Lack of organisation
7. Low technology levels
8. High labour absorption
9. Low wages, etc.

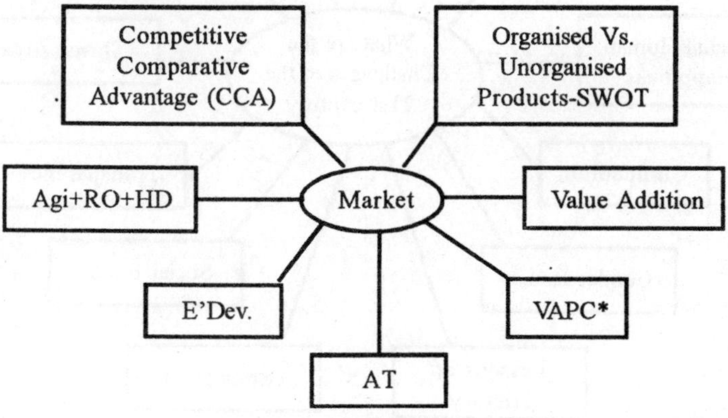

* Value Added Product Concept

CHART 9.1

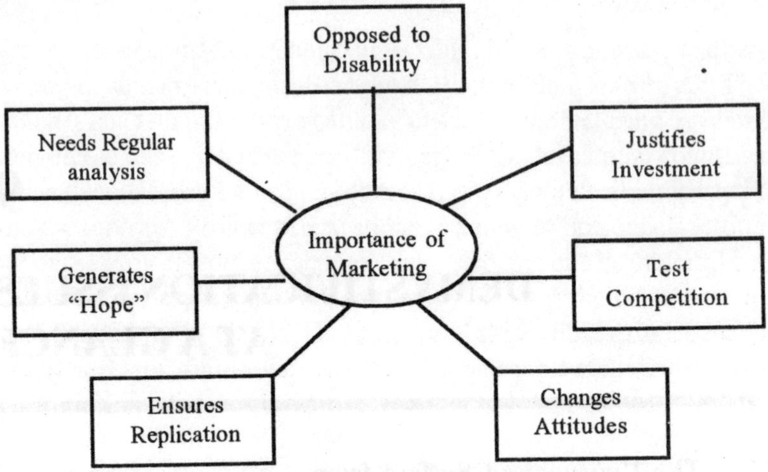

CHART 9.2

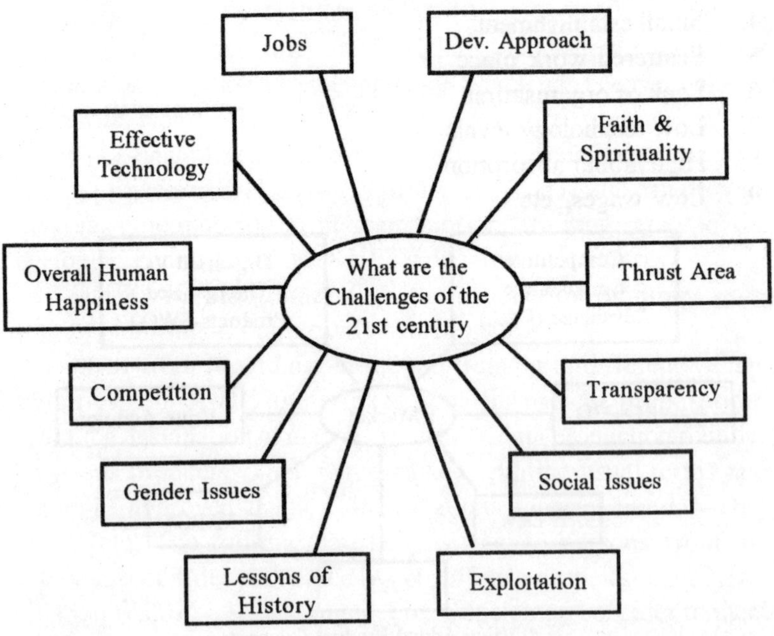

CHART 9.3

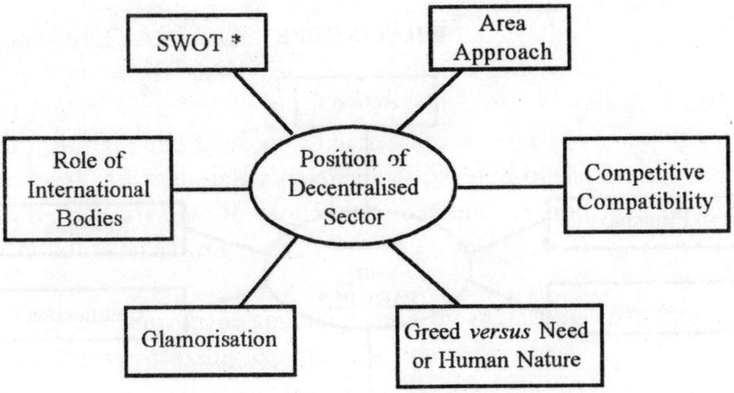

* Strength Weaknesses Opportunities threats

CHART 9.4

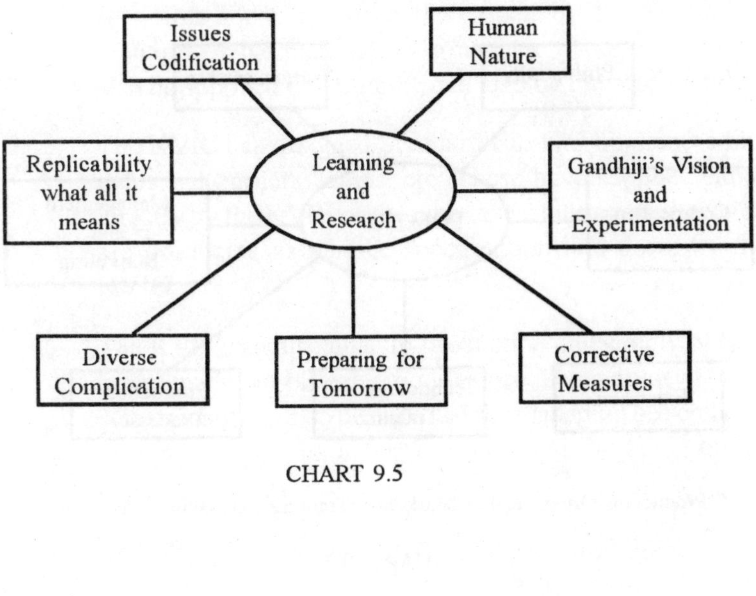

CHART 9.5

WHAT IS HOPE

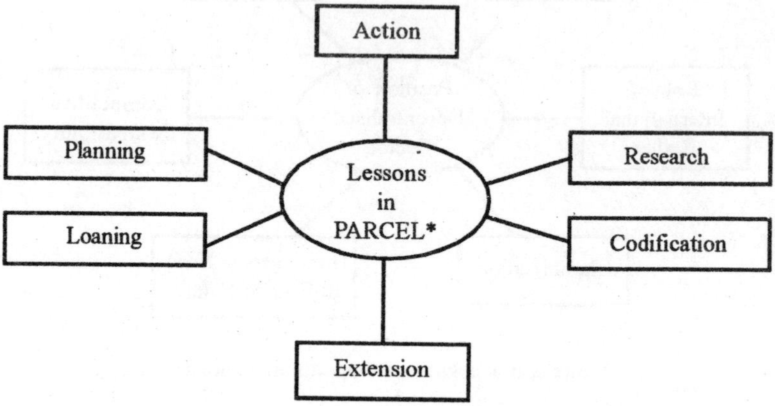

* Playing Action Research Codification Extension Loaning

CHART 9.6

ISSUES IN POMTEC

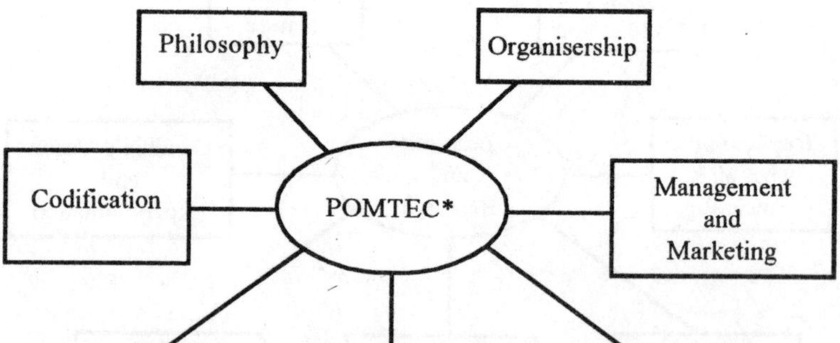

* Production Organisership Marketing Training Extension Cousultancy

CHART 9.7

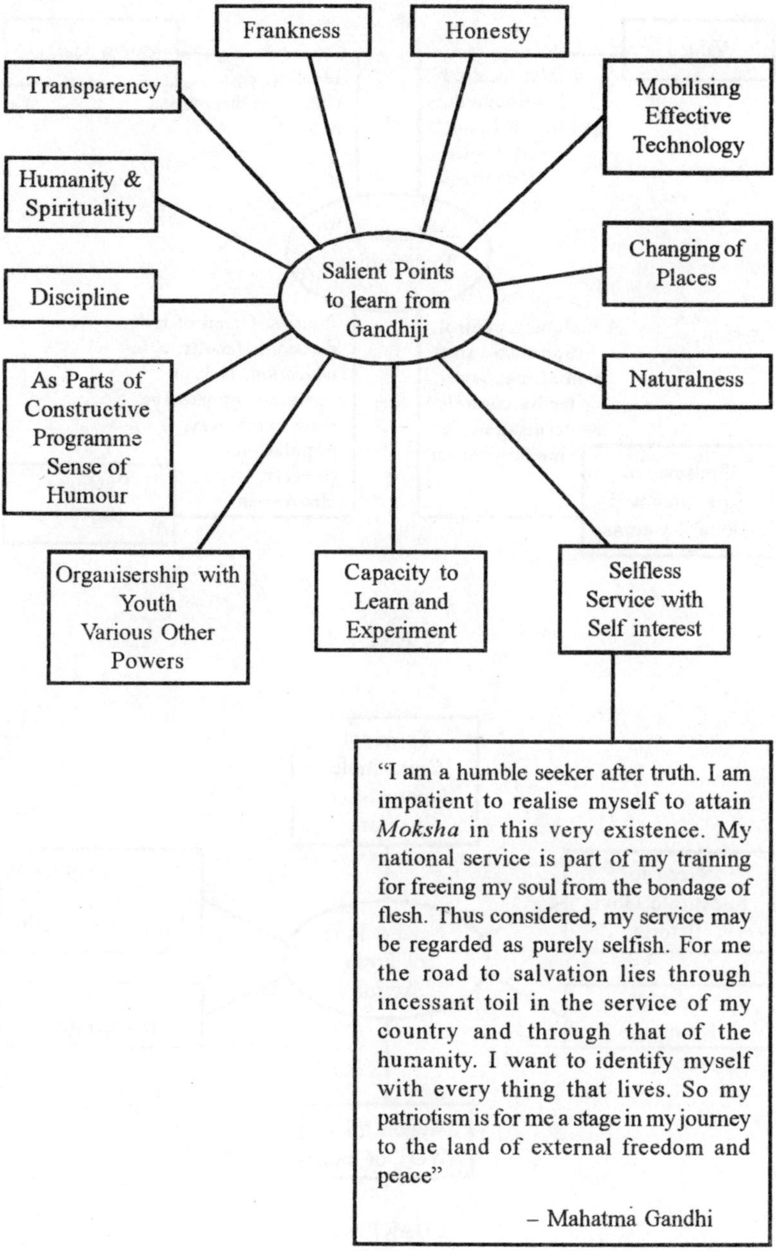
Frankness
Honesty
Transparency
Mobilising Effective Technology
Humanity & Spirituality
Changing of Places
Discipline
Salient Points to learn from Gandhiji
Naturalness
As Parts of Constructive Programme Sense of Humour
Organisership with Youth Various Other Powers
Capacity to Learn and Experiment
Selfless Service with Self interest
"I am a humble seeker after truth. I am impatient to realise myself to attain *Moksha* in this very existence. My national service is part of my training for freeing my soul from the bondage of flesh. Thus considered, my service may be regarded as purely selfish. For me the road to salvation lies through incessant toil in the service of my country and through that of the humanity. I want to identify myself with every thing that lives. So my patriotism is for me a stage in my journey to the land of external freedom and peace"
– Mahatma Gandhi

CHART 9.8

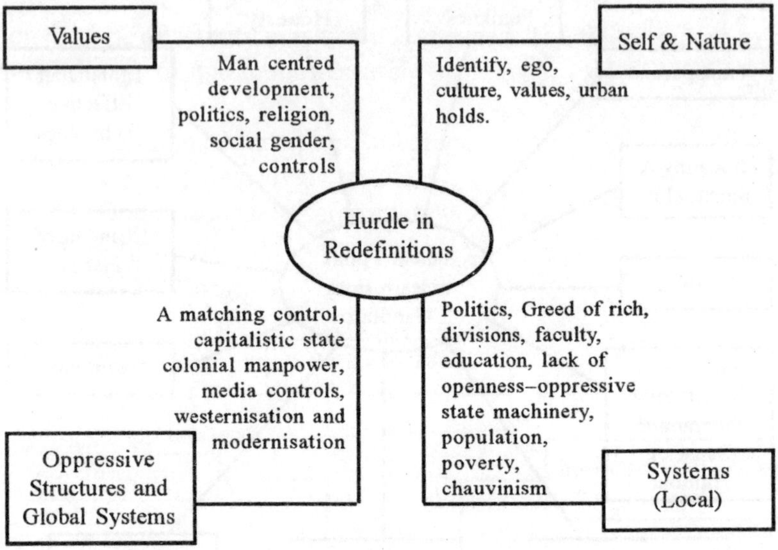

CHART 9.9

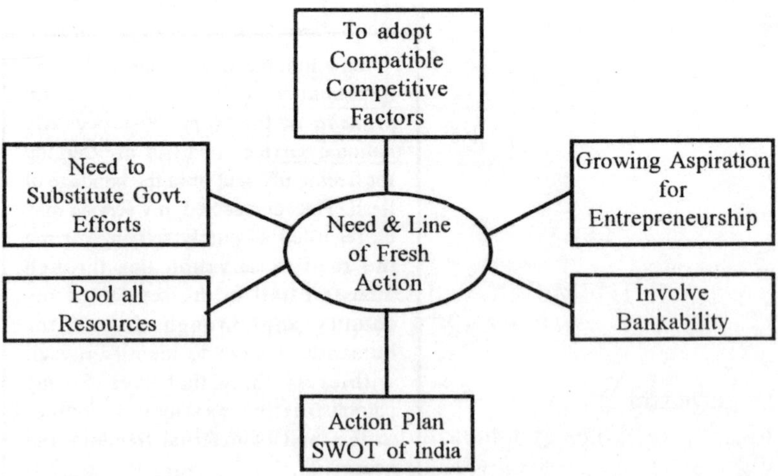

CHART 9.10

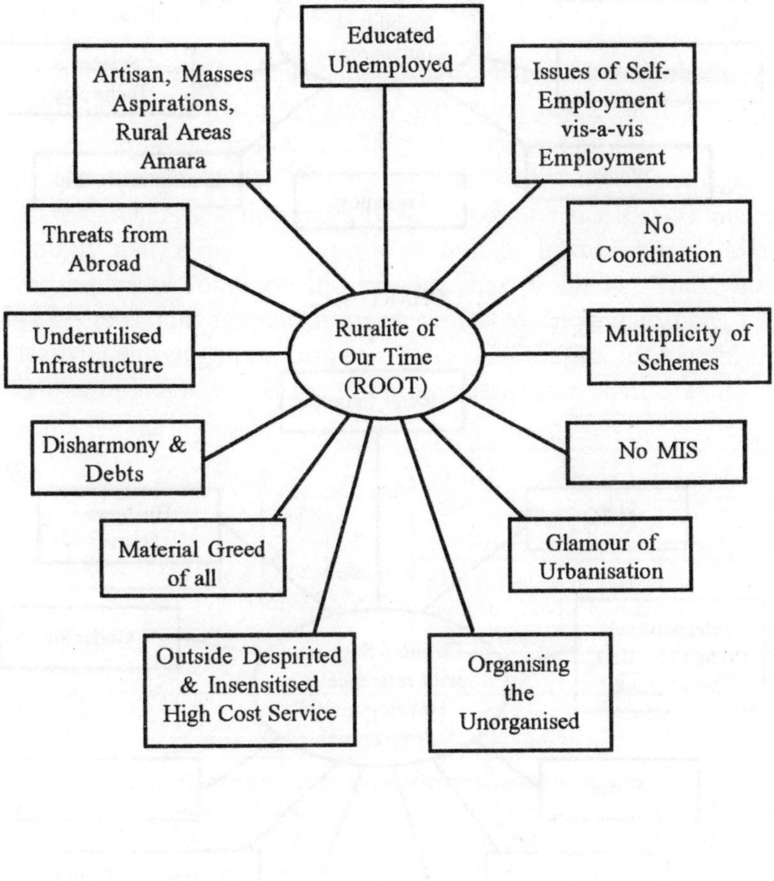
Educated Unemployed
Artisan, Masses Aspirations, Rural Areas Amara
Issues of Self-Employment vis-a-vis Employment
Threats from Abroad
No Coordination
Underutilised Infrastructure
Ruralite of Our Time (ROOT)
Multiplicity of Schemes
Disharmony & Debts
No MIS
Material Greed of all
Glamour of Urbanisation
Outside Despirited & Insensitised High Cost Service
Organising the Unorganised

CHART 9.11

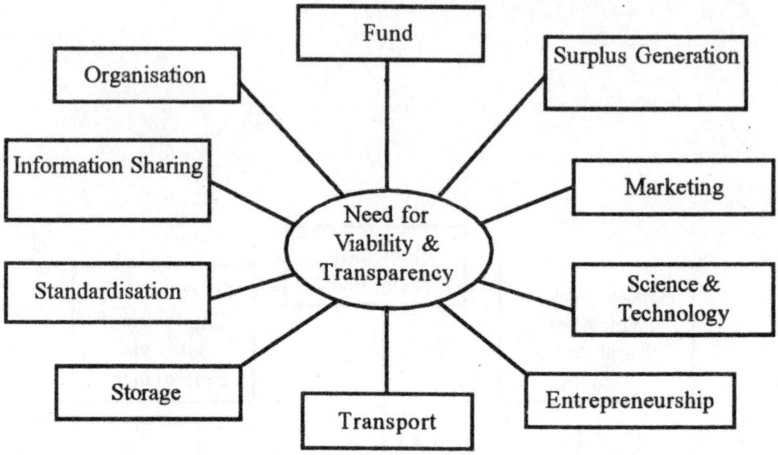

CHART 9.12

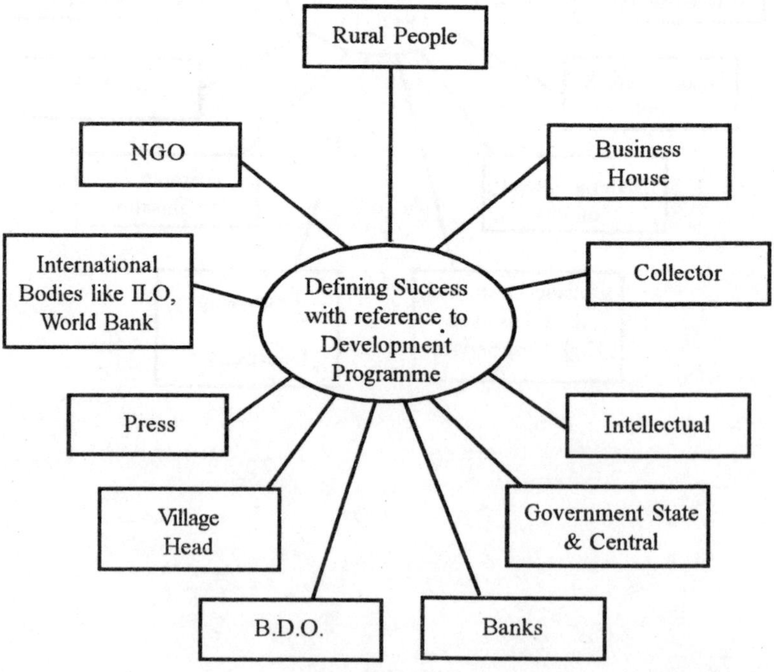

CHART 9.13

II. Basic Issues

1. Whose Plan is it?
2. For whom is it being managed?
3. Who are the evaluators?
4. Is it individual development or rural development?
5. What are the common agreement points? Or common complaint points like corruption, delay, marketing problem, less stipends, wrong selection, lack of involvement. etc.
6. Role of marketing.
7. Need for convergence points and effective communication, students and need for precautions while defining success.
8. What are the conflicting interests? Like business, philosophy *versus* mission or idealism philosophy–Mission or commission–Are they contradictory?
9. Enlightened self-interest through material harmonised interest–need for G.O. and NGO co-ordination–binding powers or convergence points in people, philosophy, purpose, projects profits or workable practices.
10. *Fait accompli* aspect like zones and realistic plan of action excepting certainties of change top-down-bottom-up economic indicators to development–demonstration impact–openness, transparency and harmonising conflicting interests–back to basic and role of values for long-term serviceable *versus* short-term commercial concerns. Have people above 40 messed up this country? Hence role of students and need for basic value orientation.

Conclusion

Defining success with reference to rural development is a holistic concept and certain common parameters need identification for a hopeful widely acceptable definition.

Factors Affecting GRA*

Against

Law & order
Ignorance
Duplicity
Lopsided
Fund flow poor
Surplus generation
Poor quality
Caste factors
Poor performance of agencies in GRA which are mostly Govt. funded
Lessons of History neglected

For

1. Multiple diverse agencies with Govt. support
2. Roads
3. Nature
4. Water
5. Housing
6. Electricity
7. Bio & Solar
8. Tourism
9. Employment creating programmes
   Agriculture
   Horticulture
   Industry, Fisheries,
   Animal Husbandry
10. Education
11. TV. Radio
12. Sports
13. Prosperous Nature

Latest Favourables

– Added thrust
– Realisation of disharmony
– Aspirations of masses
– Failure of uncoordinated efforts
– Air of freshness

* Glamourising Rural Areas

* Grants Rebates Assistance

CHART 9.14

Learning from Past Mistakes

1. Need to coordinate and provide constant linkages.
2. How markets move?
3. How Govt. supports?
4. How unorganised are discarded?
5. How grants are cornered?
6. How reports, studies, surveys remain totally uncriticised?
7. How technologies remain in pockets?
8. How pockets of prosperity develop leaving out others?
9. How present time is favourable?
10. How monitoring and identifications are carried out?
11. How R&D efforts are disseminated?
12. How specialised area develops?

CHART 9.15

Function of KVIC

Promotional

- i Organising the Beneficiaries
- ii Training-Motivation
- iii Research & Development
- iv Surveys/Studies
- v Publicity-Exhibitions
- vi Projects Formulation/ Appraisal
- vii Monitoring & Evaluation

Regulatory

- i Certification/ Registration
- ii Purity of Khadi
- iii Cost-chart
- iv Prescribed wages to Artisans
- v Quantity of Products
- vi Exemption Certificates
- vii Rebate & Interest subsidy
- viii Budget Allocation

Commercial

- i Storage and supply of Raw materials
- ii Manufacture Storage & Supply of Tools & Equipments
- iii Processing
- iv Marketing
- v Export
- vi Institutional

CHART 9.16

WHAT IS KVIC?

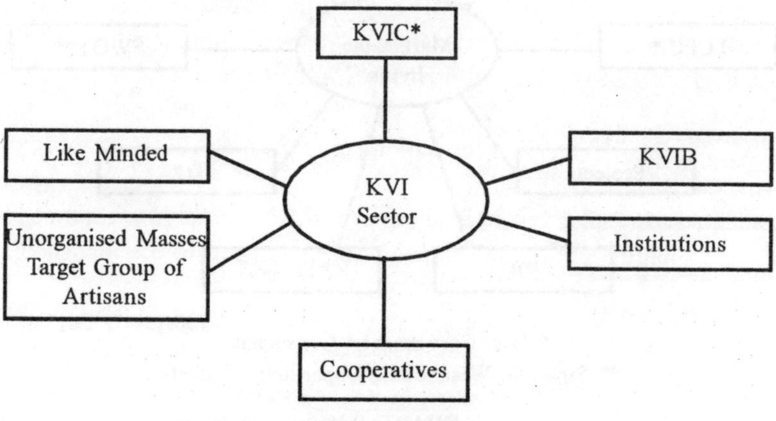

* Khadi and Village Industries Commission

CHART 9.17

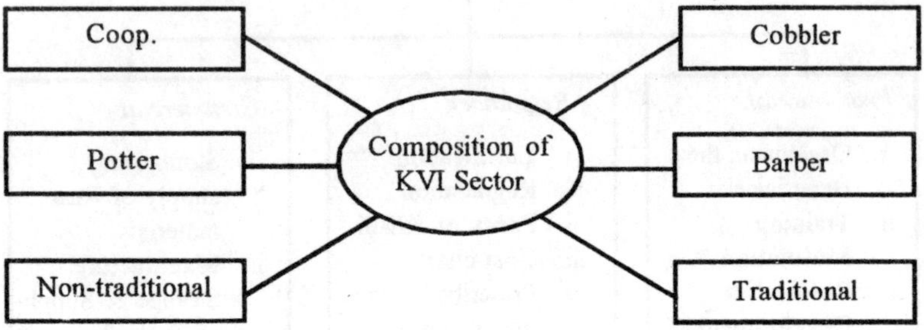

CHART 9.18

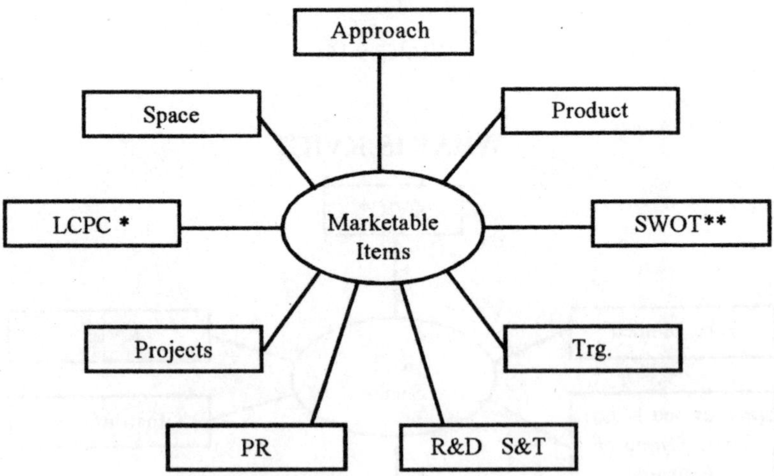

* Low Cost Practical Consultant
** Strength, Weaknesses, Opportunity, Threats

CHART 9.19

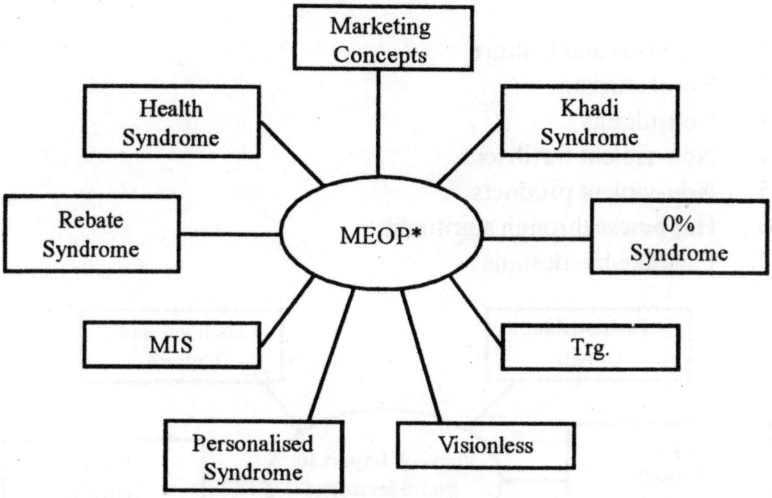

* Marketing Export Oriented Programmes

CHART 9.20

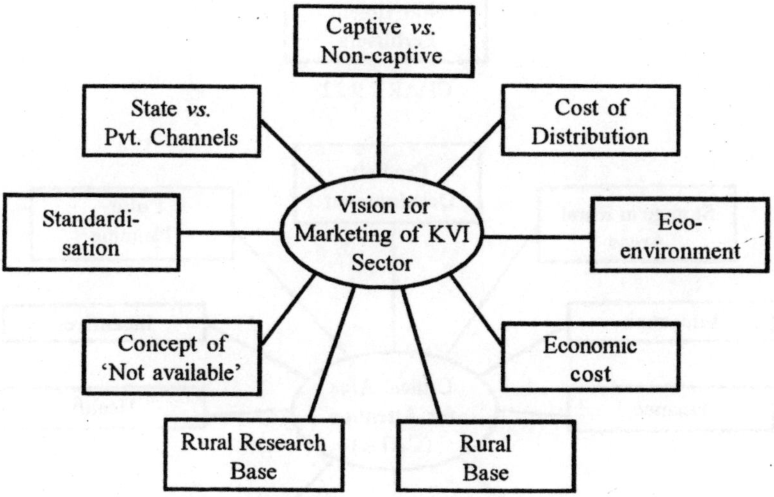

CHART 9.21

Items of Export for Rich/Developed Countries

1. Tradition and Culture
2. Rural tourism
3. Consultants
4. Non-violent fertilisers
5. Non-violent products
6. Happiness through spirituality
7. Fashionable designs

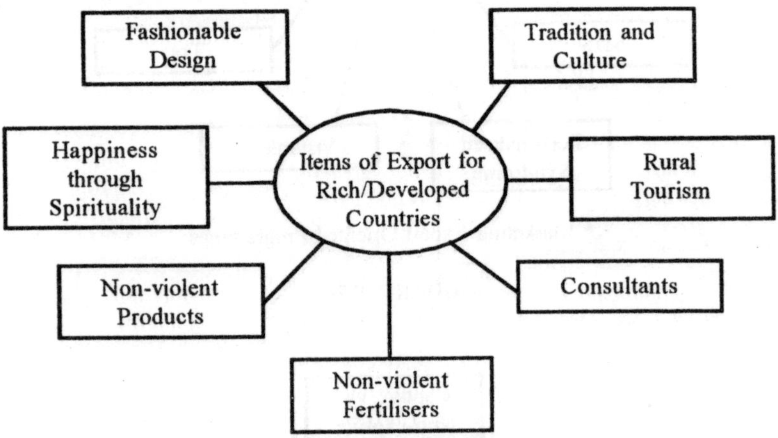

CHART 9.22

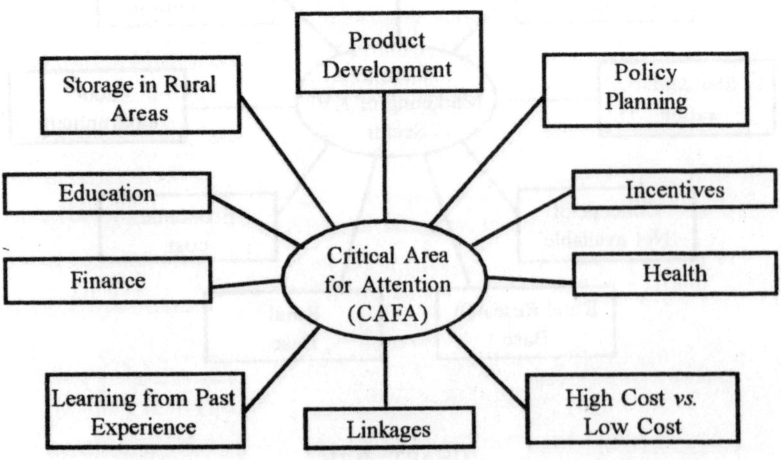

CHART 9.23

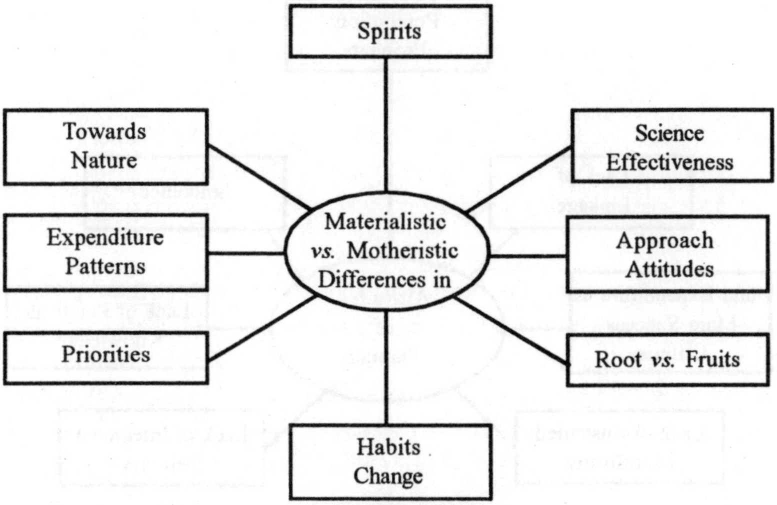

CHART 9.24

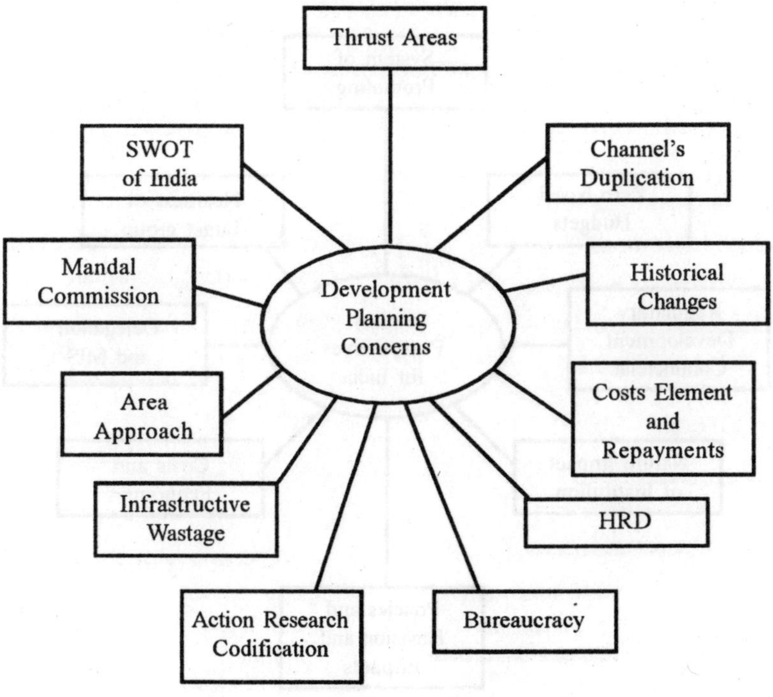

CHART 9.25

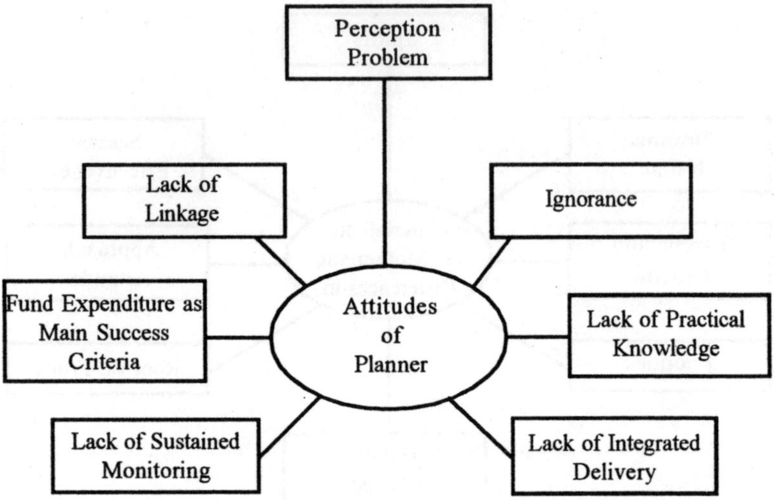

CHART 9.26

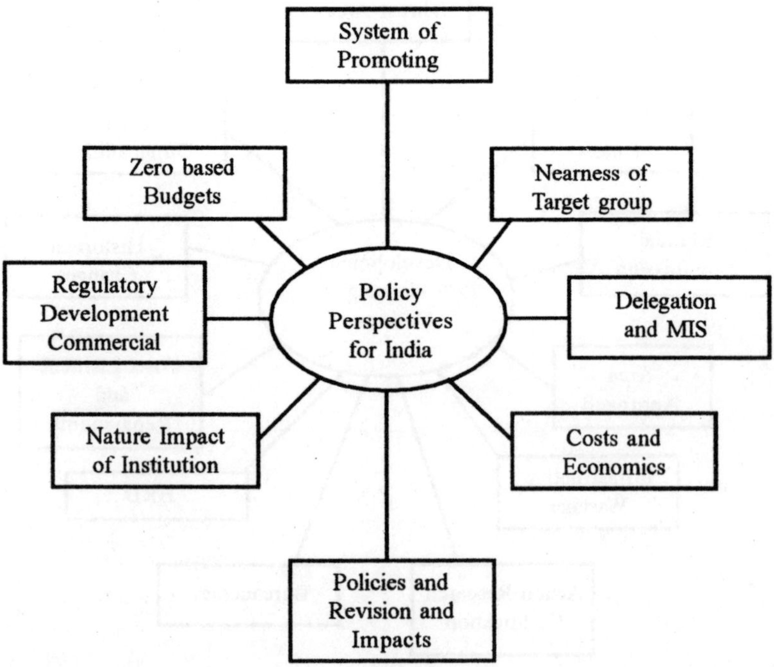

CHART 9.27

HIPPOO (Hidden Investible Potential Power of Organisation) (KVIC)

- KVIC has over 15,000 sales outlets
- It has six sliver plants all over the country
- It has 500 major institutions dealing with Khadi and Village Industries
- Roots of the organisation are 70 years old
- Participation of women in Khadi is over 90 per cent
- Infrastructure facilities are available at many places
- All KVI institutions are NGOs
- Its S&T bodies are constantly engaged in developing newer tools, equipment and production techniques
- V.I. federations ensure forward and backward linkages
- Its network is spread all over the country with special treatment to tribal, hilly and backward areas.
- Ample training facility is available
- SC/ST beneficiaries are humanly treated

CHART 9.28

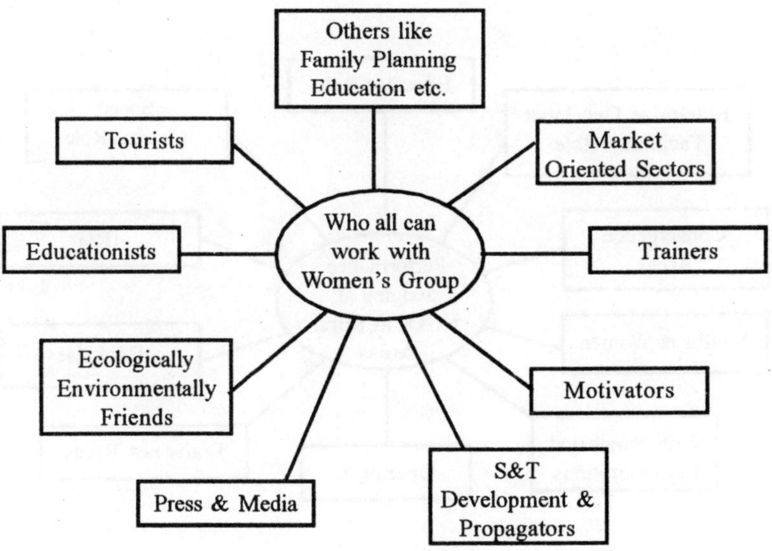

CHART 9.29

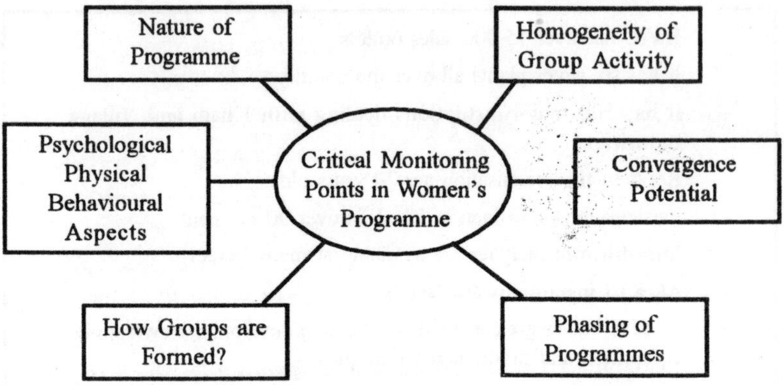

CHART 9.30

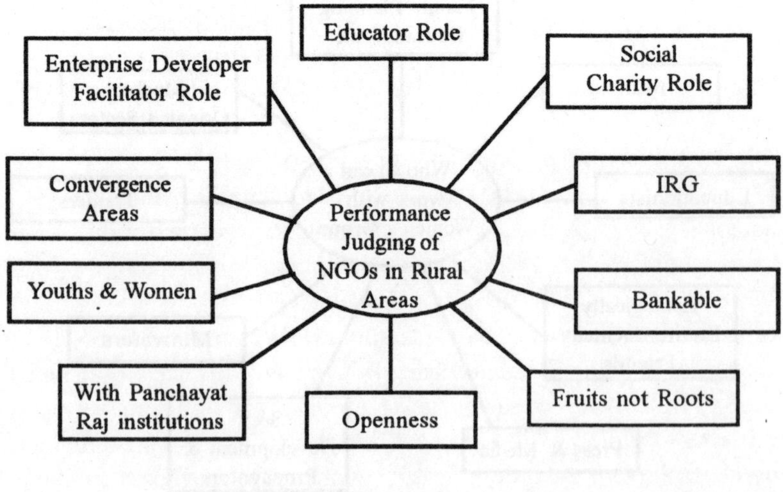

CHART 9.31

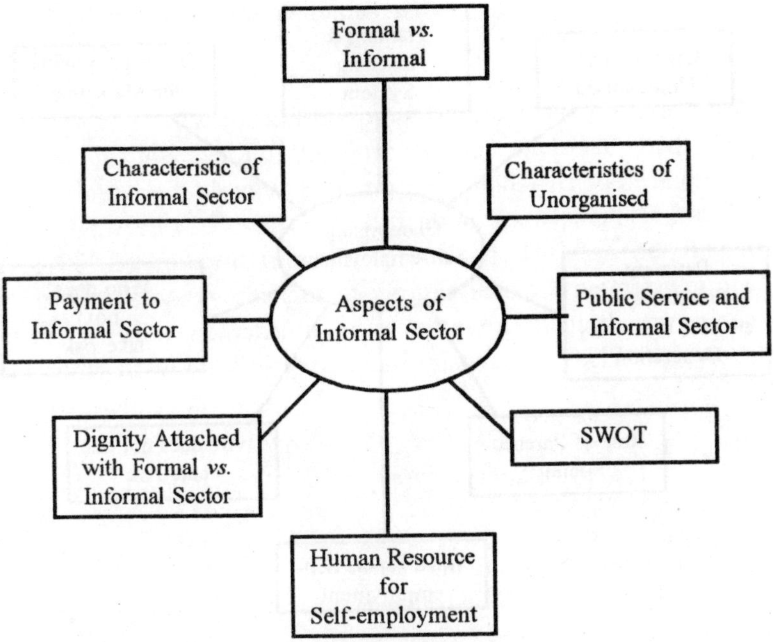

CHART 9.32

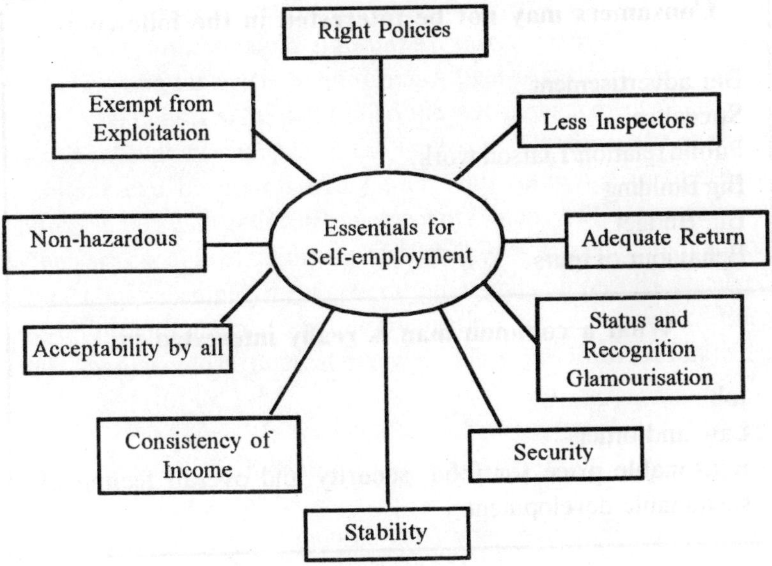

CHART 9.33

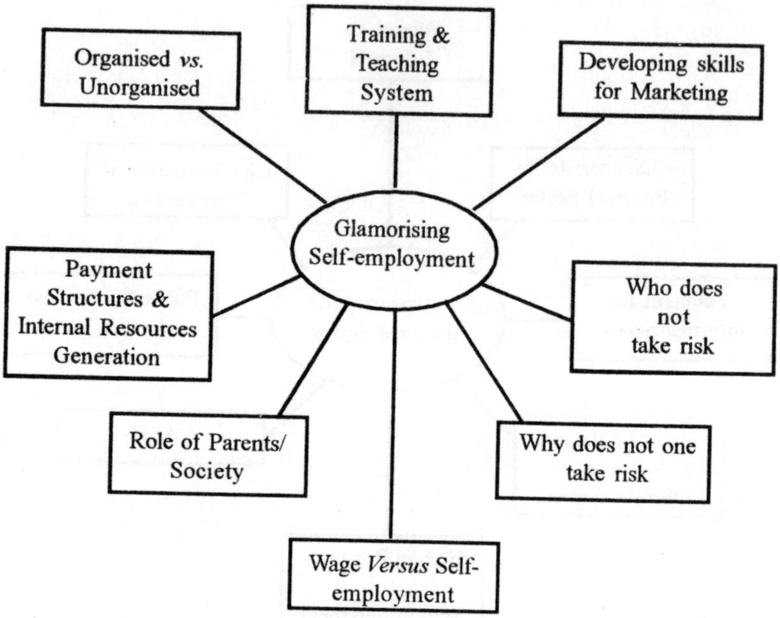

CHART 9.34

Consumers may not be interested in the following:

Big advertisement
Speeches
Public relation/Liaison work
Big Building
Big Budget
Behaviour of units

What a common man is really interested in:

Job
Law and order
Reasonable price for food, security and overall feeling of sustainable development

CHART 9.35

From Consumer's Point of View Efficiency Indicators of Central Government

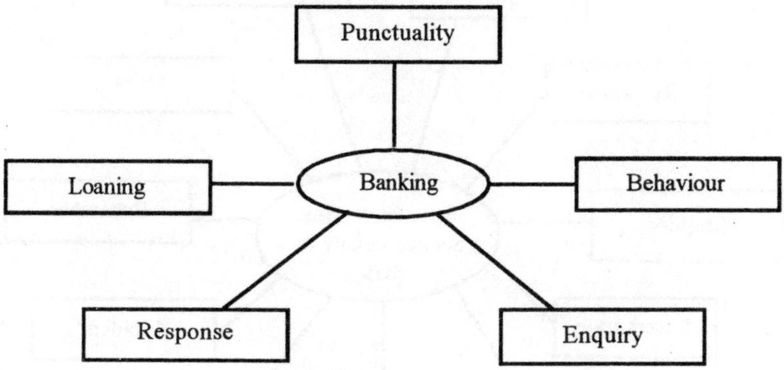

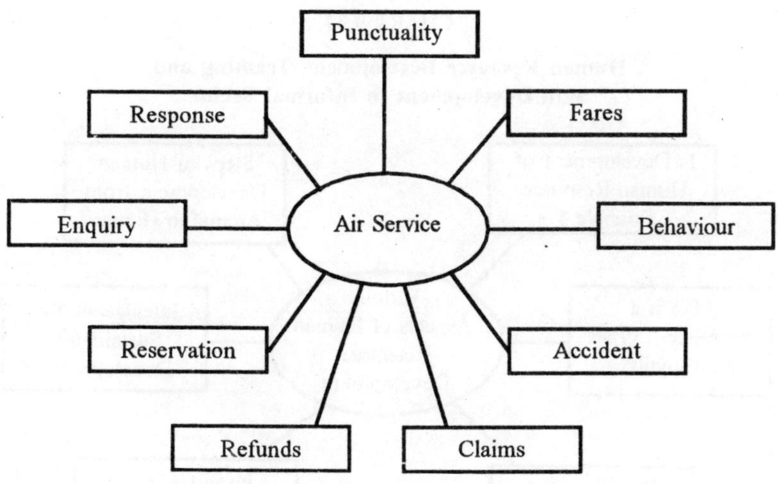

CHART 9.36

From Consumer's Point of View Efficiency Indicators of Central Government

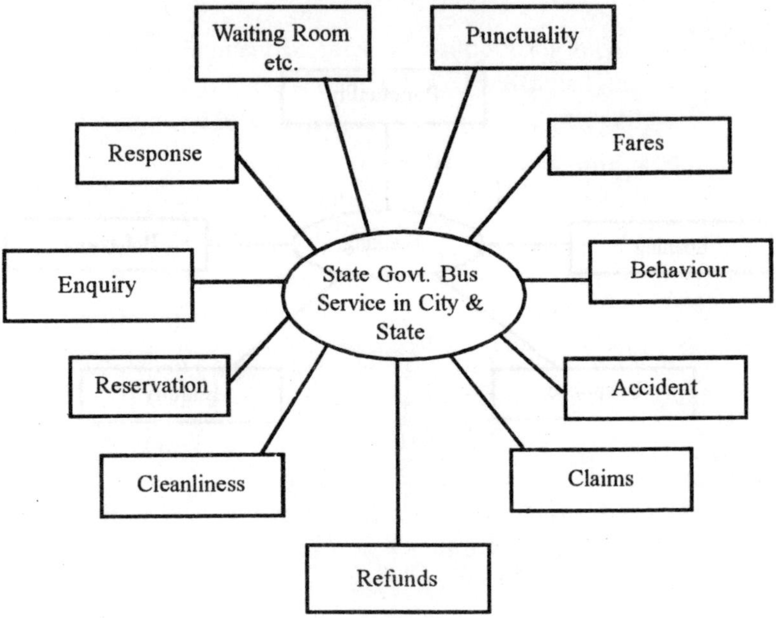

CHART 9.37

Human Resource Development, Training and Skill Development in Informal Sector

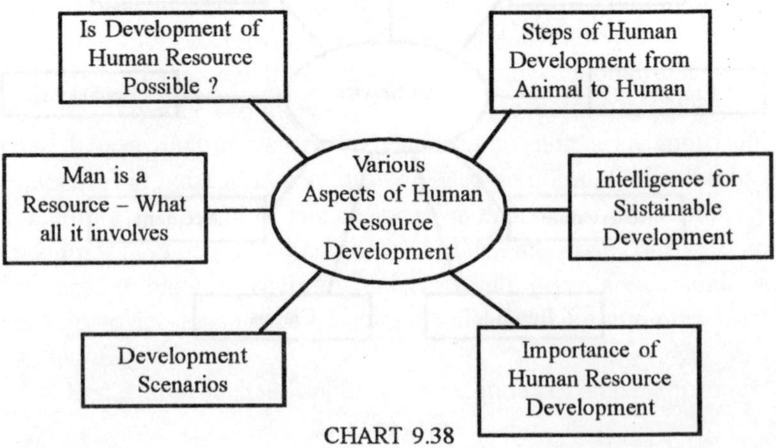

CHART 9.38

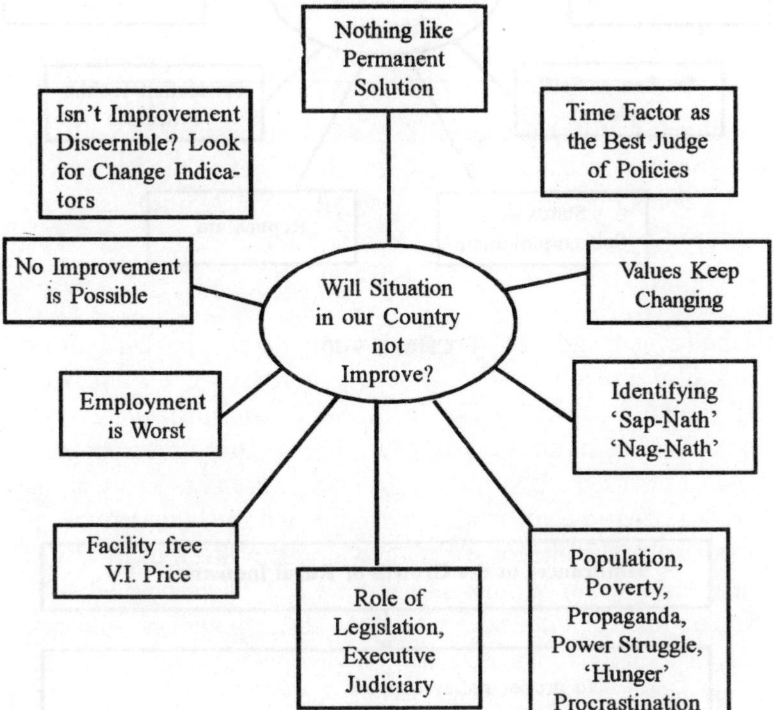
Nothing like Permanent Solution
Isn't Improvement Discernible? Look for Change Indicators
Time Factor as the Best Judge of Policies
No Improvement is Possible
Will Situation in our Country not Improve?
Values Keep Changing
Employment is Worst
Identifying 'Sap-Nath' 'Nag-Nath'
Facility free V.I. Price
Role of Legislation, Executive Judiciary
Population, Poverty, Propaganda, Power Struggle, 'Hunger' Procrastination

CHART 9.39

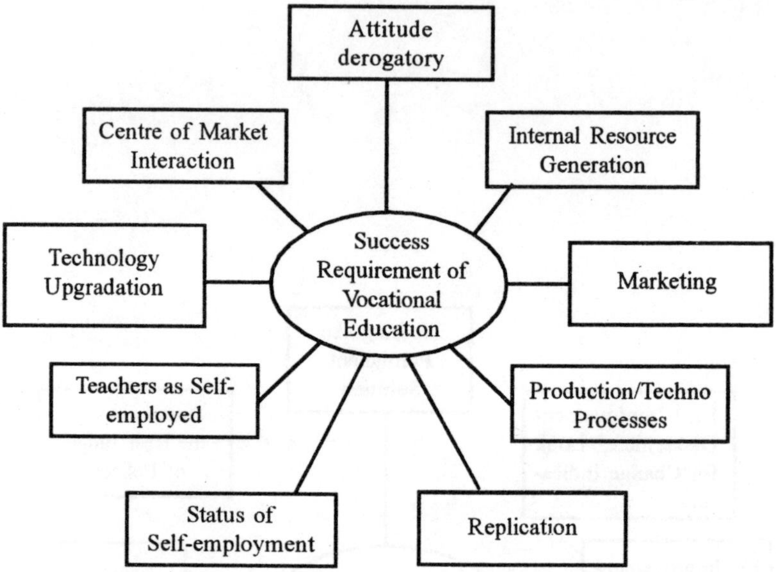

CHART 9.40

Hindrances in the Growth of Rural Industries

1. No proper policy support.
2. Inadequate and irregular supply of raw materials.
3. Lack of organised marketing channels.
4. Imperfect knowledge of market conditions.
5. Lack of effective coordination.
6. Absence of quality products.

CHART 9.41

Marketing concept is very wide and encompasses:

- Consumer orientation and satisfaction
- Study in what is good for the society
- Concept of skill
- Ideas
- Advantages of a product
- Technology
- Even problems related to a product.

Benefits of well-organised Marketing System (MIS)

- Marketing planning through reliable information on external business environment and internal company realities as well.
- Effective tapping of marketing opportunities and effective defence against marketing threats.
- Spotting trends and facilities for formulating assumptions concerning basis of economic and business conditions.
- Facilitating evolvement of action programmes for achieving set goals.
- Helping adjustment of products and services to the needs and taste of consumers.
- Provision of market intelligence
- Control of marketing activities.
- Improving quality of marketing decisions.

CHART 9.42

Present Status of Government Organisation

- High Cost, Low Impact
- Restricting governmental budgetary allocation or institutional funds to organisation results in collapse of the organisation because there are no internal resources and absence of cost effectiveness.
- Lack of marketing as a concept.
- Over obsession with budget utilisation resulting in general degradation of all that make the society alive.

CHART 9.43

Services of Marketing Organisation

- Leadership and motivational aspect to those involved in overall development of rural sector.

Resulting in:

Effectiveness in:

- Product strategy
- Cost reduction
- Integrated publicity on various costs
- Maximising overall development

Marketing Convictions Attitude

It is a result of:	And result of finding:
– Exposure	– Cost effectiveness
– Training	– Acceptability to masses
– Education	– Relevance to national needs and priorities
– Observation	– Ways and means of effective
	– Communication with
	(a) Producer and Processor

CHART 9.44

NEED OF MARKET-ORIENTED DEVELOPMENT (NOMOD)

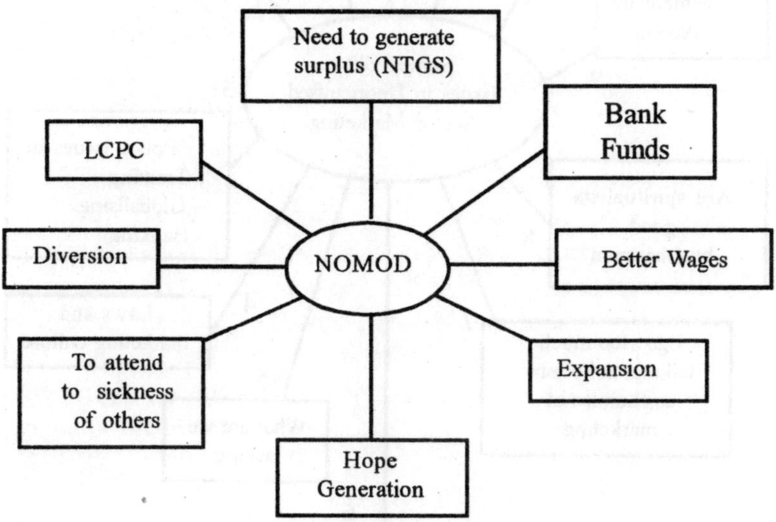

CHART 9.45

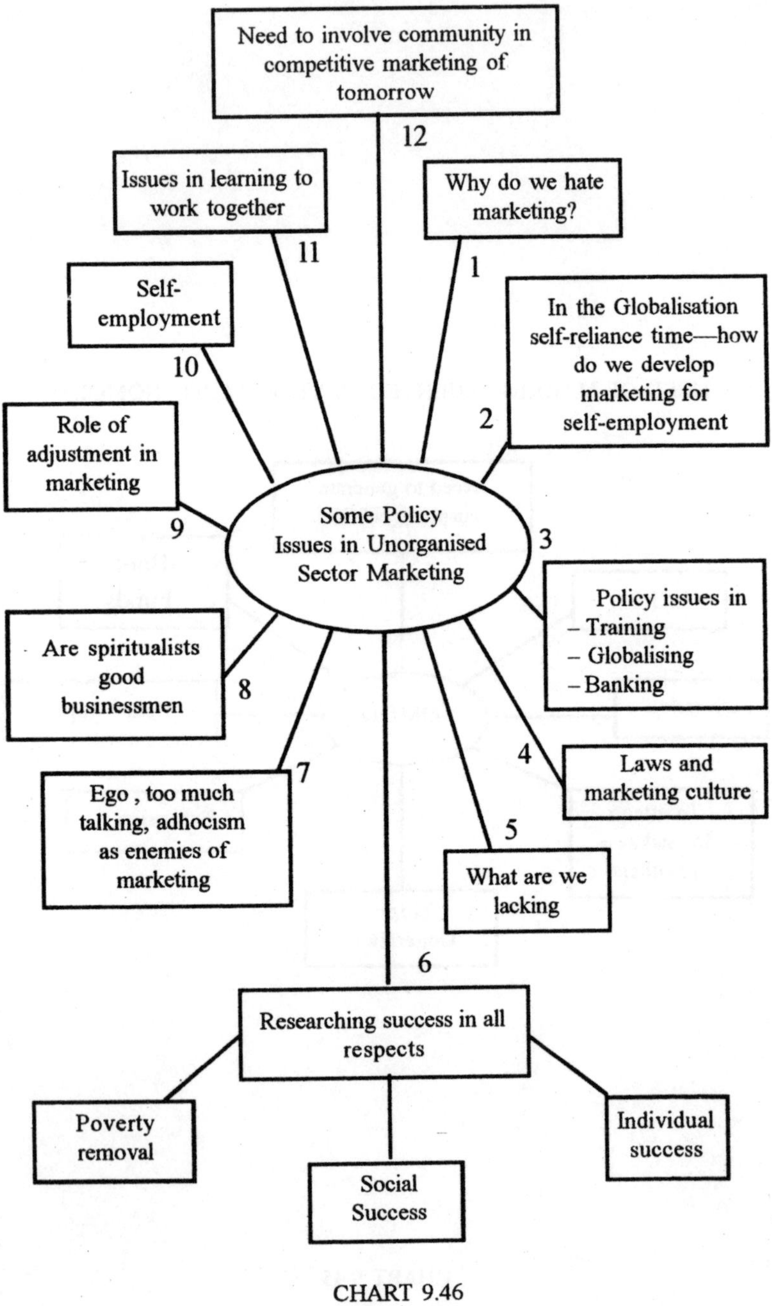
Need to involve community in competitive marketing of tomorrow
12
Issues in learning to work together
11
Why do we hate marketing?
1
Self-employment
10
In the Globalisation self-reliance time—how do we develop marketing for self-employment
2
Role of adjustment in marketing
9
Some Policy Issues in Unorganised Sector Marketing
3
Policy issues in
– Training
– Globalising
– Banking
Are spiritualists good businessmen
8
4
Laws and marketing culture
7
Ego , too much talking, adhocism as enemies of marketing
5
What are we lacking
6
Researching success in all respects
Poverty removal
Social Success
Individual success

CHART 9.46

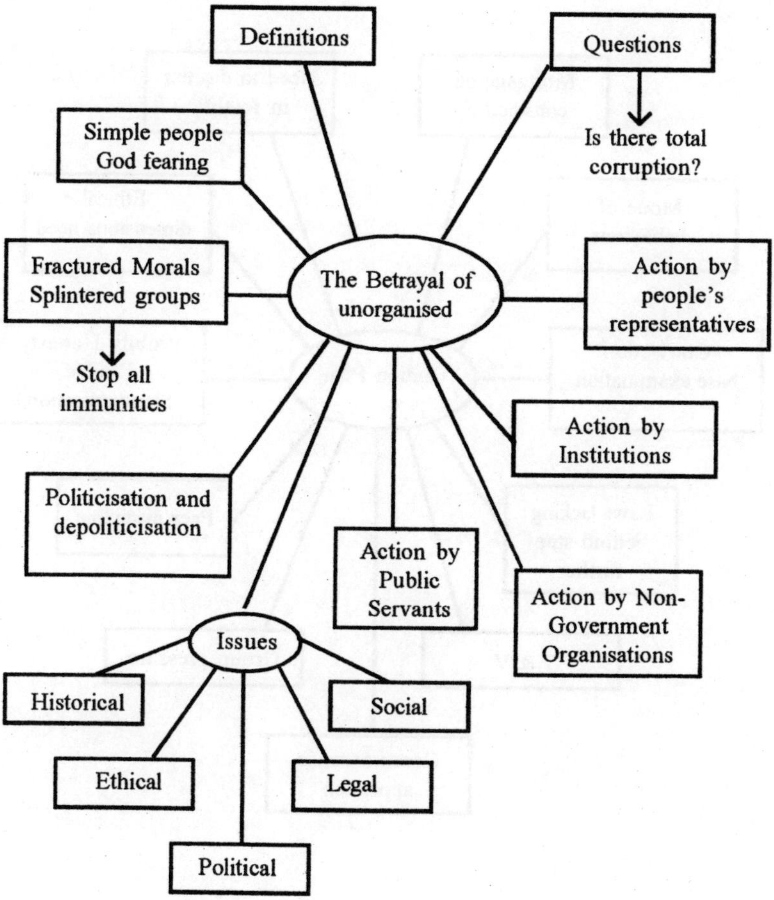
Definitions
Questions
Is there total corruption?
Simple people God fearing
Fractured Morals Splintered groups
Stop all immunities
The Betrayal of unorganised
Action by people's representatives
Action by Institutions
Politicisation and depoliticisation
Action by Public Servants
Action by Non-Government Organisations
Issues
Historical
Social
Ethical
Legal
Political

CHART 9.47

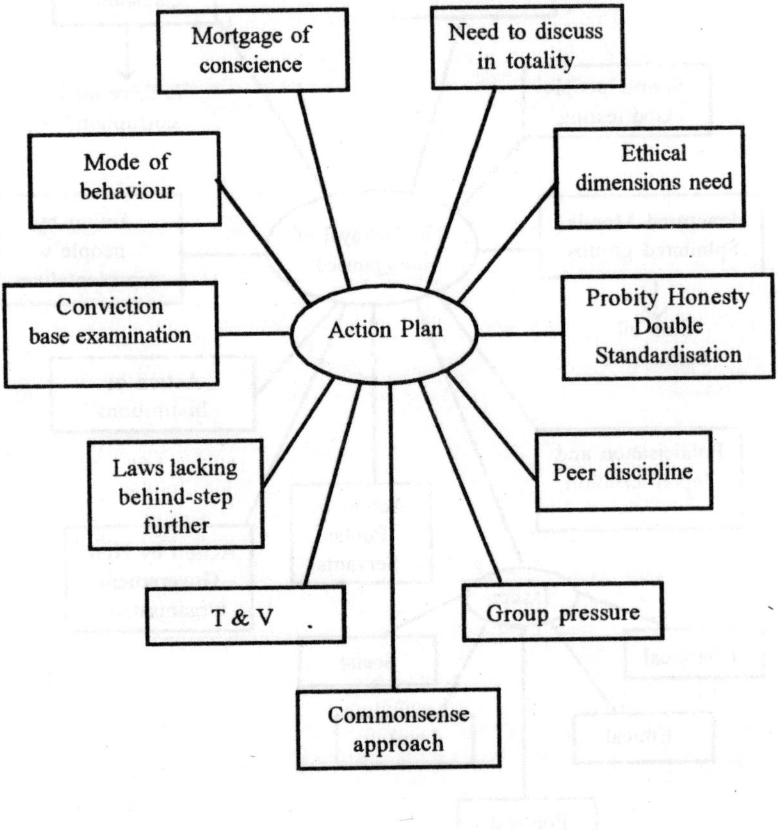
Mortgage of conscience
Need to discuss in totality
Mode of behaviour
Ethical dimensions need
Conviction base examination
Action Plan
Probity Honesty Double Standardisation
Laws lacking behind-step further
Peer discipline
T & V
Group pressure
Commonsense approach

CHART 9.48

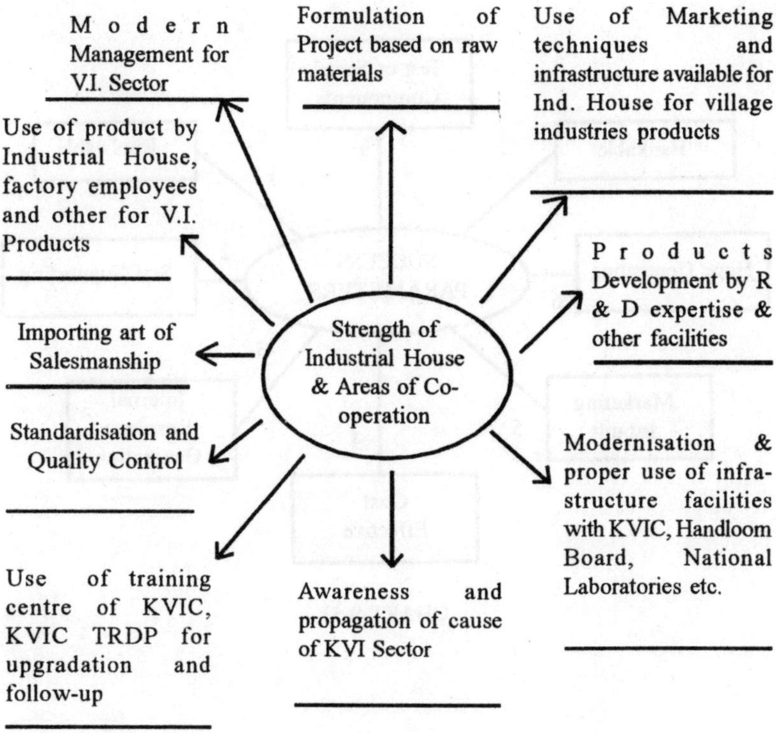

CHART 9.49

Areas of Concern
Risk Factors

1. Non-cooperation
2. Dropouts
3. Market Risks
4. Funds Availability
5. Quality Products
6. Transfers
7. Local Panchayat's Support
8. Channel of Funding

CHART 9.50

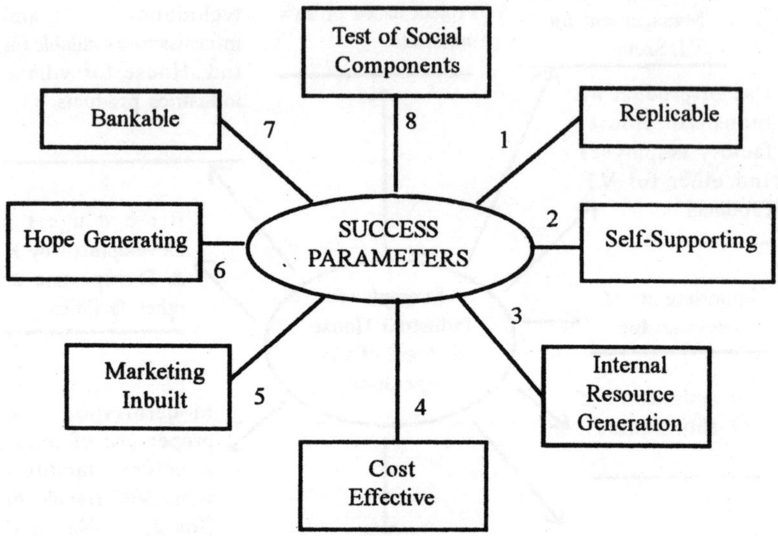

CHART 9.51

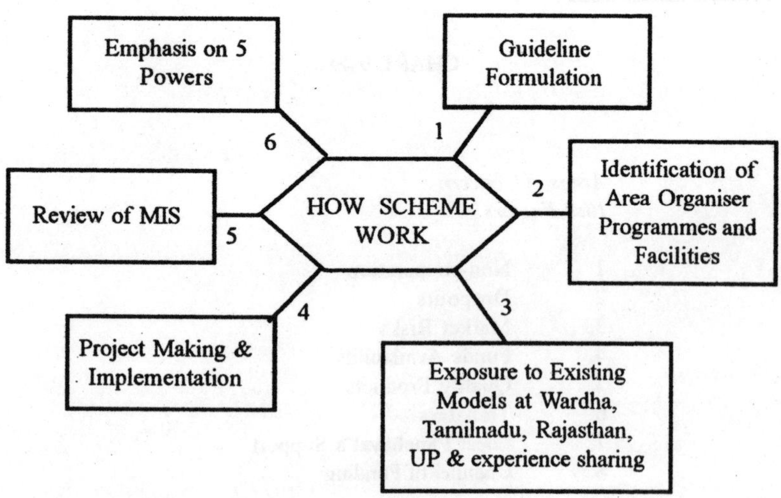

CHART 9.52

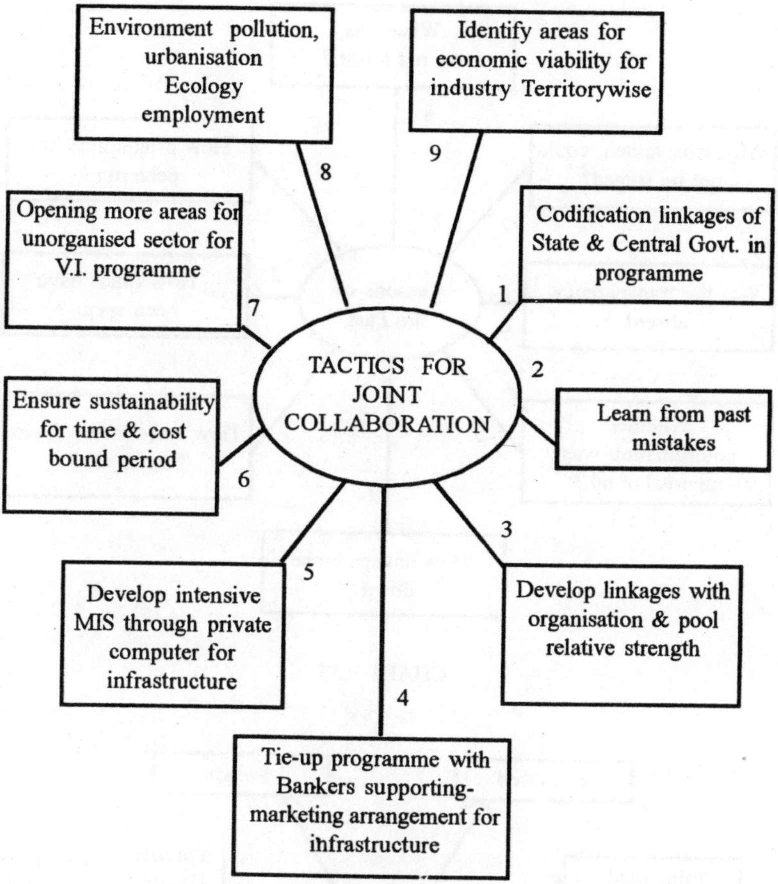

CHART 9.53

ACTION PLAN

1. Identify potential Entrepreneurs.
2. Identify SWOT.
3. Involve Bankers.
4. Involve bureaucrats, bankers planners and project implementer.
5. Codify past efforts with lessons.
6. Identify implementable short-term Action Plan.
7. Develop monitoring, follow-up mechanism.
8. Involve State Government and Panchayati Raj institutions.

CHART 9.54

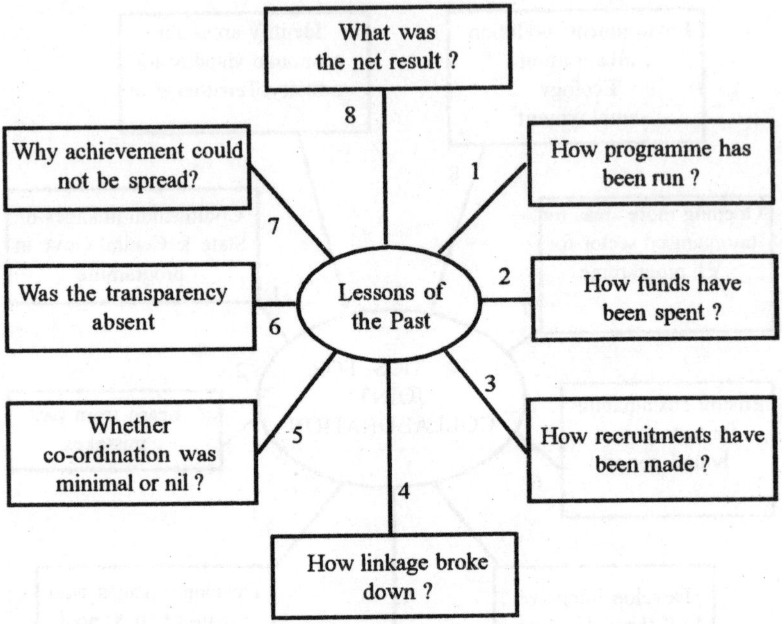

CHART 9.55

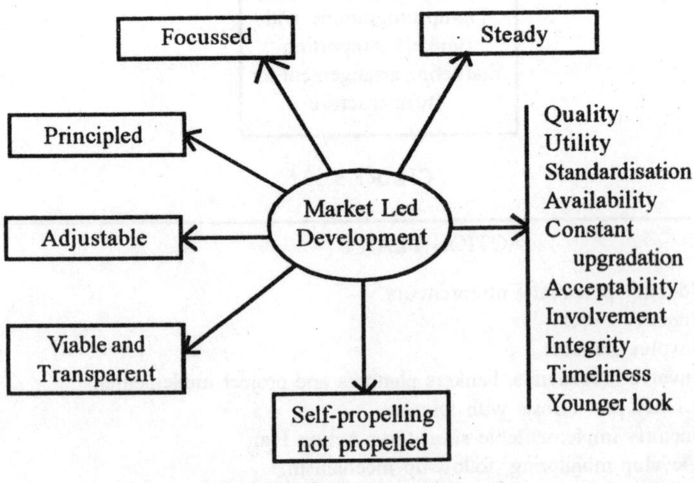

CHART 9.56

COMMON TACTICS

1. Give one lead agency a focussed area.
2. Involve as many agencies, people and stake holders.
3. Clarify issues in agriculture + rural development + rural I.S.B. + holistic self-supportary model building.
4. Thrust on women & other socially neglected but on enpowerment.
5. Bankability, viability, transparency, replicability & models.
6. Short-term objectives, Long-term objectives.
7. MIS coordination systems.
8. Periodical outputs.
9. Involve volunteers as "Peace Wagers" through confidence building and marketing approach.

CHART 9.57

WHAT TO DO?

1. Short-term Measures
2. Long-term Measures

Short-term Measures:

Objectives–Immediate results
Immediate results with maximisation of utilisation of existing infrastructure, manpower, investments made on replicable, self-supporting basis, i.e. involve technology, women force, economic principles, spirituality and faith

Long-term Measures:

Objectives–Will need attention to

a. Finance and administration
b. Academic
c. Marketing
d. Monitoring
e. Overall attitudinal change of functionaries for self-supporting programme development.

CHART 9.58

AREAS OF COOPERATION WITH OTHER DEPARTMENTS

Human Resources Development
Rural Development
Non-conventional Energy
Fruit Processing and Preservation
Health
Education
Export Promotion
Food Processing
Science & Technology
Agriculture
Leather Development Board
Training

CHART 9.59

INTERNAL RESOURCE GENERATION BY

a. Market approach
b. Pooling of Resources
c. Better servicing systems
d. Attitude changes
e. Proper appreciation:
   i. Immediately bankable
   ii. Gradually bankable
   iii. Requiring some incentives
   iv. Better systems for confidence building

CHART 9.60

MARKETING POTENTIALS OF UTTAR PRADESH

i. Tourism related
ii. Agri-business related
iii. Horticulture, Forest related
iv. Food and Fruit Processing related
v. Education, Training, Skill Upgradation related
vi. Organic Manure and Bio-gas Clusters related
vii. Co-operative and Bank Sector related.
viii. Computer and Transport related
ix. Infrastructure related

CHART 9.61

PLAN OF ACTION OR WHAT NEEDS TO BE DONE

Sharing of experience

Improving available models– Critical inputs

Identifying area specific plan of action

Locating priorities for employment generation and overall sustainable development

Monitoring systems

Need for concurrent evaluation

Identifying thrust with market orientation approach

Utilising available infrastructure resources, investments to quickly develop monitorable, replicable models of development

CHART 9.62

ESSENTIALS FOR SUCCESS OF THE PROGRAMME

1. Adequate reports to all
2. Bankability of the project
3. Linkage/tie-up
4. Regular research
5. Dissemination of all information including marketing potential, etc.

CHART 9.63

WHAT SHOULD BE EXAMINED?

a. Transparency
b. Viability
c. Marketing Approach
d. Environment friendly development process.
e. Fairness and win-win situation for all
f. Replicable model for development.

CHART 9.64

INCOME GENERATING OPPORTUNITY THROUGH RURAL ENTERPRISE

- Understanding rural development
- Critical issues in rural development
- Historical development for R.D.
- Ongoing Programmes of R.D.
- Target group on R.D.
  - (a) Direct
  - (b) Indirect
- Ruralites of our time
- SWOT of ruralite
- Problem of viability in R.D.
- Types of Programme for R.D.

CHART 9.65

A Note for Marketing Corporate Sector in Rural Development

1. What is the Corporate Sector?
2. What are its Strengths, Weaknesses, Opportunities and Threats?
3. What are the challenges of economic liberalisation, their relationship with Rural Development Programmes and how there is need to differ from charity to some commercial to full commercial gradual change?
4. What are the issues in Rural Development and who are the role players?
5. How do we define the success in Rural Development Programme?
6. What are the gradually emerging issues in the Rural Development and how Corporate Sector can influence the following:

   i. Policy issues at various levels
   ii. Financing Issues
   iii. Marketing Issues
   iv. Enterprise Development issues
   v. Science and Technology issues
   vi. Self-employment issues
   vii. Panchayati Raj or self-governance linked sustainable development issues.
   viii. Holistic Development and Rural Development.
   ix. Lessons of implementing this programme in the last 4 decades and need for innovative bold approaches.
   x. Action Plan to ensure:
      a Corporate Sector plays its judicious legitimate role without getting involved too much in charities.
      b Identifying selected areas and programme.
      c Catalyst role – prioritisation – tactic for competitive area identification–developing on the whole

bankable project with a fair amount of transparency to utilise local resort without too much dependence on outside agencies.

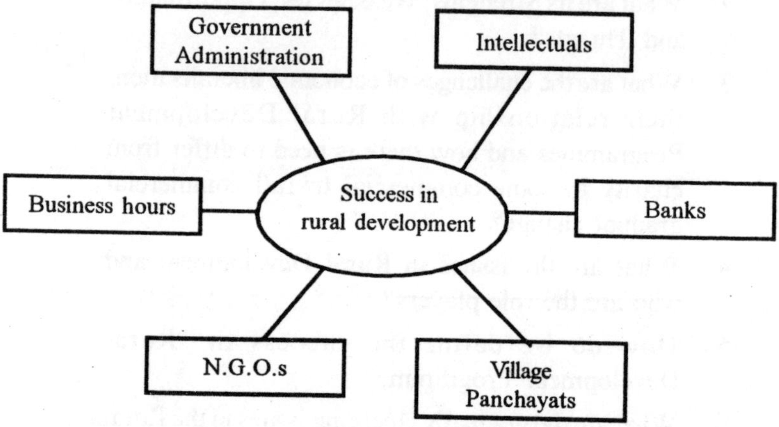

CHART 9.66

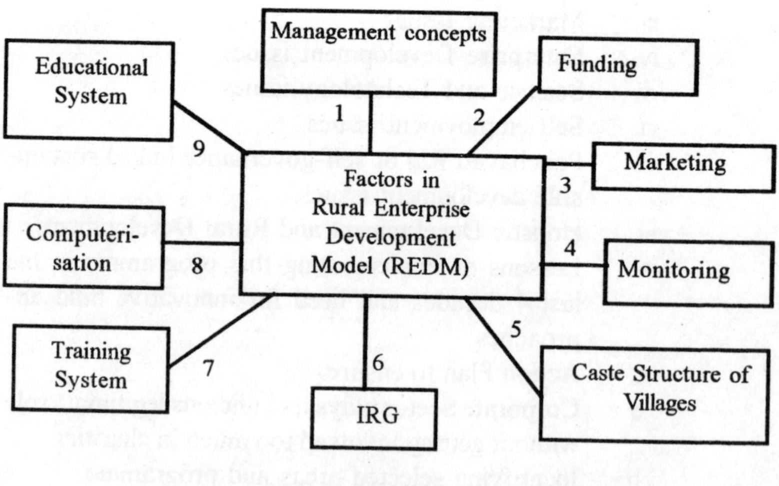

CHART 9.67

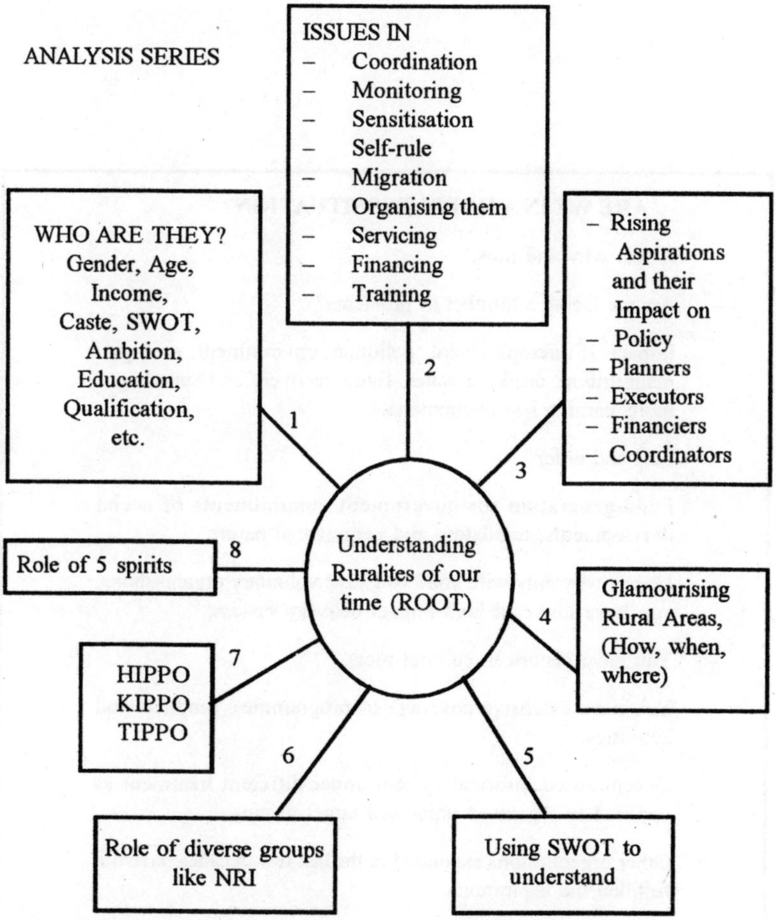

HIPPO – Hidden Investible Potential Power Organisations.
KIPPO – Known Investible Potential Power Organisations.
TIPPO – Threatening Investible Potential Power Organisations.

CHART 9.68

ARE WE IN A HOPELESS SITUATION?

- If yes, why and how?
- Are we facing a number of problems?
- Impact of unemployment, pollution, environment, ecology, malnutrition, drinking water, funds recovery and spending more, earning less phenomena.
- Law and order.
- Fund-generation for government commitments of social developments, regulatory and commercial nature.
- Hope - why only with you? you have voluntary organisations, you have low-cost high-impact delivery system.
- You have historical, cultural roots.
- You have extensive coverage of programmes, products and activities.
- Decentralised informal system under different treatment as opposed to organised unionised target groups.
- Other organisations expanded in the last few decades have not fulfilled the aspirations.
- African development model brings out you are the hope.
- Your neglect proves your importance and added attention.

CHART 9.69

LINKAGES REQUIRED

DEPARTMENTS	FOR WHAT
(1) Rural Development Department	Training, infrastructure, loan, marketing, confidence development (CD).
(2) Forest Department	Saplings, nursery, leaves, openness.
(3) Central Silk Board	Saplings, monitoring, DFLS.
(4) KVIC	Marketing quality, training, Purchases, linkages, monitoring, publicity.

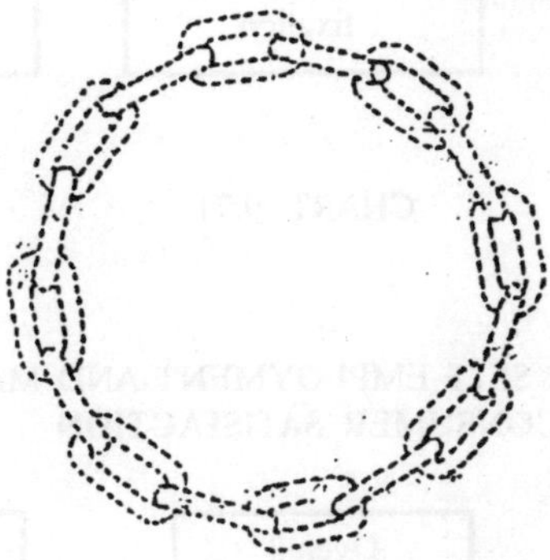

(5) Banks	Funding, Training, publicity.
(6) NABARD, SIDBI	Re-finance, studies, publicity, exposures, monitoring.
(7) NGOs	Actual work, training, marketing, saplings, exposures, exhibitions, linkages.

CHART 9.70

MISSING TACTICS

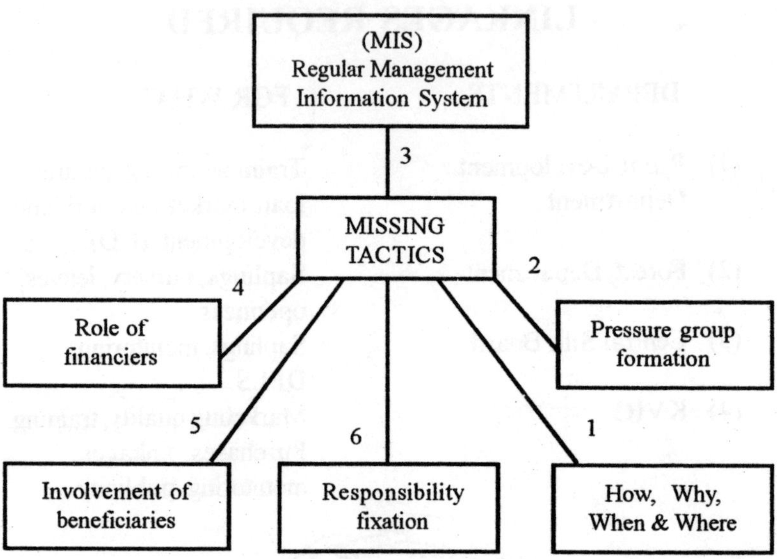

CHART 9.71

SUSTAINABLE SELF-EMPLOYMENT AND MARKETING CONSUMER SATISFACTION

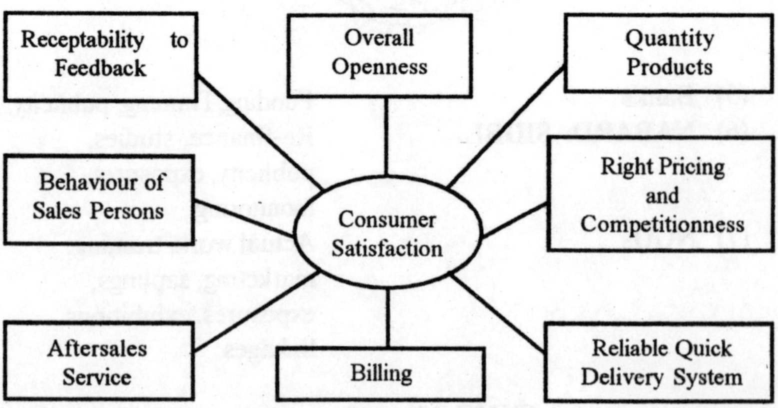

Induced Consumer - by Advertisement
Motivated Consumer - Philosophy internal urge
Captive Consumer - Reserved items, no competition, has to buy, no option
Traditional Consumer - Old friends, human approach

CHART 9.72

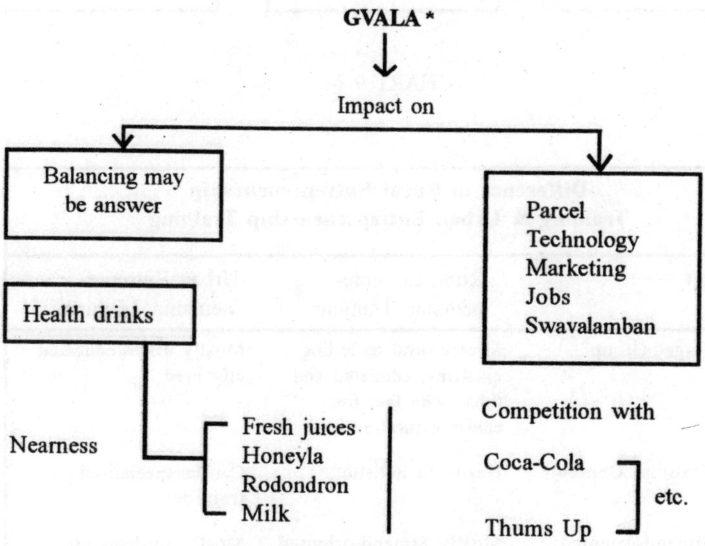

* Global Vision and Local Action

CHART 9.73

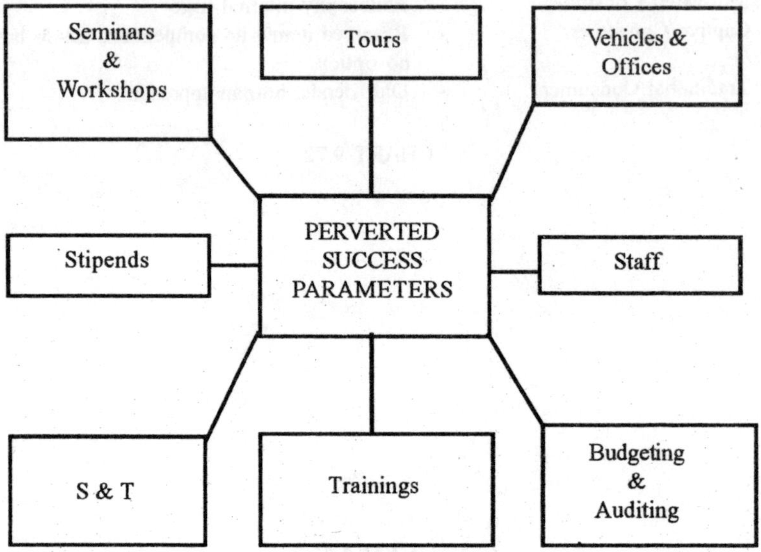

CHART 9.74

Difference in Rural Entrepreneurship Training & Urban Entrepreneurship Training		
Subject	Rural Entrepreneurship Training	Urban Entrepreneurship Training
1. Target Group	Mostly rural including ex-Army, educated and those who feel for cause of rural area.	Mostly urban/educated city bred.
2. Training Contents	Has to be holistic	Can be specialised training.
3. Stipend-oriented training/payment-oriented training (SOT/POT)	Mostly Stipend-oriented need lot of change.	Mostly students are prepared to pay.
4. Location	Must be in rural areas.	Mostly in cities.

Contd.

5.	Background of Training	Has to start from base level	His base level is already much higher.
6.	Language	Must be in local language	Mostly English.
7.	Market-oriented training *versus* production related training (PRT)	Has to be market-oriented training because demand generation would be difficult.	Can be production-oriented because he can generate demand.
8.	Capital-intensive *versus* labour-intensive (CI) or (LI)	Has to be Labour-intensive.	Can be Capital intensive.
9.	Pace of imparting training	Has to be slow.	Its mostly fast.
10.	Intensity of counselling	Has to be much more intense from Training to Production and even Marketing, accounting diversification, etc.	Can be limited since he has many specialised counsellors.
11.	Role of Bankers	Cradle to grave	Limited to financing
12.	Entrepreneur risk-taking capacity	Very limited	Comparatively large since he has many more avenues.
13.	Role of Non-Governmental Organisation	With attitudinal change, NGOs can provide excellent back-up service	Limited role of NGOs.
14.	Coordination required.	Very much	Market force can coordinate.

CHART 9.75

ACTION PLAN

1. Need for multidisciplinary project.
2. Oxygen action : (a) Principles of purity.
   (b) Project and programmes.
   (c) Demand convergence base.
3. Role of grandmother and technology.
4. Inter-connectedness and interdependence.
5. Issues in I to We.
6. Eco-action *versus* Ego-action.
7. Role of Corporate Sector.

CHART 9.76

STRATEGY FOR OPTIMISATION

Look at Limitations (LAL)

A – Money only does not help-rather...?

B – Fruit *vs.* Roots (FVR)

C – MIS

D – Incentives from output (IFO)

E – Team-work (LTWT) learning to work together

F – Host of past sad experiences (HOPSE)

G – Clarity and responsibility (C&R)

H – Cost effectiveness neglected (CEN)

I – Involve women

J – Incentives at every level

K – Openness

CHART 9.77

Policy issues for Non-farm Sector

The principles which should guide the policy development for Un-organized Sector like Non-farm Sector:

I Guiding principles:

1. Need for policy formation and its acceptance as a necessity for fighting the well-entrenched vested interest of the organised
2. This is also important for identifying models for conceptual clarity, replicability, involving beneficiaries, accepting harsh realities and learning lessons from failures
3. Tactical requirement for implementing and monitoring the policies:

- Timely reservation
- Centre for inducing industries rural areas (CFIIRA)
- Identifying strengths, weaknesses, opportunities and threats with reference to territorial peculiarities of rural and urban India
- Linkage development through redefining economies
- Building up openness
- Sensitisation of all those who matter
- Taking on the market approach
- Learning for cost effectiveness

CHART 9.78

Sustainability of Development and Non-farm Sector for a country like ours

1. Sustainable development concept
2. Emerging horizon
3. Learning from codified mistakes and revisiting successes
4. Cost effectiveness
5. Sensitisation and gender issues implication
6. Role of State organised in regulatory, developmental and commercial activities and generation and stabilisation of vested interest
7. Government as governor—implications thereof
8. If ultimate aim is happiness, can only materialistic growth fulfil it? Hence redefining impacts of :
   (i) Animal stage
   (ii) Discrete animal stage
   (iii) Enlightened animal stage

And learning their implications and stages of growth with reference to historical knowledge available today.

CHART 9.79

Reactivating the Target Group of Non-farm Sector for Policy Issues

1. Can programmes be bifurcated as per target group, for example, women, disabled, old people, ex-army people, educated unemployed and bifurcation on criteria like income, class, health, programmes
2. How privatisation or cost effectiveness can help the entrepreneurship development for optimising efficiency of non-farm sector?
3. Problems of coordination
4. Infrastructure like unutilised both in city and non-city areas
5. Local resources both of men, material, surplus funds, machines, forms
6. Identifying irritants in non-farm sector growth

- Various types of taxes
- Various regulatory authorities represented by inspectors
- Electricity problems
- Quality test problem
- Communication problem and other infrastructural problems including law and order and transport .

CHART 9.80

ROLE OF BUREAUCRATS

1. Is he sensitised to serve the target group in question?
2. His role is as–

   Planner

   Monitor

   Motivator

   Finance Provider

   Problem Solver

   Market Developer

   Codifier

   Overall Propagator and Sympathiser

CHART 9.81

AREAS OF CAUTION FOR POLICY PLANNING

1. Characteristics of organised *vs.* unorganised and organising un-organised
2. City *vs.* non-city—SWOT analysis
3. Literate *vs.* illiterate and traditions
4. Role of pressure groups

5. Impacts of frustrated society
6. Completion of vocation
7. Stipend-oriented system (SOS)
8. Parameters of evaluating effciency (POEE)
9. Role of NGOs and voluntary associations in sustainable employment generation
10. Glamourisation of life-styles or values of system
11. Marketing approach impacts

- Critical Issues—Some unknown essentials (with special reference to actual situations)
- Data Base
- Hope signals
- SAS (Sensitising Administrators for Success)
- Bankability—pricing—market structures
- Glamourisation
- Bank Finance linkages
- Low Cost High Cost
- Co-ordination and MIS
- ARCS (Action, Research, Codification Scheme)
- Attitudes and work culture
- POMPTEC (Production, organisation, Marketing Processing, Training Extension Consultancy)
- IRG and Grant *vs.* Loan (GVL)
- Learning from past historical lessons or revisiting successes
- Pooling of resources
- Common problems–corruption, percolation, fruits *vs.* roots
- Big *vs.* small–emphasis on building, staff, vehicle, petrol, tours, jobs
- LCPC (Low Cost Practical Consultancy)
- VAPC (Value Added Product Concept)
- Role of spiritual organisation
- Organised non-organised
- Privatisation/cost effective/replicable
- Human Resources
- Infrastructure resources
- Pooling
- Market approach
- Spiritual Dimensions of Development (SDD) or holistic development or sustainable development
- Role of policies (ROP)
- Effective technology *vs.* appropriate technology
- Rural entrepreneurship
- Area approach/scale
- Skill and technology upgradation as opposed to "scaling down"

CHART 9.82

Cluster Approach for Development

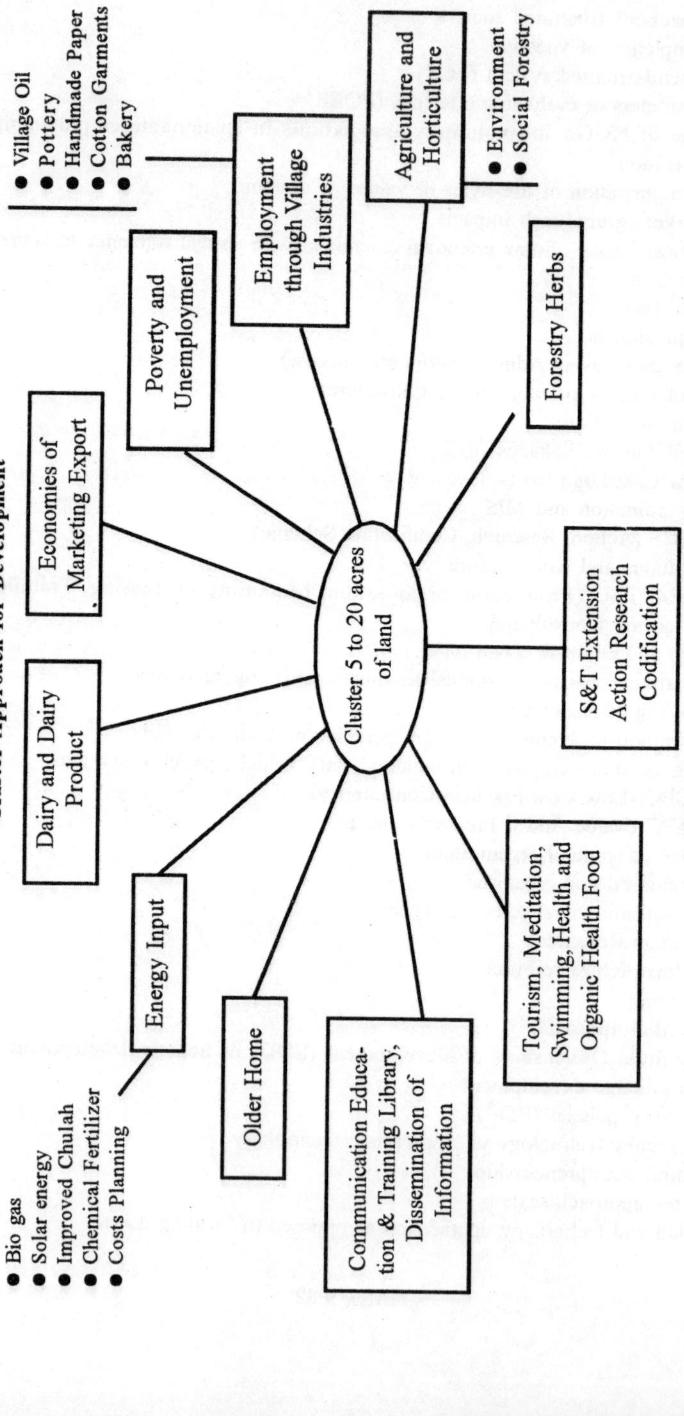

Self-supporting integrated Rural Development
"Have Fruits – Not Roots"
CHART 9.83

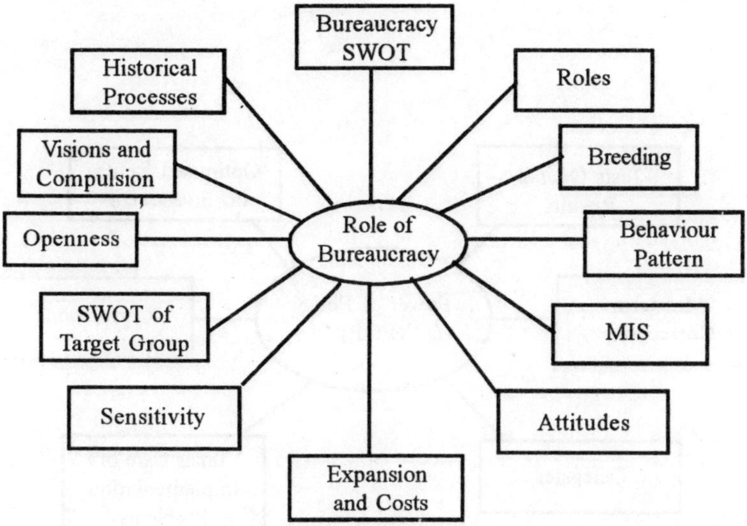

CHART 9.84

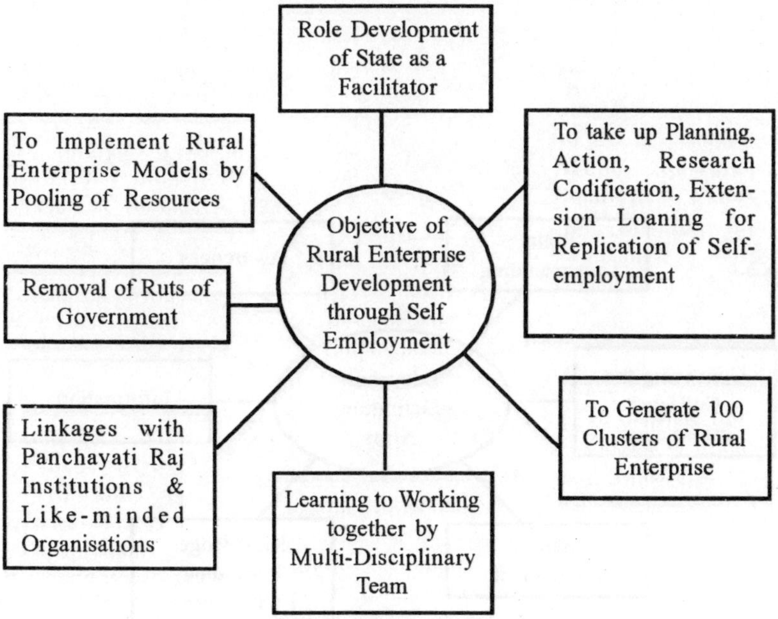

CHART 9.85

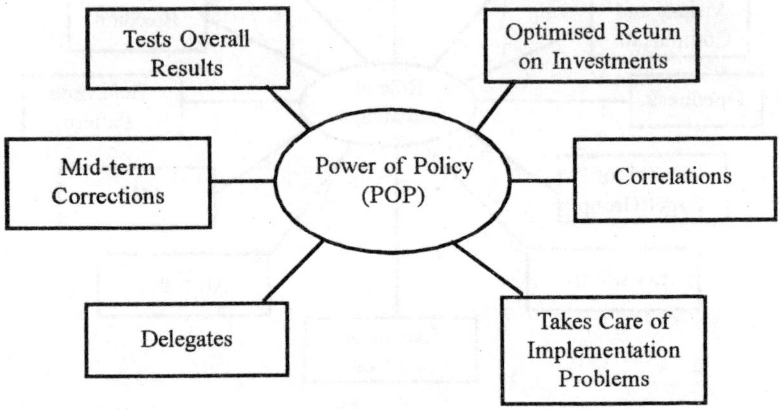

CHART 9.86

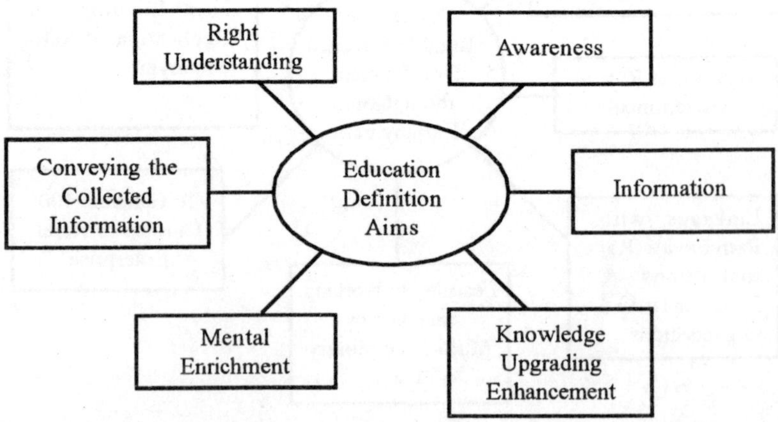

CHART 9.87

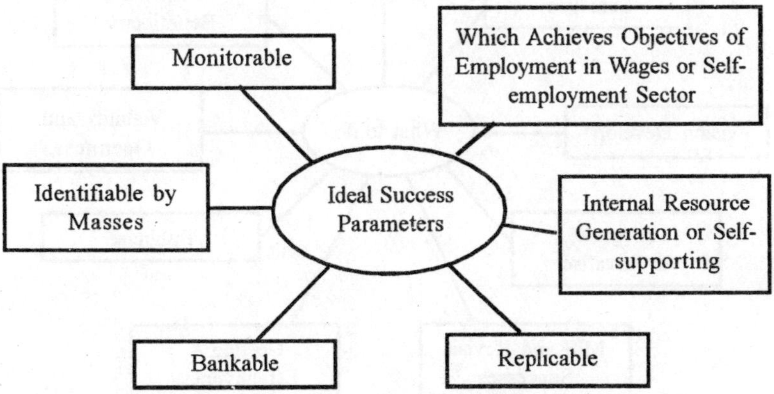

CHART 9.88

What to Do?

- Have an action plan on objectives, methodology, MIS, duties and responsibilities, inputs and outputs, studies and surveys, making the best of mistakes, motivation and HRD, production, marketing, training, publicity and involvement of communication medium and above all the costing to each programme
- Holistic approach
- Linkage with machine and philosophy
- Time is in your favour, cash it
- Be professional
- Integrate with education, economics, history, religion, military science and learn from scriptures with open mind
- Show results quantifiable in pre-determined success indicators

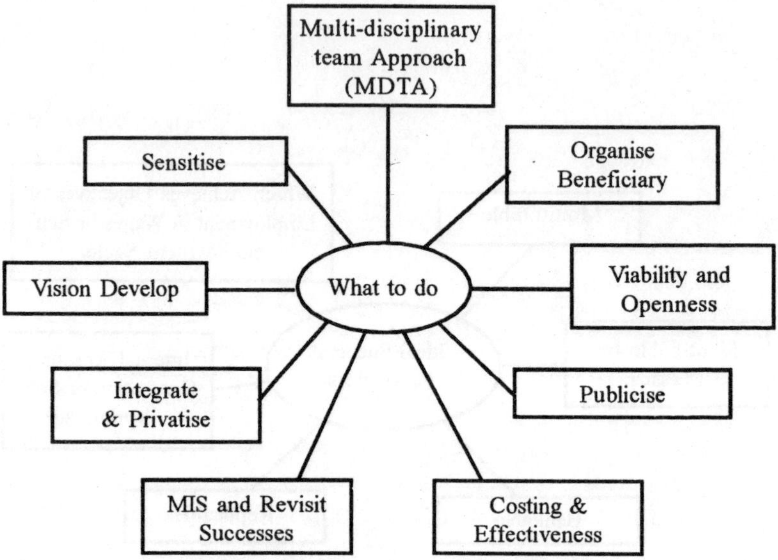

CHART 9.89

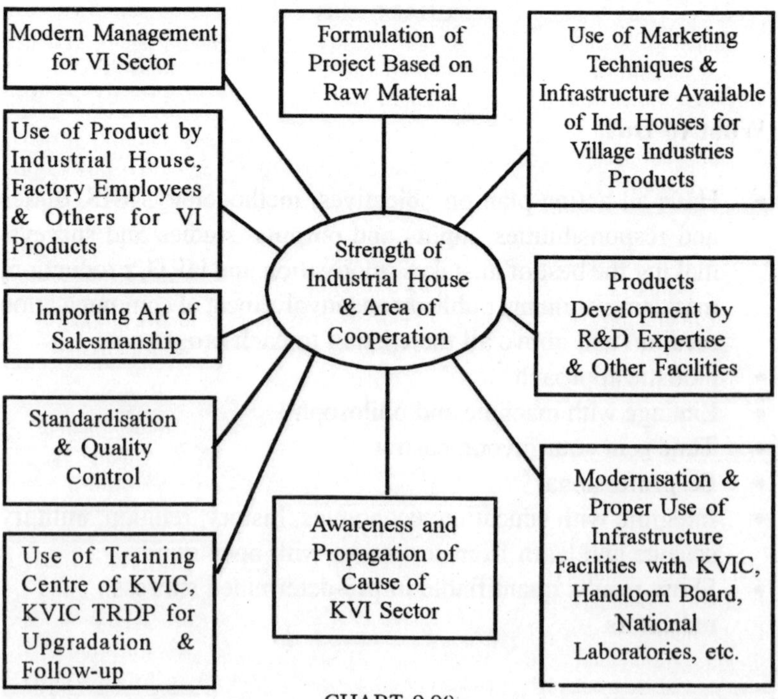

CHART 9.90

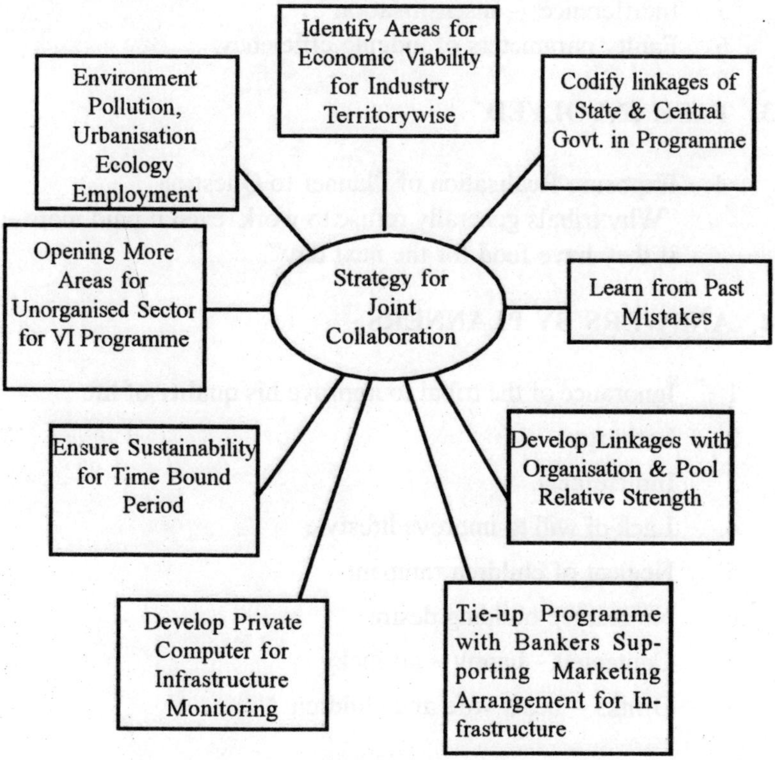

CHART 9.91

1. PROBLEM SITUATION

"Insensitivity of extension workers and planners to Tribal Problems".

2. BACKGROUND TO PROBLEM

1. The unorganised have always suffered if they can't market their products—aspirations
2. Gaps in perception
3. Wrong mindset
4. Communication gaps

5. Indifference – insensitisation
6. Faulty parameters of judging efficiency.

3. TASK INVOLVED

1. Exposure Realisation of Planner to Question
   "Why tribals generally refuse to work even if paid more – if they have food for the next day".

4. ANSWERS BY PLANNERS

1. Ignorance of the tribal to improve his quality of life
2. Lethargy
3. Indifference
4. Lack of will to improve lifestyle
5. Neglect of children rampant
6. No reserve building desire
7. Contented – happy – go-lucky
8. Drinks – beats wife and children

5. TASK II – APPRECIATING TRIBAL

When asked same question the Tribals' reply was:

We don't work because whenever we have food for next meal – we take compulsory leave – we have to work every day for our meals. We never have any fixed holidays, facilities, perks or social security and so we refuse to work whenever we have food security.

6. TASK III

Understanding implication – Two seemingly conflicting answers to same situation.

Task involved in marketing:

A. Understanding Both
B. Bridging gap
C. Better planning, action, research security programmes– "Planning to better Planning"

7. EXPERIENCE AND ITS ANALYSIS

1. For myself as Kamal Taori – IAS - a well-meaning 33 years experimentator – our perception – our approaches to tribals' attitudes
2. Our ignorance of his priorities
3. Lessons of human history
4. Priorities of planners – topdown appreciation (TDA)
5. Need to bridge gaps

8. DECIDING PRIORITY ISSUES OF TRIBALS

Basic needs
Empowerment issues
Natural laws
Historical lessons
Economic issues
SWOT analysis
Educational issues
Social issues
Political issues
Administrative issues
Work culture
Panchayat Raj issues
PARCEL issues

Action initiated

(a) As secretary-sensitised people
(b) Shared perception
(c) Better plan formulation by delegation and opening up.

9. MAJOR LEARNING FOR FUTURE

1. Need to involve masses
2. Looking from his angle
3. Pampering of government servants
4. Funding and monitoring systems
5. Ego problems
6. Issues in understanding the less understood
7. Respect for traditions
8. Transparency in programmes for unorganised
9. Monitoring and empowerment lessons
10. Overall marketing – business-like approach to servicing
11. Efficiency parameters
12. 'Maturity' in planning.

10. LESSONS FOR BETTER IMPACT OR SUCCESSFUL MARKETING

1. Expose to National Policy Maker
2. Have effective communication system
3. Make case studies
4. Select change models with replicability aspects
5. NGO's role identification.

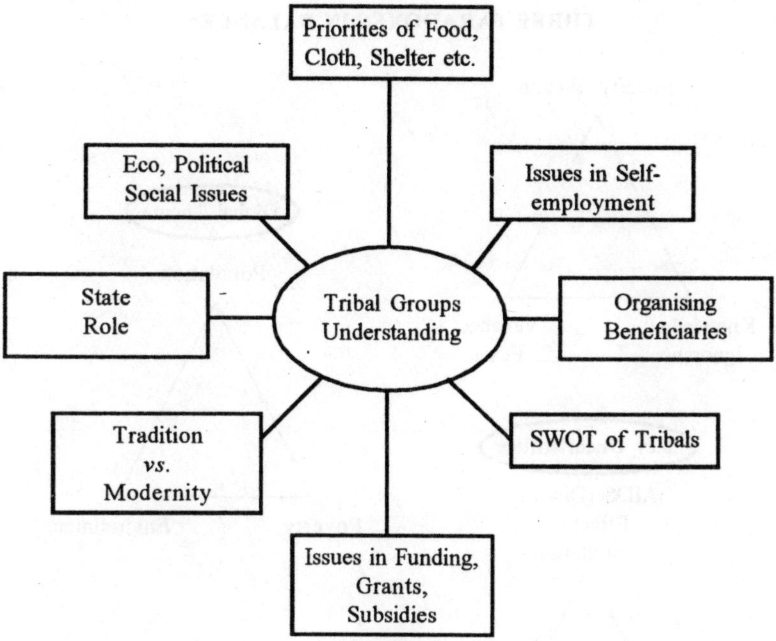

CHART 9.92

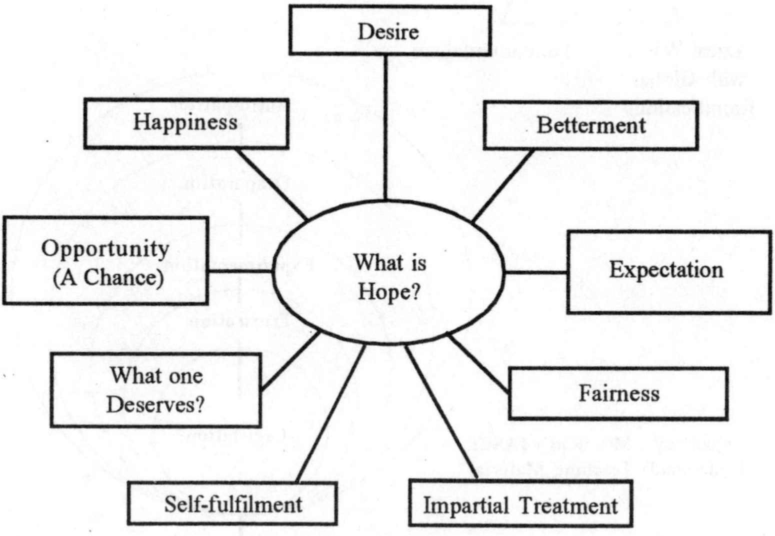

CHART 9.93

THREE PARADOXES IN BALANCE*

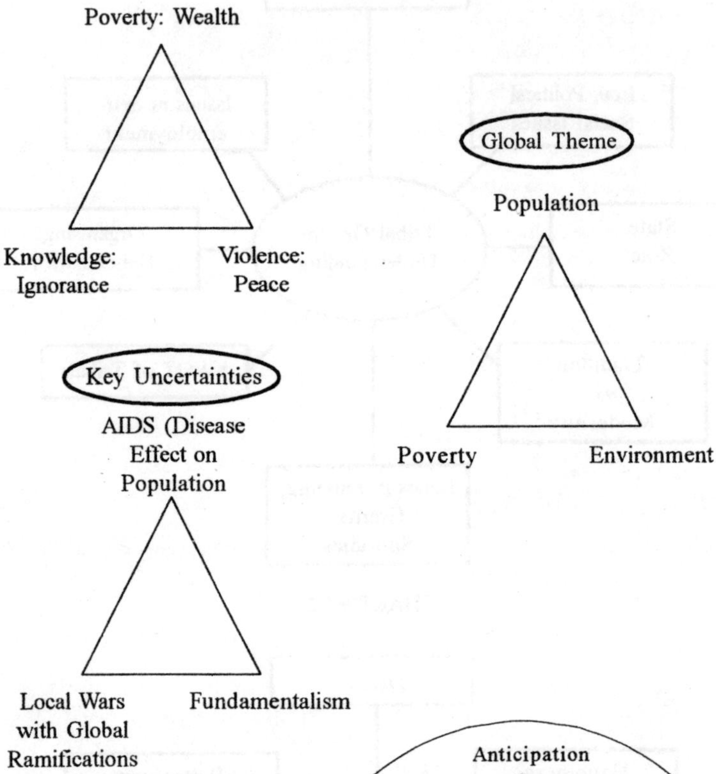

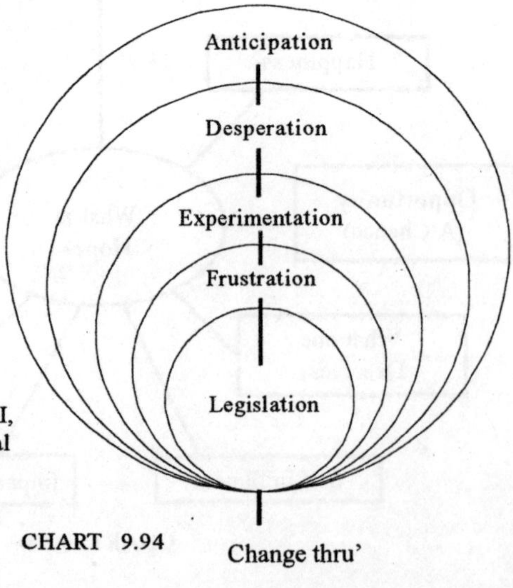

* Courtesy : Mrs. Rao's (ASCI, Hyderabad) Teaching Material

CHART 9.94

MARKETING OF DEVELOPMENT (MOD)

- Development is usually top down
- Planners decide what is good for the masses (because development is largely aid funded)
- Resources have been wasted while poverty persists
- Lack of humility and respect for the ultimate user
- Post facto evaluation of projects often delayed
- Developer never goes bankrupt
- Naive optimism and innocent assurance
- Uniformity

Needs in Developing Countries

- Socio-economic development often inhibited by problems of social change, be it in family planning or agricultural productivity.
- Therefore there is great need to change the attitudes and behaviour of people so that progressive ideas, concepts, and practices are adopted by the people.
- Many facets of rural marketing in India are similar to social marketing.
- Marketing occupies critical role in respect to the development of 'growth' areas. Marketing is the most important multiplier of such development.
- Marketing is the design, organisation and implementation of the economic and social programmes to influence public participation in a nation's development.
- Marketing delivers standard of living.

> *A good is good only if it satisfies a human want. The nature of these wants whether they spring from the stomach or from imagination is irrelevant.*
>
> — **Karl Marx**

Demand State	Marketing Task	Formal Name
No Demand	Create Demand	Stimulational Marketing
Latent Demand	Develop Demand	Development Marketing
Faltering Demand	Revitalize Demand	Remarketing
Full Demand	Maintain Demand	Maintenance Marketing
Overfull Demand	Reduce Demand	Demarketing
Unwholesome Demand	Kill Demand	Social Marketing

DEFINITION

Social Marketing is the design, implementation, and control of programme calculated to increase/influence the acceptability of social ideas and involving considerations of product planning pricing, communication, distribution and marketing research.

Product

Price

Place

Promotion

Political Power

Public Opinion

Marketing Challenge of Social Change Campaigns

- *Cause* : Social object is that change that agents believe will provide a desirable answer to a social problem
- *Change Agent* : Individual/Organisation/Alliance that attempts to bring about social change
- *Target Adopters* : Individuals/Groups/Entire populations

		who are the target of appeals for change by the social marketing
• *Channels*	:	Communication and Distribution pathways through which influence and response are exchanged and transmitted back and forth between change agents and target adopters.
• *Change Strategy*	:	Direction and PGM adopted by a change agent to effect change in target adopters' attitudes and behaviour.

CUSTOMER ORIENTED PHILOSOPHY IN SERVICE DELIVERY

- Defining the service needed by the customer
- Determining a target market and the use of market segmentation
- Taking the service to the customer rather than bringing the customer to the service source
- Emphasizing the concept or idea selling rather than providing just free services.

FOUR STAGES OF SOCIAL CHANGE

- The Crusading Phase
- The Popular Phase
- The Managerial Phase
- The Bureaucratic Phase.

WHY INTERNAL MARKETING

- Many people in the organisation do not understand programme objectives and what they mean
- Consequently, most employees do not see how their jobs have anything to do with participants or their needs.
- Most functions do not really understand the roles of the other functions in the organisation; so they have no basis for cooperation.

- Most have little or no meaningful input into the marketing direction of the organisation. This includes communicators, plan implementers, service supporters, etc.

COMPETITION: RESISTANCE FORCES TO CHANGE

Initial

- A general (emotional) opposition to any change; the inertia of a rigid system
- Rational opposition to the objectives of change
- Actual inability to change–confidence/resources
- Desire to preserve existing privileges/advantages (vested interests)
- Perception of risks—fear of consequences
- Incompatibility of the change agents negative relations.

SOCIAL MARKETING—7 Cs

- Co-ordination
- Cooperation
- Comprehensive
- Continuity
- Communication
- Community participation
- Cost effective.

EMERGENT RESISTANCE

- Reassessment of costs and difficulties (in pursuing the changed programmes)
- Loss of energy and motivation (linked to success, failure, overexposure)
- Sudden turnabout of opinion leaders (availability of resources)
- Emerged competing forces claiming time, involvement of the changed system.

INSTRUMENTS

- Logos
- Catch phrases
- Strong visuals
- Colour codes
- Usage steps

PRODUCT-CONCEPT POSITIONING

Positioning is the process of establishing and maintaining a distinctive place in the minds of the beneficiaries for a product concept.

OUTPUT

Intended Image
Positioning usually implies a segmentation commitment.

TYPES OF POSITIONING

- In relation to a product class / category
- Benefit related
- By usage occasion and time of use
- By non-functional values (great/emotional/important/fear)
- In relation to competing variables
- By price and quality
- Packaging
- By product-user.

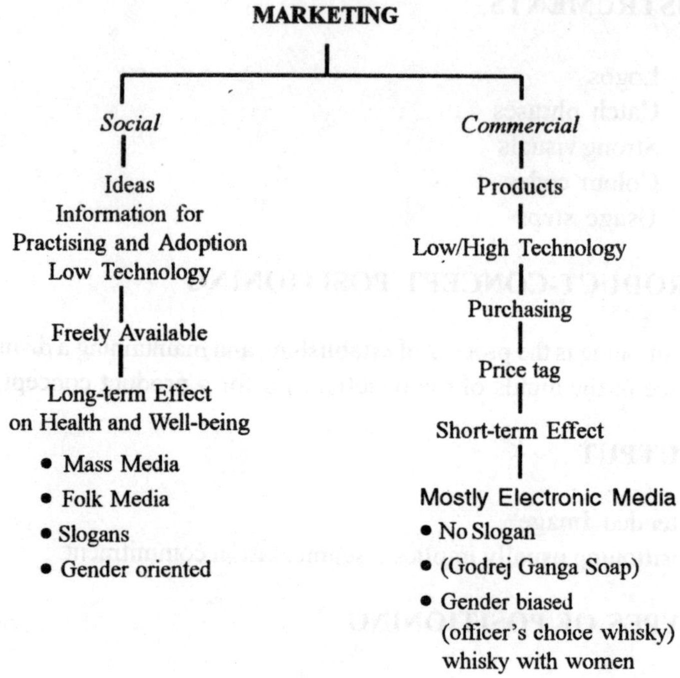
MARKETING
Social
Commercial
Ideas
Information for
Practising and Adoption
Low Technology
Freely Available
Long-term Effect
on Health and Well-being
• Mass Media
• Folk Media
• Slogans
• Gender oriented
Products
Low/High Technology
Purchasing
Price tag
Short-term Effect
Mostly Electronic Media
• No Slogan
• (Godrej Ganga Soap)
• Gender biased
(officer's choice whisky)
whisky with women

CHART 9.95

CLIENTS

Social Marketing

- Poor without Purchasing Power
- Humans

Men Women Children

Commercial Marketing

- Better purchasing power
- Specialised
- Mostly Adults

THE BOTTOM LINE

Social Marketing

Messaging the idea
Messaging Content
Resistant

- Culture Specific
- Source Authentic

Social Good of the Greatest Number

Commercial Marketing

Selling a Product at Profit
Happiness of a few

Analyze and Describe Market Segments

Bases for segmentation

- Geographic
- Demographic
- Socio-economic
- Behavioural/Psychographic

Choose Effective Strategy

Develop Product Positioning

CHART 9.96

SUSTAINABILITY ISSUES

Economic Viability

- Input
- Budgeting
- Productivity
- MIS
- R&D
- Marketing Information
- Planning
- Finance — Bank, NBC
- Management
- TQM
- Policy

Recoveries
Management Information System (MIS)
Caste
Marketing
Organising the Beneficiaries (OB)
Training/Human Resource Development (HRD)
Foreign funding
Funding Science and Technology (S&T)

Social Viability

- Values
- Comm ORG
- Volunteers
- People Partnership
- Community discipline

CHART 9.97

APPENDICES

APPENDIX-I

Recommendations of Ramakrishniah Committee on Marketing of KVI Products

154. The Directorate of Marketing is in no position to devote attention to Marketing Policy and Planning, or for that matter any work other than of a routine nature. (9.3)

155. It would be correct to describe the activities of KVIC as sales-oriented rather than marketing-oriented. This has happened despite the caution and advice given from time to time by experts engaged by itself. (9.9)

156. It is clear that although several expert groups before us had presented detailed blue-prints for reorganising and strengthening the marketing set-up of KVIC, neither the Government nor for the KVIC, had been able to take the necessary basic decisions. (9.19)

157. It is essential to set up a nodal agency under KVIC for the performance of all the marketing tasks. As the previous attempts to make suitable adjustments within the present administrative set-up have failed, it would be advisable to make a clean break and create a separate corporation under the aegis of KVIC. This could take the form of a statutory corporation or a company under the Companies Act. As

the success of the corporation will depend greatly on the leadership to be provided by the Managing Director, it should be ensured that he has the necessary ability, experience and qualification in marketing by offering attractive terms. To facilitate co-ordination, the Chairman, KVIC, may be made the Chairman of the Corporation and the Managing Director of the Corporation, a Member of the KVIC. The Board of Directors of the Corporation may consist of five others, bringing up the total to 7. The five may include the Chief Executive Officer, KVIC, three representatives of the KVI organisations running the Bhavans and Bhandars and one Marketing Expert from a reputed academic organisation. (9.20)

158. The functions of the Corporation will be: (i) to organise market research: (ii) to supply market intelligence to all selling and producing organisations in the KVI sector; (iii) to set up infrastructural facilities for sales outlets; (iv) to manage sales outlets at important selected centres; (v) to establish and manage common facilities for processing and finishing wherever necessary; (vi) to prepare marketing plans; (vii) to arrange supply of raw materials in accordance with the marketing plans; (viii) to establish standards of quality and enforce compliance therewith; and (ix) to take all steps necessary for promoting exports of KVI products (9.21)

159. The Corporation must be suitably funded for carrying out its functions. To start with, it may have a capital of Rs. 10 crores for investment in the physical facilities that are essential. It should be possible for the Corporation to plan its working capital needs from the banks. We have been given to understand that the Corporation's scheme to assist the dispersed rural artisans in upgrading their products and in marketing them will be favourably viewed by friendly foreign Governments for bilateral aid under the broad heading "Rural Development". This avenue deserves to be explored, once the basic decisions on the marketing set-up are taken. (9.22)

160. To begin with, the Corporation will have three departments– Commercial Operations, Marketing Services and Marketing Planning. (9.23)

161. One of the first steps to be taken by the Corporation is to organise the market information system. It would be worthwhile to engage an expert to draw up the details in the light of the latest developments. (9.24)

162. The importance of Market Research cannot be overemphasized. A systematic survey should be conducted, with a view to discovering the characteristics of the present patrons and their expectations as well as the points that will attract new consumers. The readymade garments of cotton khadi which have already captured the imagination of the customers have a bright future. This segment of the market can be expanded, if reliable information is available about consumer attitudes while organising market research. In the case of village industries products, research cells should be at the State level, so that they can pay adequate attention to the peculiarities of the different industries and the artisans engaged in them. (9.25)

163. The Corporation should draw up a time-bound programme to ensure opening of sales outlets in all urban centres and all villages with a population of 2,000 and above. It may directly manage the outlets in the metropolitan cities and other important centres. As regards the remaining, the aim should be to entrust the management to local institutions to form federations at the State level and provide common services, including marketing. There is great scope for experimenting with the terms on which such agencies can be granted. Considering the exorbitant costs involved in acquiring shopping space in urban centres, it is abvisable to try the mobile outlet scheme. Tricycles are useful and may be tried. (9.26)

164. The Corporation should minimise its role in physical handling of goods. It should be possible for the Corporation to provide the necessary information of stocks at different places in

the country and facilitate the establishment of direct contacts between different organisations managing the outlets. (9.27)

165. In regard to cotton khadi and other goods which are in need of processing (such as dyeing, printing, finishing, etc.), the Corporation may also set up and manage such common facilities for the use of producers or the sales outlets in the area. The old scheme of Vastragars should be revived, after making suitable modifications. A Vastragar is not a mere store of goods or even the manager of certain physical facilities, but a centre of market intelligence. Considering that nearly 75 per cent of cotton khadi is now being sold in the form of printed, dyed and fabricated products in some Bhavans, the Vastragars are bound to play a very important role. In the case of village industries also a similar organisation should be evolved for post-production processing, wherever necessary. Adequate margins, say 4 per cent for Central Vastragars at State level and 3 per cent for regional Vastragars must be provided. (9.28)

166. As regards readymade garments, the Corporation may take the initiative in supplying designs and appropriate advice, leaving the actual tailoring and the procurement of materials to the outlets concerned. This is an area which has a vast scope for development. (9.29)

167. The Corporation should bring the Managers of the outlets and the producing institutions together at least once a year, say, in June, so that the producers will come to know the consumer preference in time and plan their production accordingly. If necessary, such conferences may be arranged twice in a year. (9.30)

168. As one of the main difficulties of the artisans employed in village industries related to supply of raw materials, the Corporation should undertake a programme for ensuring adequate and timely supply. Past experience of KVIC should be carefully evaluated before embarking on a new scheme for procurement and storage of raw materials. The concept of Village Industries Supply Development Centre

prima facie appears to be attractive. It is worthwhile to try it out in some Districts on a pilot basis. (9.31)

169. As present KVIC operates a cotton supply scheme and a Merino wool import scheme. It is logical to transfer these schemes to the Corporation. Similar action is called for in the case of mother units for processing cotton and supplying slivers to spinners and soap base to soap workers. (9.32)

170. There should be no objection of the KVIC sales outlets dealing in non-competitive non-KVI goods. Care may be taken to study the implications of this step in regard to liability under income tax and sales tax laws, before actual implementation. As stocking involved working capital and concessional financial assistance, a list of these goods may be drawn up and kept under constant review. (9.33)

171. On the pricing policy of KVI goods, there is no particular merit in strictly adhering to the cost plus formula, and in refraining from fixing prices in accordance with the principle of what the traffic can bear. The sales outlets must be enabled to adopt a rational pricing policy product-wise and take resort to pooling, if necessary. It should not be beyond the ingenuity of the Corporation to evolve a system by which surpluses generated as a result of the adoption of the principle, 'what the traffic can bear' , are shared by the sales outlets on the one hand and the producing institutions which have supplied the goods on the other. This may be tried on selective basis. (9.34)

172. While the sale of khadi products should continue to confine to recognised outlets in view of the need to ensure purity of the product and to avoid malpractices in regard to rebates, there should be no objection to allowing the normal trade channels to deal in the products of village industries. Further, some khadi readymade garments may be released for sale through selected trade channels on an experimental basis, after taking adequate steps in regard to brand name, logo, etc. It is not difficult to find a suitable procedure for avoiding abuse of the rebate provision. Some other khadi products

may also be thrown open in due course, after gaining some experience. Further, the outlets of similar organisations like Handloom Co-operatives, General Co-operative Stores and the public distribution system may be permitted to sell KVI goods. (9.35)

173. The new Corporation should think in terms of utilising the existing channels, irrespective of the nature of their ownership, provided suitable commercial terms can be settled. As the village industries products present a wide variety, it will not be correct for the Corporation to think of undertaking their marketing entirely through its own channels. Different marketing strategies have to be evolved for different products of village industries. (9.36)

174. The Corporation has to organise training in salesmanship and display (interior as well as window). The second kind of training has not received much attention so far. The existing training courses for salesmen have to be revamped so that all salesmen are put through a refresher course of a short duration of three months in the major emporia. (9.37)

175. Sales promotion, through well-planned publicity, holding of exhibitions and special campaigns is an area in which a great deal remains to be done. It is essential that a certain percentage is earmarked for this purpose. Exhibitions have to be held at different levels, District, State and All India. It is desirable to locate exhibition units at the State level instead of concentrating them at the level of the KVIC. The Exhibition wing will have to be equipped not only with the usual kits but also audio-visual materials, particularly relating to important activities of the institutions which have successfully implemented the programme. There is scope for holding small exhibition-cum-sales in selected industrial establishments, educational institutions and in local fairs and festivals. Suitable grants will have to be made available to the registered institutions or other agencies that are entrusted with the task of holding these exhibitions. (9.38)

176. Rebate on sales is an important sales promotion device. (9.39)

177. As regards establishment of standards of quality, the arrangements for testing are not satisfactory. There is no statistical quality control system worth the name. Very little work has been done in respect of packaging which in several cases would be the best method for ensuring faithfully that the declared quality has been presented. It is no doubt true that quality control is a complex subject and it has become even more complex for KVIC due to the fact that the number of products is large, their production is dispersed widely in the country among small units with few resources and the cost of enforcement per unit of product is often prohibitive. It is against this background that the KVIC and the Marketing Organisation will have to examine afresh how to create and maintain the reputation that the sales outlets recognised by the KVIC do in fact offer goods of quality. (9.40)

178. The first step is, of course, to lay down standards which are verifiable. For this purpose, it should adopt comparable standards, if any, laid down by other organisations like ISI and AGMARK. Stages of caution to be observed in the production process, drawing of samples for testing and the utility of maintaining the testing equipment etc., are some of the points on which emphasis has to be laid during the training of the artisans and the Managers to ensure that at the time of procurement for sale in the departmental or certified outlets, samples are drawn regularly and got tested in recognised laboratories. The Central Testing Laboratory at Nasik and the Regional Laboratories that KVIC set up should be carefully reviewed for the adequacy of their facilities and procedures. The need is for introducing the system under which failures to adhere to the standards should be invariably followed by penalties. At any rate, the Corporation to be set up by the KVIC should set an example by not accepting for sale in its outlets any items which fail

to pass the standard tests. Such firm action will send proper signals to all persons and will trigger greater awareness and respect for quality. (9.41)

179. There were 137 trading units in 1985-86, 28 of them having been classified as dead. When the Marketing Corporation comes into being, it will be logical to transfer the relevant activity to it. But before doing so, it is desirable to take appropriate decisions about the continuance of each of these units. No unit that has no justification for continuance should be transferred to the Corporation. Further, the earlier the so-called dead units are closed, the better for KVIC. (9.42)

APPENDIX-II

Marketing Strategies for Decentralised Sector—SIDBI Round Table Meet

January 10–12, 1994, New Delhi

EXECUTIVE SUMMARY

A three-day Round Table meet was sponsored by SIDBI with the objective of giving a boost to the decentralised sector by evolving effective marketing strategies.

The congregation comprising experienced people from the decentralised sector, particularly rural marketing, saw some significant and very relevant points being raised and discussed. Many concrete suggestions emerged from the meet and an action plan was prepared based on the following:

1. Promotion of Decentralised Sector

The importance of decentralised sector in the economy of the country was clearly realised and stressed, considering that 100 million job seekers will enter the employment market in the current decade with little hope of getting absorbed in either agriculture or industry. More and more people are expected to seek livelihood in the non-farm or the decentralised sector. The following issues and action plans have emerged:

1.1 Identification of high potential sub sectors (activities) which can play a significant role in providing employment.
1.2 Promotion of innovative income generation activities with suitable financial package to generate employment opportunities.
1.3 Development of a database bank for dissemination of relevant information and technologies for application in this sector.
1.4 Realisation that the craft sector is a minuscule role player in providing employment in the vast non-farm sector.
1.5 Critical need for Entrepreneur Training of the producers in the decentralised sector.

2. Role of NGOs in Income Generation Activities

Quite a few NGOs have moved into the income generation sector without adequate knowledge and orientation in business, skills, resulting in half-baked income generation programmes which rely heavily on subsidy props. This issue came up for a detailed discussion and it was felt that there is a need for a guiding policy for the NGOs engaged in income generation activities.

2.1 Need for demarcation between the developmental activities and income generation activities by the NGOs.
2.2 A business like approach to be adopted by the NGOs in implementing their IG Activities.
2.3 Evaluation of the IG activities should be based on more quantifiable economic input-output ratios as against the subjective "social indicators".
2.4 NGOs should stress more on the facilitation of the process than total implementation of the scheme.

2.5 In the wake of liberalisation of the economy and the withdrawal of the commercial banks from the non-viable rural sector, NGOs may consider setting up rural banks.

3. Resource Pooling for Economies of Scale

Duplication and working in isolation is a typical problem in the developmental sector. This not only drains the limited resources but also proves uneconomical and ineffective in the long run. The following major areas of pooling were identified to foster optimal utilisation of resources specially in the wake of onslaught by the organised sector.

3.1 Common branding and advertising for similar products.
3.2 Pooling of available specialised services.
3.3 Development and promotion of innovative marketing systems.
3.4 Induction of professionals in the rural sector.

4. Co-ordination and Networking

Need for co-ordination and networking among the various promotional institutions and their activities was emphasised and felt strongly. Potential organisations must take up this important role at regional levels.

5. Exploration of Traditional *Melas* and *Haats*

The traditional *melas* and *haats* which are an integral part of the country's culture have much to offer as major marketing outlets. This channel of sale has been tapped only in a limited way and a lot needs to be done to promote these low cost relevant and socially acceptable mediums for rural marketing.

6. Role of Corporate Sector in Rural Development

The corporate world can play a significant role in promoting the rural economy. Some of the significant areas where they can contribute are:

6.1 Initiate developmental programmes
6.2 Sponsor and support developmental activities
6.3 Provide forward linkages to rural production system
6.4 Render the much needed management skills to the tiny industries.

7. Utilisation of Dormant Infrastructure

The dormant infrastructure and resources of the promotional agencies (e.g. CSIR Labs, KVIC Training Centres, Weaver's Service Centres, etc.) need to be utilised optimally to reduce the problem of scarcity of funds.

ACTION PLAN

As the very purpose of the meet was to be able to evolve strategies which can be implemented, an action plan was prepared to follow up the recommendations of the meet. The significant decision taken at this juncture was to form a three-member core group. This group has been given the short-term task to:

1. Organise a study of traditional marketing systems (*Melas* and *Haats*),
2. Identify a few suitable agencies for disseminating information on potential technologies,
3. Initiate a dialogue with the corporate sector, and
4. Reach findings on the NFS sector to the developmental organisations so that they can explore more gainful sectors of employment other than crafts.

MARKETING STRATEGIES FOR DECENTRALISED SECTOR

Objective : To evolve location specific, viable, effective

		marketing strategies for decentralised sector.
Participation	:	Senior representatives of credit and marketing institutions, heads of NGOs engaged in IGP, marketing research organisations, donor agencies, autonomous bodies and knowledgeable individuals.
Location	:	USO House, Special institutional Area, New Delhi
Duration	:	3 days
Dates	:	January 10-12,1994
Timings	:	
Format		9.30 a.m. to 6.00 p.m.

Each speaker was assigned a topic (based on specific experience and in relation to the organisation's work) and requested to make a presentation. This was followed by round-table discussions on that specific subject. A facilitator/ moderator was nominated for each session as chairperson, who also summed up the discussions at the end in the form of recommendations.

Topics of Discussion

- Rural credit
- High growth sectors and appropriate product choices
- Product design
- Quality
- Standardization
- Packaging
- Umbrella brands
- Market research for ascertaining consumer taste, choice and preferences
- Marketing systems
  - Sales outlets
  - Trade channels
  - Institutional buyers
  - Traditional selling systems like *melas* and *haats*
  - Export

- Institutional linkages for strengthening sale of decentralised sector products
- Enterprise management training
- Sales promotion and advertising
- New initiatives and directions
- Networking-coordination
- Pooling of resources for economies of scale

Output : Location specific, sector specific marketing strategy recommendations.

INDIAN ECONOMY–AN EMERGING SCENARIO

The opening up of the macro economy as a consequence of the liberalisation policy has rendered the decentralised (tiny and cottage) sector more vulnerable than ever before. In this context, it is of immense importance to examine the relevance of this sector in the Indian economy. Let us consider the following facts:

(a) 100 million people will enter the employment market in search of livelihood during the current decade.

(b) The rate of absorption of labour in the economy has been declining over the years mainly because of land fragmentation, mechanization and computerisation in the agriculture and the organized sector.

(c) There is a gradual move towards freeing of the commercial banks from priority (agriculture and related activities) sector lending, which will further slow down employment opportunities in this sector which accounts for over two-thirds of the country's total work-force.

(d) During the current decade there is a prospect of a zero growth in the farming, organised industry and the public sectors.

The above facts clearly bring out the gigantic employment problem the country has on its hands.

NON-FARM SECTOR–AN OVERVIEW

We need to study the current situation in the Non-farm sector (NFS) to be able to examine the existence of large-scale employment opportunities in this so far neglected sector.

The Decentralised (Non-Farm) Sector

This sector comprises of all non-agricultural economic activities in the decentralised sector—household and non-household manufacturing, construction, transport, trade and services.

Status

This sector is most vulnerable and requires modern marketing and production technology to increase the value addition and sustainability. It is becoming increasingly difficult for its products to compete effectively with mass produced factory counterparts because of low productivity, poor designs, unattractive packaging, lack of standardization and absence of strong brands. In fact, there has not been much effort made in promoting this sector.

The Task

The problems being faced by the decentralised NF sector need to be understood and worked upon in great detail. The sector requires focus on finance, technology, skill training, entrepreneurship training, raw material, infrastructure and marketing. Marketing, which by itself embraces the wide spectrum ranging from product designing, branding and advertising to sell, is the most important area which has to be taken care of, to give it a meaningful thrust.

SIDBI Round Table Meet

This meet was organised to find ways to give a boost to the decentralised sector by evolving effective marketing strategies. The deliberations, attended by about 25 participants, focused on the above-stated problems and raised some very important issues.

The next few pages contain a summary of the discussions held during each of the sessions.

January 10, 1994

Introductory Session

The meet began with an introductory session where the objective of the workshop, 'providing opportunities for employment in the decentralised non-farm sector through developing the marketing linkages' was laid down by Brij Mohan, Deputy General Manager of SIDBI.

Pradeep Kashyap, brought out the relevance of the objective to the Indian economy by way of a quantitative analysis (see Table 1) , from which it becomes abundantly clear that not many new employment opportunities will be possible in the agriculture, organised and public sectors.

Table 1 : Employment Status

	Total (in millions)	
Total Working Population		315
Rural Working Population		249
Agriculture	205	
Non-Farm Sector	44	
Urban Working Population		66
Private Industry	34	
Government (including PSU)	18	
Self-employed/others	14	
Additional Job Seekers in 90's		100

Session 1 *Decentralised Sector : Towards a Common Understanding*

Chairperson Brij Mohan, SIDBI

Speakers 1. Vijay Mahajan

Decentralised sector : An overview—profile, dynamics, economics

2. Jaya Jaitly, Dastkari Haat Samiti
Marketing crafts : Learning from the past and seeking new directions

This session laid stress on the importance of the decentralised non-farm sector in the national economy.

Vijay Mahajan, who is in the process of completing a major study on the rural non-farm sector, shared some of his major findings. He said that the crafts sector employs less than 1 per cent of all rural jobs. In fact, the beedi industry alone provides more employment than the crafts sector. There is thus a need to look beyond the glamorous crafts sector and seek employment opportunities in other activities, such as flour mills, bidi making, sweets and confectionery which have registered high growth rates. The contribution of NGOs/Government in marketing of decentralised sector products is not even 1 per cent of the total marketing effort. This brings out the importance of the 'open market' operations and hence a need to promote more private initiatives.

In terms of employment opportunities, he concluded that the crafts sector has been showing an overall decline with some segments like pottery and blacksmithy registering a negative employment growth rate. On the other hand during the same period between 1977 and 1988, sub-sectors like construction (11 per cent annual growth rate), sweets and confectionery and a few others have registered impressive growth rates. Establishments employing between 6-20 people have registered the highest growth rate whereas individual self-employed have not grown at any significant rate. Looking at it from another angle, the highest growth rate has been registered in manufacturing clusters engaged in the same livelihood (Khurja for potteries or Moradabad for brass) and hence any strategy formulation must keep this important finding in mind (Table 2). Further, demand for mass produced goods is declining whereas niche markets (Kanchivaram sarees in the handloom sector as opposed to Janta dhotis) are growing.

Jaya Jaitly stressed the need for deglamourising the rural sector.

We need to widen our vision and identify and develop new prospects. For example, innovative practices in standardization and packaging can find solutions through traditional methods rather than looking at industrial packaging materials. She also mentioned the need for being guided by the potential and not the plight of the rural people. There was a call for reducing the subsidy props also.

She felt that protectionism had done more damage than good to the crafts sector. She, therefore, suggested market driven approaches like eco-friendly, people-friendly and employment themes for boosting sale of products from the decentralised sector.

She cautioned against the capitalistic model of the West which though appeared attractive and seemed to offer solutions is itself registering a decline in employment in many industrialised countries and even recession in some cases.

While summing up the deliberations, Brij Mohan agreed with the points made by the speakers and said that there was a need for differentiating between craft preservation and providing livelihoods. Distribution channels for crafts marketing needs to be widened for better availability and further utility (and not just decorative) products must be promoted for expansion of markets. Crafts people should be trained to become entrepreneurs.

Table 2 : Employment Scenario (1991-2001)

Sub-Sector	Growth Rate	
	Pessimistic	Optimistic
Grain Milling	4.00	6.00
Bidi Manufacture	3.00	5.00
Handlooms Cotton	-1.00	2.00
Textile Garments	6.00	12.00
Structural Wooden	2.00	4.00
Construction Building	10.00	15.00
Freight Transport (Vehicle)	12.00	16.00
Passenger Transport	12.00	16.00
Confectionery	10.00	15.00
Iron and Steel	10.00	15.00
Embroidery	10.00	16.00
Powerlooms	10.00	16.00
Repair of Motor Vehicle	10.00	16.00
Hotels/Rooming	10.00	16.00

Session 2 *Market Research/Action Research*

Chairperson	Kamal Taori
Speakers	1. Barneyo Choudhary / Raghu Roy, ORG Role of market research and market information systems in promoting decentralised sector products
	2. Kamal Taori, KVIC Government Promotional Agencies: Need to professionalise and shift from State-led to market-led strategies

Barneyo Choudhary explained at length the type of researches that can be conducted and their relevance to the promotion of the decentralised sector. Raghu Roy spoke on the support that the various sectors can provide to the development of this sector. Centralised and decentralised, private and Government initiatives working in a well-coordinated way can provide excellent support by way of knowledge/expertise, skill development infrastructure creation, networking, providing market information, creating distribution channels, etc.

Kamal Taori touched upon a very crucial issue of revitalising the dormant infrastructure and the resources of Government Institutions and NGOs. He stressed on the need for a systematic approach in taking up any activity through planning, action, research and codification. Internal resource generation which can come about by releasing the hidden, uptapped potential of organisations, professionalism in providing marketing linkages and bringing the like-minded people together were a few of his suggestions for the sector.

Action-oriented and continuous research can make research more meaningful. A well-designed system for buyer, seller and producer interaction can also be very useful for providing the missing linkages in the production-marketing systems.

Session 3 *Marketing Support Systems in the Development Sector*

Chairperson . Raghu Roy, ORG

Speakers

1. Laila Tyabji, Dastkar
   Marketing initiatives in the NGO sector: Need, problems, government support
2. Binu Gianchandani, Karukriti
   Marketing outlets in the NGO sector—problems of viability

Laila Tyabji brought out the importance of exhibitions in exploring new marketing possibilities but felt that agencies should pool their resources to upscale efforts rather than having too many small isolated efforts. Lack of planning, proper packaging, standardization, pricing, quality, etc., are some of the problems being faced by rural products. She said that institutional marketing of utility items has a good potential for enhancing the sales of rural products. Marginalisation of crafts people is taking place due to elitism through designer products resulting in shrinking market size. She also cautioned against alternative marketing which would not result in isolation from the mainstream marketing.

Binu Gianchandani narrated her experiences of running a craft sales outlet and the difficulties connected with it. Some of the points brought out by her were very educative and useful for people wanting to start similar ventures. Involvement of the producers, proper location, commission linked salary and competitive prices are crucial factors in ensuring success of retail outlets.

Lack of a professional approach, dependence on subsidies, incorrect costing, lack of stake in business and a "welfare" approach are the reasons which contribute to the limited success of NGO income generation activities. The ideological barrier, that profit is a dirty word, is detrimental to the business activity whereas there is nothing wrong with charging customers what they are willing to pay. This is a sound marketing principle.

A few very relevant and challenging suggestions came out from this session.

- Successful marketing outlets like SEWA (Self-Employed Women's Organisation) and Dastkar can consider branding some of their products as they have a good reputation with customers.
- The existing private outlets also need to be utilised by the NGOs in selling their products.
- Proper networking and infrastructural support from funding agencies rather than subsidies can go a long way in improving sales.
- Expansion of distribution channels and customer oriented product development is a must.
- Mail order system, mobile vans and other innovative marketing methods need to be considered.

January 11

Session 4	*Grassroots Marketing Initiatives*
Chairperson	M.P. Ranjan
Speakers	1. B.L.Tripathi, Jawaja Grassroots production groups: coping with market realities–lessons for the future 2. Jolly Rohatgi, OXFAM Struggles of a single marginalised producers in finding an edge in their local markets 3. M.P. Jhalla, SWRC Organising grassroots producers for crafts marketing: the process and strategy

This session witnessed the 'non-business' like approach most NGOs adopt. NGOs need to have a different approach when dealing in business activities, since a 'welfarist' approach does not succeed in the competitive marketplace.

B.L. Tripathi narrated his Jawaja experience which is already well known to most people. The group felt that the inputs of IIM, NID and others over a period of 17 years were disproportionate to the results in providing help to a mere 40 artisans.

Jolly Rohatgi drew on her experience from the field and advised

NGOs against becoming jack of all trades. The lack of any risk is the main cause for the 'non-business like' approach of the NGOs. The role of funding agencies was also discussed and it was felt that there is a need for them to put a check on the proliferation in the activities of the NGOs. Consolidification as also demarcation between the pure developmental role and the support role for economic activities is also necessary.

M.S. Jhalla spoke of his experience in working with rural artisans. He felt that there is a need to train the local people on all aspects of business management so that they can become self-sufficient.

Motivation of the producers and building upon their initiatives is very important as can be seen from the success of Grameen Bank, Bangladesh.

The role of NGOs entering the income generation sector must be clearly defined and they need to develop a business like working.

Rather than make a beeline for the glamorous city markets over which NGOs have no control and artisans find it difficult to understand taste, choice and preference of urban buyers, there is a need to look at products under IGP programmes (beyond crafts) for which a steady local market exists. Recent studies by ORG, NCAER and IMRB have established that the rural markets grew at twice the rate of the urban markets during 1984-89. Also the number of middle class in rural areas is the same as in urban areas, with perhaps greater purchasing power.

NGOs need to frame a withdrawal strategy so that they start pulling out gradually by transferring more and more responsibilities to the groups and withdraw completely over a period of few years.

Session 5 — *Role of Private Sector in Decentralised Sector Marketing*

Chairperson — Jaya Jaitly

Speakers

1. Sita Ram Gupta, LUPIN
   Private sector initiatives in promoting decentralised sector products
2. Kishore Rao, Action Aid
   Scope of corporate partnership

Sitaram Gupta in presenting his organisation's work showed how they have been creating a balance between the developmental and economic role of the NGO both of which are interrelated. Specialization may not always be possible when we are talking about a wide and varied subject like rural development which needs a holistic approach. NGOs cannot be ruthless with the craftsmen and leave them to their fate in case of economic non-viability but need to transfer management and ownership gradually to the producers so as to strengthen them. He said that a judicious mixture of sincerity and dedication of NGO, management strength of the corporate sector and the infrastructure and network of the government can do wonders for the development of the country. Such a pooling of strengths has a better chance of bringing about mass-scale employment.

He outlined a method by which large business houses can adopt one district each for development and exhibited confidence that such a gesture can go a long way in providing the necessary thrust to the development of the villages.

Kishore Rao discussed the prospects of corporate partnership in rural development and laid down the mutual advantages of such an arrangement. This will be useful to the corporate sector in enhancing their image. In many cases the corporate sector is keen to extend their support but are unaware of the possibilities and method. Their co-operation must be solicited not on charitable grounds but on a win-win situation, where the industry also gains through such a partnership in terms of enhancement of corporate image, getting acceptance and goodwill with the community where they are putting up their industries or a sense of pride.

It was decided to initiate a dialogue with the Chambers of Commerce and Industry to involve the corporate sector in decentralised sector marketing.

Session 6 *Product Design and Brand Promotion*

Chairperson Laila Tyabji, Dastkar

Speakers 1. M.P. Ranjan/Swati Mitra, NID
Role of design in value addition of products

and expansion of markets.

2. Arun Kumar, Development Alternatives
The role of product design in marketing.

The role and importance of product designing and brand promotion was brought out during this session.

M.P. Ranjan showed that development of designs was interconnected with imbibing business sense in the development sector. It is only due to stiff competition in the past couple of years that efforts are being made to improve designs. He felt craft must be seen as an industrial activity and not a cultural process if we have to make it succeed in the market. Product designing must be linked with the customers choice and not the other way round. He explicitly brought out the fact that design input is not merely to improve aesthetics. There are many functional elements to design–usage, operation, handling, protection, etc. Design can also add substantial value to the product–particularly craft (e.g. Shyam Ahuja, durries).

Arun Kumar drew from the experience of the development of the micro concrete roofing. The lengthy and gradual process required in disseminating the new technologies was evident from this. Proper networking between all the concerned organisations for gaining experience from each other is very important. Very often we need to sell a concept and system and not merely products, e.g. selling roof tiles was not as successful as marketing roofing systems using these tiles.

Session 7 *Institutional Support Systems*

Chairperson Pradeep Kashyap

Speakers

1. Lalit Mathur, CAPART
CAPART's role in promoting IGP efforts in the NGO sector
2. R.K. Singh, HIMCON
Role of specialised agencies in promotion of production systems in decentralised sector

Lalit Mathur brought out the crucial points necessary for the success of IGP in rural areas. Need for promotion of non-land-based (Non-farm Sector) activities. Coordination among various inputs as envisaged by the VISHWA Cell (Karnataka) was also suggested. There is a need to bring down the increasing dependence of people on institutional support and increase inter-dependence. Value-added production and induction of new technologies are important for finding viable solutions for prospective IGPs.

R.K. Singh stressed the need for technological, qualitative and training input in this sector. A rural producer is as much into business as any other urban producer and there is a need for entrepreneurship training.

Collaboration among various marketing efforts was put forward as an important requirement. Better compensation for rural development professionals was also recommended.

January 12

Session 8 *Traditional Marketing Systems*

Chairperson Sita Ram Gupta, Lupin

Speakers
1. Jaya Jaitly, Dastkari Haat Samiti
   The *Haat*–a low-cost, effective sales outlet
2. Pradeep Kashyap
   Rural *mela* and its modern urban counterpart

Jaya Jaitly brought out the long-term cost effectiveness and advantages of permanent infrastructures for holding urban *haats* as against raising temporary structures for urban *melas* at substantial costs which have to be written off.

Pradeep Kashyap emphasised the importance of the traditional *melas* and rural *haats*. Their strength is that they are sturdy, low cost and their relevance is evident from the fact that they have survived the onslaught of the Mughals and the British Raj. The timings of these *melas* and *haats* are also very appropriate as they are held just when the people have a lot of money after a hectic harvest season or to coincide with a religious occasion. These *melas* do not require much expenses on publicity. They already have a high visitor turnout since they are held in the same location and during the same month every year.

He also explained that the costs of many simple traditional products are transparent as they are easy to estimate unlike the cost of multi-component and mechanised corporate products (VCR, Refrigerator, etc.). Thus the selling price of rural products cannot be fixed vey high, resulting in small margins for sellers. Besides the inherent inefficiency of government marketing, this factor alone explains why the 50,000 odd showrooms run by KVIC, Handloom and Handicrafts Corporations, Jute, Leather and Coir Boards incur losses year after year when all hidden costs and subsidies are included in the expenses.

He emphasised the need to introduce modern marketing concepts to make these existing channels of selling for decentralised sector products even more effective.

APPENDIX-III

Some Reflections–On Past Innovation

A request was made to an old Gandhian who had worked in the Commission also to give his reflections on some innovative schemes which were started in the past. Reflections on the issues as answered by him are given in original.

The issues raised are:

1. Why the Grama Swaraj project and integrated development project failed ?
2. Why prohibition failed in Wardha district and Gujarat State?
3. Why the efforts to transform Wardha district into Gandhi district failed? and
4. How long should rebate be continued for Khadi products?

I. Why the Grama Swaraj Project and I.D.P. failed ?

At the outset, I refuse to accept that they failed. I accept that they did not give the results desired by us. In my view, the reason is we aimed too high. Neither the workers engaged in the projects nor the people responded to our efforts to our intent and purpose. It is natural to aim high though we may not wholly succeed than to aim low and claim success.

The Grama Swaraj Movement had the blessings of Pujya Acharya Vinoba Bhave. The project was intended to strengthen the Gramadan Movement and make Gramadan villages to blossom into Grama Swaraj units. Details of the projects were finalised after discussing with Sarva Sri Shankar Rao, Deo Dhirendra Mazumdar, Annasaheb Sahasrabuddhe and Dada Dharmadhikari. They were great leaders by themselves and had much experience in field activities in constructive work in rural areas on Gandhian lines. Hence, it must be admitted that the projects were planned by experts.

It is true that Gramadan Movement itself was an utopian idea. It was intended to bring about a new social order. All the great leaders of the day solemnly assured Vinobaji to work for it and contribute their efforts to make it successful accepting the utility of the movement and its urgency. It is a different matter that they did not do their best or the movement could not be carried further. It only proves that either the time was not opportune or the effort made was inadequate or the people were not prepared for such a socio-economic change over. It does not mean that the programme was wrong, deficient or inappropriate. Rightly has it been said that failure is a stepping stone to success. Even now, we can take it up to work it to success. Adi Sankara gave the *mantra* "Aham Brahmaswami". How many Advaitis have realised the import of it or act up to its concept? Bhagwan Buddha gave us the message of *Karuna.* How many Buddhists act up to it or try to practise it? Bhagwan Mahavira called upon the people to practise *Ahimsa*, Do Jains follow it ? Do others practise it? The whole world today is full of violence. So did Jesus, Zoroaster, Mohammed, Bhagwan Ramakrishna, and recently Mahatma Gandhi, each one of them gave us messages. The world is far from them. That does not mean that the messages were wrong. We should only conclude that we should continue to endeavour till success comes to us. Rightly did Nehru say "Success comes to those who dare and act".

II. Why Prohibition Failed in Wardha District and Gujarat State?

Again, I should say that the prohibition policy is not wrong. There has been deficiency in implementing it. Let us learn a lesson from the failure. Let us endeavour to get over those causes. Not only prohibition failed in Wardha town and district. Gandhiji spent nearly 12 long years in Sevagram. No one can deny that he served the people of Sevagram village as best as possible. But did they follow him? He served the Harijans in Nalwadi. It is well known that those Harijans discarded Gandhiji and respected Ambedkar. It only proves how superficial is the understanding of the common people. We cannot, therefore, give up endearing them still further. We should continue to serve them. Much more difficult is the problem relating to the drink evil .

III. Why the Efforts to Make Wardha District into Gandhi District Failed ?

C.R. (Rajaji) was the Prime Minister of composite Madras State in the pre-Independence days (now the same position is known as Chief Minister). He was born in Salem district. Naturally he desired to make it a dry district. And he made it. But today perhaps illicit distillation is rampant there. Can we say, he erred in selecting Salem for introducing prohibition in that district? So also Vinobaji was not wrong in calling upon the workers to make Wardha district a Gandhi District. If it is not Wardha, where both he and Gandhiji lived and worked for long years and put in dedicated service, which other district can he select?

Only six months after Rajaji introduced prohibition in Salem district, when the Excise budget for the next year was brought for voting in the then Legislative Council of Madras State the then District Collector of Salem District, not a confirmed prohibitionist, an English man, a true civilian officer, sent his report on the working of the prohibition policy in the District to the then P.M. of the State, which Rajaji read in the Council Session. The district collector commended the policy and programme and reported that the poor people of the district had largely benefited by it, they were having better food and better standard of life. I myself am personal witness to the benefit of prohibition in Sarvail village, Nalganda district in Andhra Pradesh, in the then Hyderabad State when it was in force in that village for a year. But unfortunately, the Government of Hyderabad State would not agree to continue it subsequently. Therefore, I emphasise that prohibition with all the shortcomings is really beneficial to the common man. I shall not like to comment on why the State Government do not desire to enforce it.

Theft, burglary, murder, gambling, adultery, rape and corruption have not been eliminated from the society, in spite of a number of legislations in force and the police force maintained by the Government. That is no excuse to do away with those Acts or to disband or reduce the police personnel. It is the moral duty of a Government established by law to give every protection to the people from all that are injurious to the people.

IV. How Long Should Rebate for Khadi Production be Continued?

Personally, I am not for subsidy for any business transaction or industrial production. I am of the opinion that every industry or business should be able to stand on its own legs. Otherwise, it should be buried deep.

But, there is a proviso to it. That is, it must have a free scope to compete in the market. It must not be made to face competition by giant industries, which are assisted in a number of ways by the Government. The researches in technology, maintenance of roads, railways by the Government and provision of concessional tariff to large-scale industries are indirect subsidies offered to such industries. Because of the adoption of higher technologies, they throw out of employment a number of unskilled labourers. A responsible Government has a moral duty to provide alternative employment and help them to exist. Many schemes for rural employment are indeed indirect subsidies for those large-scale industry sectors, which drive the rural industries to the wall. So, I am unable to accept the argument that only Khadi is being subsidised by the Governments.

But I concede that Khadi should soon forgo this luxury of subsidy. This will become possible when Khadi is purchased and used by the villagers, where carding, slivering, spinning, weaving and all other allied activities are pursued, thus providing employment to the rural unemployed or underemployed and help them to have a better standard of life. The villagers must be made to realise this economy. Intensive education in this direction is necessary . This was attempted upon through the Grama Swaraj, I.D.P. Department in the past. I have already explained under Item No. 1, why that good work did not give the desired result. Reviving that work and concentrating greater attention is the only sure way to end subsidy on Khadi.

Note : Since old habits die hard, it is difficult to draw pointed conclusions and clear the path for hope. However, as the author sees it the answer to success lies in developing a wider horizon and accepting realities of human behaviour and lessons of history. Good intentions cannot be translated into good results by mere wishful thinking. Hard facts for internal resource generation have to be kept in view.

APPENDIX – IV

My Guru–Raghavulu, Doyen of Marketing

My association with Raghavulu is hardly three years old. But as a man of dynamism, vision, openness and practical wisdom, I have no words to express his contribution to the field of village industries and Khadi. He is always looking for new opportunities. In a cluster where the holistic picture of the sector can be projected has been his dream. Programmes which are replicable, self-supporting and capable of multiplying hope has been receiving special attention. In the Gopalapuram area of Madras it is an experience to see tailoring, production, marketing, coordination, mediation. Guest house, hall and offices of KVIC and institutions, etc., are working in a cluster. In a system where everybody is trying to run away from others it is a pleasant surprise to see heterogeneous activities and organisation working for a cause.

The vision of the following makes us understand the importance of marketing. As has been brought out earlier, marketing is not confined only to that of products. The concepts, problems, good points, awareness also needs sustained marketing. Grant rebate, subsidies are anti-sustained marketing. They leave a bad taste and overdependence on State funds. Hence as a practical missionary, Shri Raghavulu's case needs indepth analysis and action plan conversion. His views on some of the important issues which have direct bearing on hope generation must be analysed.

Regarding the sustainability and development extendability of the programme, Shri Raghavulu has been feeling that linkage building and coordination would be the crucial factor in times to come. Funding is only one aspect. More important is sustainability, employment generationability, getting away from slums and cities and developing a man and a nation confident and vibrant. This can come only through a decentralized programme wherein dependence on State and others is minimum. The youth has to be the centre and idealism has to be the guiding principle. Gandhi, Kumarappa, Kumaraj, Meerabai, Vivekananda, Mother Teresa should be interpreted in the light of the present situation. This interpretation has to be holistic and again sustainable. The science and technology and their massive communication capacity has to be re-examined with reference to experience. The export potential of various programmes has to be coordinated. Woman power, faith and spiritually, technology have revolutionised the entire psychology of man towards nature. The definition of economics of profit, capital-output ratio, incremental capacity, bankability of project have undergone unimaginable changes. In this situation, programmes have to become sustainable. This means new and new innovative methods must be developed to reduce cost of production and distribution on the one hand and to develop comparative choosy markets on the other. This follows non-traditional approach to marketing not only of the products but also other related aspects which makes products acceptable and competitive. The new experiences of coordination with schools, economists, thinkers, bankers and like-minded organizations (LMO) makes an interesting study of sustainability of programmes.

When we talk of structural reforms, liberalisation, competitive capacities, isolated or borrowed pump-sets will not solve the problem of a massive rich traditional God-fearing country of ours. The behaviour of the country and concerned target groups must be appreciated with reference to experience and aspirations. The low-cost high-impact system building cannot be always a substitute for high-cost high-impact system. Hence while for some products and processes, man-driven bicycle and tricycle may be a solution, developing supply system for others, the big van may be the answer. The objective is to reach the target group effectively and economically. The choices which are available are diverse and depending on the capacity of repaying, a method will have to be adopted. What applies to the delivery system equally applies to the total marketing system. TV or Radio may not be the answer for publicity for all the products all the time. Khadi can be publicised on TV during the rebate period bemoaning consumers to buy khadi because there is rebate in the name of the Father of the Nation. But the same media and the cost can be utilised to highlight the strength of khadi with reference to environment, sick assistance, equity and distribution of money spent. Same principles can be applied to various other products and system building. But the real self-supporting system development will come through surplus generation and making programmes widely acceptable. While youth may look for security and better returns, he also looks for a brighter future. How do we ensure it happening? Obviously, successful models like those of Raghavuluji can be an answer in the right direction. With reference to economics, bankability, sustainability, youths' involvements and low-cost publicity measures, there may be, hardly any substitute for what he has done. By involving the office of Governor and other VIPs in propagating the cause, he has developed a system to compete with UNICEF. There may be many more areas in future where his innovative dynamism and youthful professionalism would open up new vistas. The need is replication. By exposing others to the experience, a long-term solution for many of our problems relating to marketing attitudes may be found.

APPENDIX-V

A Case Study for Sustainable Development of Handmade Paper Industry through Market Approach

PREFACE

As it is well known, Handmade Paper Industry is one of the oldest traditional industries in India. With sustained efforts of the KVIC during the past four decades the industry had gained importance and had been recognised as one of the potential industries under the KVIC despite its sickness in several pockets of the country. With better planning, monitoring, coordination and pooling of resources it is possible not only to revive the sick units but also expand the activities throughout the length and breadth of the country.

The experience so far gained in the industry has indicated distinct possibilities to develop this industry as a replicable model for other sectors. This is one of those decentralized industries which have a very bright future because of their eco-friendly nature. Time and tide wait for nobody, so the same time also makes people, industries, projects relevant or irrelevant in the given situation. Hence with this background, it is proposed to examine the case study of

Handmade Paper Industry in India by adopting a holistic market approach with the active involvement of entrepreneurs, artisans, dealers, printers and merchant exporters, NGOs, etc., since time is in favour for development of this otherwise low profile industry until a few years back into a viable, transparent and bankable sector.

PRESENT STATUS OF HANDMADE PAPER INDUSTRY IN INDIA

In 1953 when the All India Khadi and Village Industries Board took up the revival programme of the industry there were only 35 units with an annual production of around Rs. 5 lakhs. Today after 39 years of sustained efforts, the industry with its present 438 working units (231 handmade paper and 207 paper machine units) has achieved a production of paper-board to the tune of 12,356 tons handmade paper/board valued at over Rs. 1,506 lakhs (Rs. 1,445 lakhs handmade paper and 61 lakhs papier mache) during the year 1993-94. The industry has provided gainful direct employment to around 6,820 persons of whom around 40 per cent constitute women workers and persons from the weaker sections of the society. Wages earned by these workers were to the tune of Rs. 426 lakhs during the same year.

The pattern of total production may be analysed as under:

1.	High-grade paper	20%
2.	Writing and printing	05%
3.	Fancy and decorative paper	10%
4.	Filter paper and Filter pad	05%
5.	Card sheets (200 GSM and above) and Board	35%
6.	Cover and Stationery	20%
7.	Industrial paper	05%

The conventional raw materials used by the industry are old and new cotton rags, waste-paper. Jute, grass and straws are also used but on a very meagre scale.

The net disbursement under Handmade Paper Industry including paper converted schemes as on 31st March 1993, is around 14.76 crores. Besides, it is estimated that around Rs. 5 crores is invested by 80 direct hand-made paper units recognised by the KVIC as genuine handmade paper units. However, the total capital investment in the working units (since more than 150 units are dormant/defunct) is estimated at Rs. 15 crores only and the production is also to the order of Rs. 15.06 crores during the year 1993-94. Thus the production and investment ratio stands in this industry at 1:1 for the last several years.

Improvement in the Machinery and Technology

The industry which started with primitive equipment like hand knives, dhanki for pulping, pumice-stone for hand-glassing in its early days has gradually been equipped with modern power-operated equipments such as rag chopper, hollendar beater, hydraulic press, calendering machine and cutting machine besides peddle-operated uni-vats in place of dipping method vats for sheet lifting. With the introduction of these machines it has been possible to diversify the production by the use of cotton rags and agro-fibres.

With a view to increasing the productivity and reducing the drudgery of the workers, KVIC approved a few years back introduction of power-operated sheet, making machine, namely Cylinder Mould Vat up to 30 face size, as a part of adopting intermediate technology. The experience so far with the CMV is that higher grammage paper (over 150 GSM) is possible to be real substitute to the handmade paper only by hand-lifting or on Auto-Vats. It is, therefore, necessary to explore possibilities of devising a better but simplified mechanism to improve the sheet lifting process.

Efforts have been made in utilizing agro fibres in the HMP Sector with the pilot plant trials conducted at Dehradun, Pune, Wardha and other places in the past. However, no systematic action has been taken to extend the results into the field in order to make use of agro fibres on a sustainable basis. Thus as on today the industry mainly depends on cotton rags and recycled waste paper for its raw material requirement.

BACKGROUND INFORMATION OF HMP-UNDP PROJECT

During the 1970s Mr. Judte, Industrial Development Officer from UNIDO, Vienna, used to participate in IPPTA Conferences in India when he could interact with Shri. S.N. Singh, the then Development Officer of Handmade Paper Industry, who was representing the HMP Directorate in such meetings. During the course of such interactions between Mr. Judte and Shri S.N. Singh while recognizing the immense potential the HMP Industry had in India, it was proposed that efforts should be made for an overall strengthening of the industry in the country. Keeping in view this broad objective Mr. Judte had arranged a "Fact finding mission" on the request of the Commission to study the problems in the Indian Handmade Paper Industry. It was in furtherance of this proposal that Mr. Simon B. Green, Chief Technical Advisor to the HMP-UNDP Project, was deputed to India as a fact finding mission in February, 1985. On the basis of Mr. Green's initial report a Project was forwarded by the UNIDO to the Indian Government which however remained unimplemented till 1989 due to protracted correspondence at various levels.

Team Responsible for Grounding the HMP-UNDP Project

At this crucial stage I having worked as Chief Executive Officer of the U.P. KVI Board assumed Office of CEO of the Khadi and Village Industries Commission in May, 1989. I have a great conviction and devotion to the KVI Sector and in particular to the development of Handmade Paper Industry in which I found immense potential to grow and contribute its share to the environmental protection measures. My assumption as CEO, KVIC, coincided with the presence of another devoted senior IAS Officer, Shri Ramchandran, in UNDP Office at Delhi on deputation from the Government of India. We two top Executives together with senior officers in UNIDO and UNDP Branch at New Delhi notable among them being Ms. R.M.V. Assumpcao, Mr. Nerul Islam, Mr. E. Dessau and Mr. Vivek Rao with their vision and zeal were responsible for the expeditious implementation of the long-pending HMP Project. Our efforts were strengthened with the presence of another senior IAS Officer, Shri Vardachari, in the Ministry of Economic Affairs who had extended his full support to the objectives of the Project and accorded necessary financial clearance for the Project.

I found in Shri S.N. Singh, who was then Industrial Advisor to the U.P. Government and who was associated with him in the U.P. Board for the development of the HMP Industry, a suitable person in all respects to shape the destiny of the UNDP Project. Shri S.N. Singh (who had since voluntarily retired from the services of KVIC) was inducted in September, 1991, for leading the Project by appointing him as its National Project Coordinator for a period of three years. Final approval of the project document with UNDP inputs of 6.86 lakhs U.S. Dollars and Rs. 55 lakhs as KVIC input initially was communicated by the Ministry to the KVIC in September, 1991. The broad objectives of the Project were:

(a) To study the demand pattern of handmade paper and board in India and abroad with a view of determining the grades of paper and board on which the handmade paper industry should concentrate for its economic viability.
(b) To set up a testing laboratory for pulp and paper and a paper-making demonstration plant as part of the handmade paper industry to give advice on how to produce improved product qualities and greater varieties of higher value handmade paper/board and products for the home and export market and to assist in creating capabilities in Indian villages to produce good quality handmade paper and board.
(c) To enhance the capabilities of the handmade paper directorate/centres in the areas or training, consultancy and information services to serve the Indian handmade paper industry.

Progress of the Project

Mrs. Bordia, the then secretary, Ministry of SSI and ARI, favoured allocation of the Project at Sanganer near Jaipur, a place known for growth of traditional Kagzi Centres since the Mughal period, in order to extend the project benefits to the Kagzies and other artisans engaged in the development of Handmade Paper Industry. A small piece of land was also acquired by the KVIC near Sanganer from the Rajasthan Housing Board which was inspected by Mr. Simon B. Green, CTA appointed by UNIDO (United Nations Industrial Development Organisation). Mr. Green, however, did not approve the site considering it as inadequate and preferred a larger plot to develop the project for taking up multifarious activities in the long run. Therefore, efforts were made to acquire a larger piece of land.

Role of Rajasthan Housing Board

It was at this juncture that the Rajasthan Housing Board which had considered the fresh proposals sympathetically and had been generous enough to donate a bigger land of three acres area free of cost to the KVIC in their Housing Board Zone which is known as Sikarpura in the outskirts of Sanganer. Efforts made by Shri S.N. Singh in this transaction have been noteworthy and also the role played by the then Secretary of the Rajasthan Housing Board, Mr. Salauddin Ahmad, allotting the land as a freehold deserves full appreciation.

Construction of Building

By acquiring the above land the project requirements of the building which were earlier planned for about 6,000 sq. ft. were reconsidered and at the instance of CTA a much large building admeasuring over 14,000 sq. ft. area was conceived. The estimated cost of the building which was originally planned at Rs. 20 lakhs gradually increased and with additions and alterations proposed by CTA from time to time during his visits, the building finally had taken shape to such a large size that its financial costs went up to over Rs. 51 lakhs to be met from KVI inputs. This resulted in delay at various levels in the KVIC also in sanctioning the required funds and thus the grounding of the project got inordinately delayed.

SUSTAINABLE DEVELOPMENT THROUGH MARKET APPROACH

Realizing the above situation and the inherent delay involved at various stages in commencing the pilot plant of the project, NPD of the project gave a serious thought to the problems and with his dynamism and determination followed by close cooperation from the Director of HMPI, NPC, Shri S.N. Singh, All India Handmade Paper Industries Association, Kagzies of Sanganer offered a strategy for market development as the immediate objective of the project was initiated. As a part of this objective UNIDO through UNDP was convinced of the necessity to give exposure to the project in the international forum and the first successful attempt was the project's participation in the New York Paper Stationery Show, in May, 1992. More than half a dozen persons representing the industry from India, besides some officers of the KVIC participated in the said show on a cost-sharing basis. This participation had indeed given for the first time, a good international exposure to the Industry, so much so that the Handmade Paper and Board Industries, Sanganer, whose products have been displayed there in a big way through the efforts of Ms. Alexandra Soteriou, the consultant of UNIDO, had built up its international reputation and today it has become 100 per cent EOU in the country.

Participation in Other International Trade Fairs

Influenced by the encouraging response at New York Paper Stationery show, the KVIC had participated in international exhibitions and trade fairs followed later at London, Ghana and Singapore which had also helped the Industry in harnessing the export potential of other units as well.

MARKET STUDIES

International market studies have been conducted by the Consultants of UNIDO, namely, Mr. Serlachius and Ms. Alexandra Soteriou, besides Dr. Kamal Taori, NPD of the project.

Their reports point out the vast unexplored market for the Indian handmade paper and its converted products.

A domestic market survey was also undertaken by the Operational Research Group on behalf of UNDP and their report also revealed substantial domestic market for paper converted specialities. Participation in two Workshops at Delhi in March 1993 and October 1994 besides first ever international trade fair on paper known as "Paperex" at New Delhi, in the exhibition at Nehru Centre, Bombay, have also given adequate exposure to the Industry in the corporate sector and other Industrial Houses.

Technical Study Tours and Fellowship Training

A team of two senior technical persons from the HMP Directorate, Shri S.N. Singh, NPC of the project, besides the then President of the HMP Federation have visited a few countries on a study tour led by CTA and studied both Japanese and European technology in making handmade paper, during May-June 1992. Five technical staff at junior level management have also completed their fellowship training in Japan, U.K. and Czech and three in the Philippines and the U.S.A. to fulfil the desired objectives of the fellowship training. Their reports also indirectly suggest a vast market potential both abroad and within the country by introducing certain measures for quality upgradation in some of the Indian handmade paper varieties.

The Effect of Market Approach in its Totality

The cumulative effect of the above market approach as a part of the objectives of the Project which has been taken up as a mid-term correction considering the delay in grounding the Project for the reasons already stated may be summarised as under:

(a) Except Handmade Paper Department, Sri Aurobindo Ashram, Pondicherry, Handmade Paper Institute, Poona and the Directorate of HMPI (in its meagre contribution) none other HMP Units was directly exporting handmade paper and its converted products before concerted market efforts were made under the banner of UNDP Project.

(b) The Handmade Paper and Board Industries, Sanganer, had grown to the stature of a total export, oriented unit as a result of participation of its representatives on a cost-sharing basis in the New York Paper Stationery Show for the first time. This unit is reported to have achieved an impressive Rs. 2.14 crores export turnover during the year 1993-94.

(c) Product development and market research in the shape of diversified products and made roots into the industry which otherwise had been making mostly conventional varieties. As a result of demand from the creative customers, artists, printers in the line, new products like grass, flower, algae, tea, bagasse, coir mottled papers have been developed to the customer taste by the units without any major efforts for quality consciousness or adoption of technological upgradation measures. The total effect of these efforts on the industry as a whole is that during the year 1993-94 both direct and indirect exports are reported to have crossed Rs. 6 crores value as against the paltry sum of Rs. 60 lakhs three years back. More and more trade enquiries are also pouring in and the HMP-UNDP Project as well as the Director of HMP Industry are seriously engaged in motivating more units to take up export oriented production.

(d) M/s Shanker Gramodyog Seva Sansthan, Hapur, has started direct exports consequent to their participation in Singapore Fair which was arranged by the KVIC. Other units like Kagzi Industries, Sanganer, A.L. Paper House, Sanganer, Pavan Patram, Kalpi, Swastik HMP Unit, Ladwa, Shivneer Handmade Paper Junnar have also diversified their products and started exporting substantial goods through Merchant Exporters like Sakar International Export India of Delhi, Kardmagic of Bombay and others who have assessed the international requirement and introduced a host of converted products.

(e) Capacity Utilisation : The impact of the market demand has been clearly visible by the fact that it helped even a number of KVIC/KVIB financed (List in Annexure-I) units substantially increase their capacity which had remained greatly under-utilized all these years. This is evident from the overall performance of the Industry which had recorded Rs. 15.06 crores production during the year 1993-94 compared to Rs. 12 crores during the preceding year.

SPIRIT OF HEALTHY COMPETITION

As indicated above with the improved performance of a number of units for a few years, a spirit of healthy competition has grown among the well-established handmade paper units and this has led to the in-flow of more and more orders. This is a very healthy sign for the industry and augurs well for sustained efforts to bring consumer awareness and encash the favourable environmental factors for the growth of the industry.

ROLE OF PRIVATE UNITS

There are around 80 private handmade paper units in the country which have been financed by other financing institutions like Banks, S.F.Cs., etc., and are only recognised as genuine handmade paper units in order to help them avail certain fiscal concessions like Central Excise Exemption and State Sales Tax wherever applicable. The notable among them are three major producing kagzi units in Sanganer besides small private units functioning in Kalpi, Latur and other places. With the increased export prospects in the early 1990s the demand from the domestic market has also substantially grown and some of the private units in Kalpi and others like Kalpakala HMP Unit, Latur, have shown phenomenal growth in meeting their local demand. This is also directly attributed to the marketing awareness brought by the UNDP Project.

AREAS OF CONCERN VIS-À-VIS SUSTAINABILITY OF PROJECT

The HMP-UNDP Project was formerly inaugurated by the Hon'ble Chief Minister of Rajasthan on 28th May, 1994 when the former

Chairman, Dr. Yashveer Singh, and the present Chairman of the KVIC Shri Naval Kishore Sharma, were also present. Although, work in the laboratory with machines imported by UNDP has begun the pilot plant is yet to commence its regular activities. With the machines fabricated in India under the advice of CTA and approved by UNIDO being installed, the pilot plant is expected to start its regular activities from 1st June, 1995. The tenure of the project and also the services of NPC, Shri S.N. Singh, stand extended till September, 1995. As such during the next 9 months it is essential that all efforts are made to consolidate and realise the fruits of marketing awareness already brought out by the Project not only in the country but also abroad. Many of the areas of concern for the sustainability of the Project like quality control, technology upgradation, entrepreneurship, training, cost effectiveness, self-reliance through PMT concept national programme for HMP development, incremental cost ratio, involving youth for providing additional employment generation as per the High Power Committee recommendations, etc., are briefly discussed in the following paragraphs:

Marketing, Production and Training Programme

There is a need to integrate marketing, production, and training as a part of diversification and increase utility of the trainees and the trainers. Traditionally the training in the industry has remained confined to organising the managerial and artisan training. The time has come to understand the utility of giving marketing linked entrepreneurial training for this industry. This becomes important because of the growing unemployment of educated persons. Vocationalisation of education can very well be lined with handmade paper on 100 per cent entrepreneurial capacity to develop the programme. For this, on experimental basis coordination can be well established with Handmade Paper Training Centre, Pune, Kumarappa National institute of Handmade Paper, Sanganer, Aurobindo Ashram, Pondicherry and even with private units at Latur, Sanganer, Pune and Kalpi where training would be much more useful practically and can be capable of ensuring sustainable jobs.

An effort was made in this direction in Kalpi but due to lack of sustained monitoring it could not succeed. Vocational education may have to play an important role in the future educational system. This industry can definitely provide an ideal place for linkages provided a marketing tie-up could also be developed. Other training institutions like the I.I.T.s, Polytechnics, etc. will also have to be suitably motivated to reorient their efforts to develop linkages. It is worth trying if this linkage could be developed on an experimental basis with institutions working in the field of vocational education on a selected basis.

Glamourisation

The industry which is fast approaching its take-off stage with its market potential already picking up should strive to bring glamour to the sector for its long-term sustainability. This can be brought about by involving youth both men and women, corporate sector, NGOs and qualified entrepreneurs as already mentioned. Some of the areas which can bring glamour are meeting the demand of exclusive items of eco-friendly handmade paper through International Hotels, Air-port Authorities, Tourism Development, etc. This can be better achieved by promoting modern showrooms with the help of the corporate sector where exclusive items with decent packaging are displayed.

Search for Alternative Raw Materials

Presently main raw materials for the industry are recycled cotton rags and waste paper. Some of the agro-fibres are used mostly for mottling and blending with the above main raw materials. However, looking to the future growth of the industry on the one hand and possibility of its diversified uses on the other scarcity of rags is a certainty. It is, therefore, imperative that alternative raw materials are brought into greater use in a phased manner. Agro-fibres such as wheat straw, paddy straw, jute waste, banana fibre, sun-hemp, etc., can be gainfully used by blending with cotton rags for producing a good lot of varieties. It will be in the interest of the industry to promote establishment of mother pulping units for agro-fibres pulping taking all precautions for affluent treatment and ensure supply of pulp sheets to the small handmade paper units throughout the country to avoid any pollution problem at individual unit level and thus bring down their capital costs. The HMP-UNDP Project should take up this issue also seriously as a part of its objective.

National Programme on Handmade Paper

The HMP-UNDP Project had already prepared tentative project profiles for a national programme of the handmade paper industry which envisages setting up of 1,000 HMP Units throughout the

COMMUNICATION FOR HANDMADE PAPER

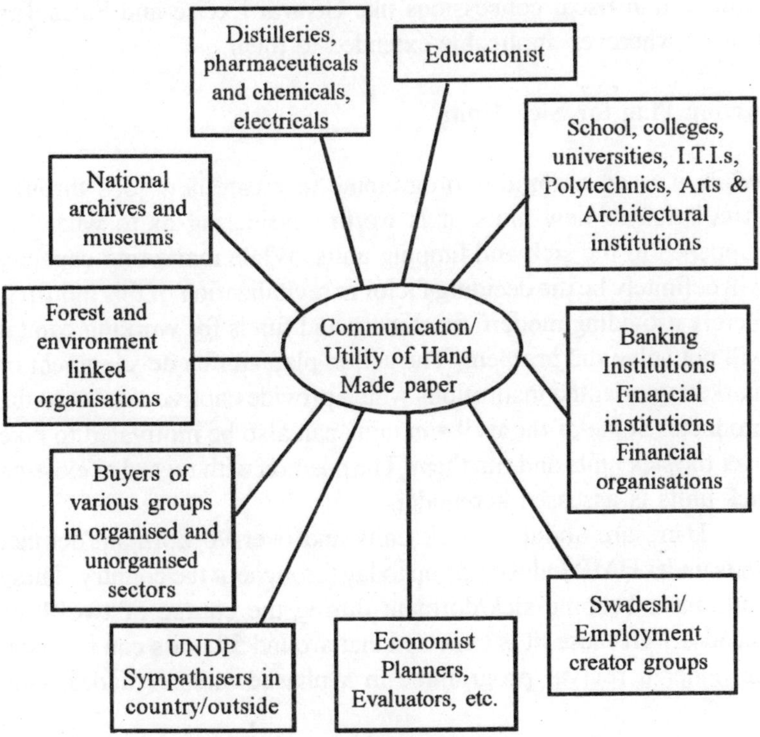

CHART 1

country in a period of five years both as cluster units and also as individual units. In order to achieve this massive programme concerted efforts involving various implementing agencies like entrepreneurs, NGOs and others besides several financing institutions, Corporate Sector, SC/ST Corporation, Women's Welfare and other Socio-Economic Development Organisations have to be made. The Project should motivate retired technical staff of the Industry and experienced representatives of the units besides its own technical staff in order to extend Low Cost Project Consultancy services to those interested in setting up handmade paper units through bank finance. The economic viability of the industry has been proved with the success stories of several HMP Units established by Individuals, partnership concerns (List in Annexure-II) and therefore units promoted with quality control and standardization measures can very well sustain bank rate of interest with certain fiscal concessions like Central Excise and Sales Tax benefit wherever applicable extended to them.

Action Plan for Sick Units

While it is an ambitious programme to create new jobs through installation of new units, it is worth considering as to what has happened to the sick and limping units. While marketing capacity will definitely be the deciding factor in revitalization of this industry, merely providing modern machinery and funds for working capital will not solve the problem. The action plan can be development of marketing oriented institutions which provide captive market to the products. Some of the well-run units can also be motivated to take over the sick units and run them. The position with regard to existing sick units is assessed hereunder.

There are about 35 sick units and over 90 dormant/defunct units under HMP Industry as on today throughout the country. These units have become sick/dormant during the course of two-three decades. "Of these, it is expected that around 50 units can be taken up under a revival programme in a phased manner under bank finance, motivating capable entrepreneurs also for the purpose. Taking into consideration production of 20 tonnes per annum from each unit after their revival, their performance would add to the industry's overall growth as indicated below:

	Additional Investment	Per annum
(a)	Investment already made in sick units Rs. 2 lakhs on an average each	Rs. 1 crore
(b)	Additional estimated investment under revival programme Rs. 2 lakhs each on an average	Rs. 1 crore
(c)	Average production of 50 units at 20 tonnes per annum of file covers, card sheets, etc.	1000 tonnes
(d)	Value at Rs. 30/kg. on an average	Rs. 3 crores
(e)	Direct/indirect employment	300 men 200 women
(f)	Earnings/Annum	Rs. 60 lakhs

The Kumarappa National Handmade Paper Project, Jaipur which is offering consultancy services as a part of its extension programme can co-ordinate in the revival of these sick units.

While all the above issues have a much important role to play in a planning, monitoring and funding process, one cannot undermine the role of organizational support. KVIC with its multifarious activities and existing products may not be able to do justice in the future competitive market. The regulations, developmental and commercial needs are bound to be different. In an open liberalised competitive system when barriers are breaking down need for proper SWOT analysis of any industry can never be overlooked. The industry has to build up its overall capacity to sustain and grow in spite of the reduction in the concessional finance. But if the market favours this can be a turning point. Hence apart from a national project on Handmade Paper as brought out separately, there may be a need for separate organizations to fully exploit the potential of this industry on bankable, replicable pattern of development.

LESSONS FOR OTHER RURAL INDUSTRIES LIKE SOAP, FIBRE, LEATHER

From the significant progress achieved during the last three years in generating domestic and international market for eco-friendly handmade paper through HMP-UNDP Project even before its pilot project could take up its regular plant activities the following two lessons are worth considering by other environment friendly industries like Soap, Fibre, Leather, Marble, Beekeeping, etc., to adopt market oriented measures.

1. Once market demand is created on a sustainable basis the artisans/production units themselves would rise to the occasion and find out their own ways and means to manufacture the goods acceptable to the market. Thus market approach takes priority over other inputs.
2. Therefore, the technological inputs or technological upgradation is a secondary aspect.

Strength for Handmade Paper

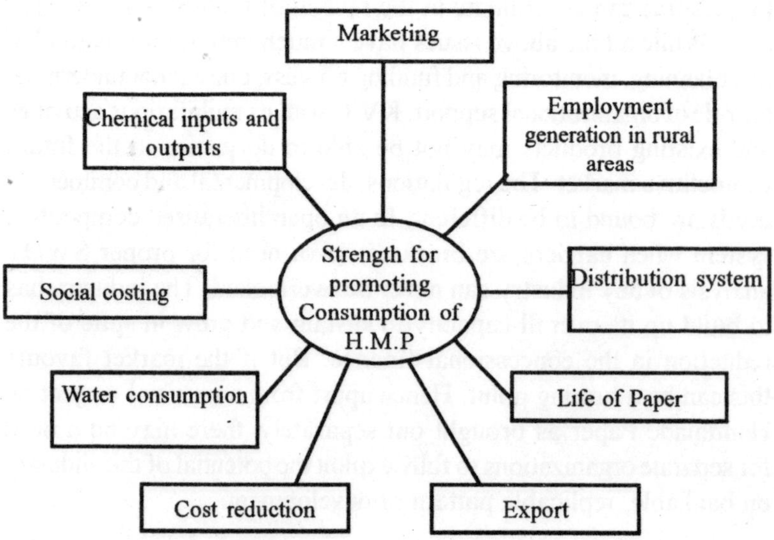

CHART 2

FUTURE AREAS OF POTENTIAL IN HANDMADE PAPER INDUSTRIES

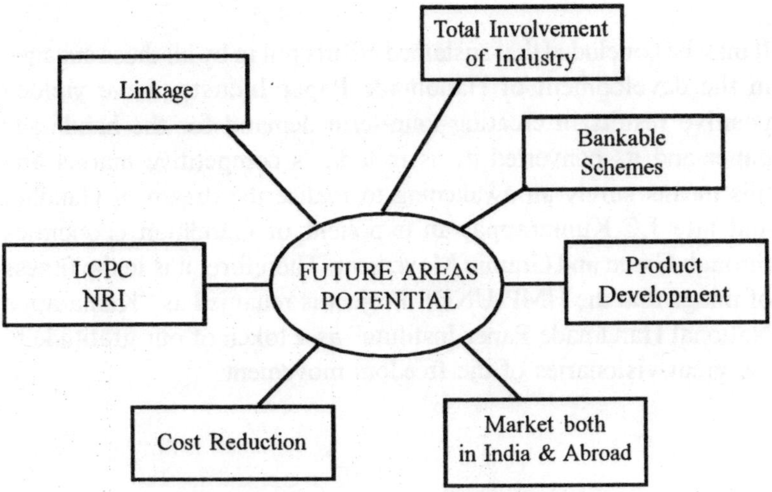

LCPC: Low Cost Practical Consultancy
NRI: Non-Resident Indian

CHART 3

Leading to Social Development for:

- Competitive atmosphere to learn from mistakes
- And to badly utilise the buyers psychology

Products : Requirements that they should fulfil

- Should be in accordance to the taste of the buyers
- Should meet the expectations of the buyers in terms of quality, price and presentation

CHART 4

REALISATION OF DREAM OF GANDHIJI AND LATE SHRI KUMARAPPA

It may be concluded that sustained efforts put in by all those engaged in the development of Handmade Paper Industry have yielded positive results in creating long-term demand for the handmade paper and its converted items in today's competitive market and this means surely an awakening to realise the dream of Gandhiji and late J.C.Kumarappa, an exponent of Gandhian economics through Green and Gramin Movement. Therefore, it is in the fitness of things that the HMP-UNDP Project is renamed as "Kumarappa National Handmade Paper Institute" as a token of our gratitude to the great visionaries of the freedom movement.

APPENDIX–VI

A Marketing Role for Planning Commission Specially in Unplanned Areas

The Planning Commission had brought out in May, 1994 a discussion paper prepared in the Perspective Planning Division of the Planning Commission titled 'Indian Planning Processing and an Agenda' for its reorientation. Recently the Planning Commission had deliberated with economists its role in the new economic set-up. As is well known the new economic policy enjoins liberalization, opening up, building up competitive capacity, permitting the closure of inefficient and, on the whole, developing new concept for cost effective systems including privatisation. This has initiated a chain reaction. Whether in the field of share market, banking, new investment, entrepreneurship development or even new added thrust of rural development programmes along with subsidies, grants, work cultures a new ethos seems to be prevailing all around. There are many who feel that the market should be the planner. The discussion paper brings out the historical paradigms and their adverse consequences of earlier action. Whether it was dominated by public sector or over dependence on State or policies of protection or urbanization have all led to an imbalance in growth. The organized have managed to corner the best. Hence the dismantling of controls, regulation and administrated prices are already under way. The role of public enterprises is being redefined and even investments divested. The market is being permitted liberally and freely to play its role in terms of investments, policies, perspectives. However, in areas of social welfare, population control, environmental protection, health and education, the Government will have to continue to play its responsible role. In this situation the natural question arises as to what is the role of planning processes and how in times to come, the traditional role of resource allocator and fixer of priorities will be decided. It is a fact that the planning interventions definitely be required in areas where free market game will be disastrous for protecting the weak and for reduction in the regional imbalances planning will have to still play numerous roles.

In this situation when it comes to programmes for the unorganised or decentralized, one would like to mention about the competitive compatible areas of advantage to a country like ours. While paying attention to human development inducts, priorities, attention to neglected areas, etc., the most important area of concern is learning from lessons and codifying a plan of action for sustainable development based on equity, justice and all that which makes countries great. It is here that the vision and clarity in the role of Planning Commission can be very useful. Many feel that the traditional planning has been allocating 8 to 10 per cent extra than the previous year's expenditure. Depending upon the Strengths, Weaknesses, Opportunities and Threat analysis the resources or priorities have hardly been emphasized. If that was so, the initial angle of Rural Development Programme would not have been there. It is only for the last few years or decades that various experiments have been carried out in terms of Rural Development. It is not the question of funds or machinery rather than many feel it is the question of over-manning of Rural Development Programmes. What is missing is the enterprise development which has direct linkages with marketing, policy issues, return of investments and overall creating conditions through policy and again issues where rural areas get glamourised. This glamourisation has been the missing link but as the cities become overcrowded, polluted, unsafe, there is an awareness towards rural, natural, eco-friendly, lifestyles. This means pooling of various programmes through Enterprise Development concepts to usher in any change processes on a self-supporting basis. Ultimately the success parameters of Rural Development Programmes have to be principled as opposed to personalities. The principles have to be widely acceptable not only to the target group but also to the planner, evaluator, banker, analyzer, public leader and even the Press. It has to have an in-built replicability. Despite realization, the helpless feeling amongst the senior bureaucrats or even planners needs to be clarified, analysed and suitable plan of action needs development. It is here the *inter se* priorities with linkages, area approaches have to be planned and acted upon by the Planning Commission. The dichotomy of data-base in the rural areas or even the overlapping nature all needs redefinition with reference to success. It is here as resource allocator, codifier, protector of the rationalist, watchdog of duplication, question raiser, that the Planning Commission can play the role which nobody else is able to play. The problems of our time (POOT) have to be blended with opportunities of our time (OOOT). This can be done only with a holistic view and area specific programme with the Panchayat Raj fully developed. The inputs have to be based on matching contributions and also regional SWOT analysis, the performance and enterprise development to make projects replicable, self-supporting and competitive. The role of technology has to be area specific and effective in turn to the target group. There can be no generalization. Depending upon the level of development, overall absorption, capacity, manpower capabilities the shift has to take place immediately to boost the masses inbuilt capacity and willingness to do better and to improve their self-confidence through self-enterprise or developing competitive capacity to manage self-managed institutions. This is the need of the day. The sustainability of the development coupled with Human Development has to encompass the Gandhi-Vinoba-Kumarappa model as an essential aspect. Various organizations have massive infrastructures lying underutilized in the far-flung areas. But having linkages with marketing need not only be supported with funds, but also developing them for further competitive capabilities. The KVI sector is one of those institutions having about 5 decades' experience in running rural employment programmes. With better training, management practices, return on investment, bankability of projects and fully tapping in turn and ecological factors which are in their favour are in an ideal position to take off. The fact has to be shed. The old guards have to be awakened to take up new challenges by actively involving inbuild. It is a golden opportunity not only for the Planning Commission but also for many neglected organizations like the KVIC to realize their potential investible hidden power and rise to the occasion. We are in the new millennium and it is time to give practical shape to the dream of the Father of the Nation. Let us give a greater thrust by arousing entrepreneurial capacity of the masses by working together. Let the resources be pooled. Let the market along with efficient systems be the guided force. Let the competitive advantages through SWOT which our present time offers be our channelling agent. These are no bias scopes, but plan, action, research oriented necessities of our time, whose time has come. The Planning Commission can definitely give a clear direction at this stage when best utilization of the manpower resource, infrastructure, funds is called for. Let there be wider discussion before the action is launched.

APPENDIX—VII

MARKETING PEACE
Non-Violence as a Strategy for Holistic Development

Introduction

With the advent of twenty-first century some of the challenges of our time compel us to look at issue of peace, sustainability of development, and many other neglected dimensions from a different angle. With the collapse of socialism, big question on capitalism, humanism emerges as the only viable and sustainable long term option. It is here various dimensions of violence, conflict, learning to staying and working together, peace and many other areas of strategies for making win-win situations for all becomes priority and concern. Social transformations have their own compulsions. The political, the economic, cultural, social and various other dimensions of social transformations must ensure equity and fairness in opportunities and probe to everybody. The human rights, gender inequality, religious revivalism, unequal access to goods and services, proliferation of arms and simultaneously urge and clamour for peace and sustainable development with environmental considerations have to be looked into.

Challenges of our time

- Massive awakening
- Failure of past development models
- Collapse of socialism, doubts on capitalism and unavoidability to humanism
- Redundancy of established institutions
- All round lack of faith
- Dwindling resources of the State
- Overstaffing and poor work culture around State organisations
- Neglect of community and traditional hereditary practices
- Realisation that State cannot be held together on religious or armament factors
- Massive codification of examples of failures and successes
- Humanity and human rights becoming supreme
- Compulsions of global vision and local action (GVALA)
- Awareness of women and neglected/exploited groups
- Insistence on money as the biggest wealth at every level
- Need for regional and local authorities to take responsibilities and play their legitimate role with transparency and viability
- Poor infrastructure and attention to unorganised, dispersed and decentralised sectors and its harsh realities acceptance.
- Need to involve people, community and all role players

It will be clear that many of these challenges are unique and unparalleled. There is no historical semblance hence we have to look for new models for effective functioning, timely corrections and self-supporting planning and research systems for using all development potential.

Compulsions and Dimensions of Peace

If we accept the chellenges of our time and the urgency to look at various strategies and tactics for sustianable peace not only in few pockets or areas of the world but everywhere, in every nook and corner then obviously the massive awakening, the widespread information technology and free flow of information also compels us to try to look at various dimensions and compulsions of peace.

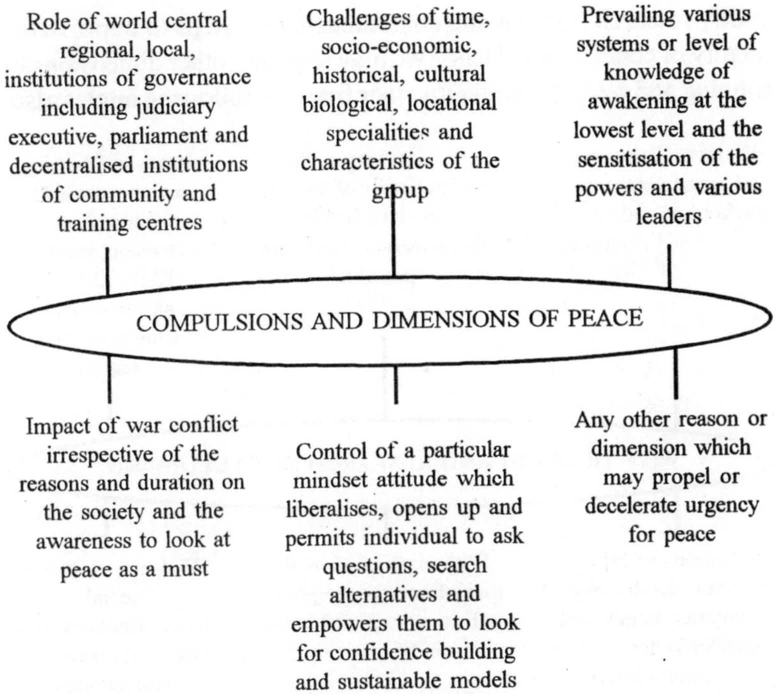

From the above analysis we will be able to draw some patterns, compulsions, imperatives and also dimensions which will enable us to look into various angles of conflict peace and social transformation. This will also facilitate identification of role players and stake holders so that a long term and short term plan of action could be drawn with certain parameters of milestones, checks and balances and also parameters of successes with risk factors.

Role of Training and Research

By compartmentalised treatment of research and training tremendous harm has been done. The disastor which it has inflicted on the well meaning individuals and also the society can be corrected only when the aspects of training and research which includes condification, planning, learning lessons from others involving various stake holders and also carrying out continuous learning and training processes. This also means multidimensional approach to analyse codify research training and continuously take steps to improve the quality of conclusions. Hence we may look into other dimensions of training and research going together from the following angles also.

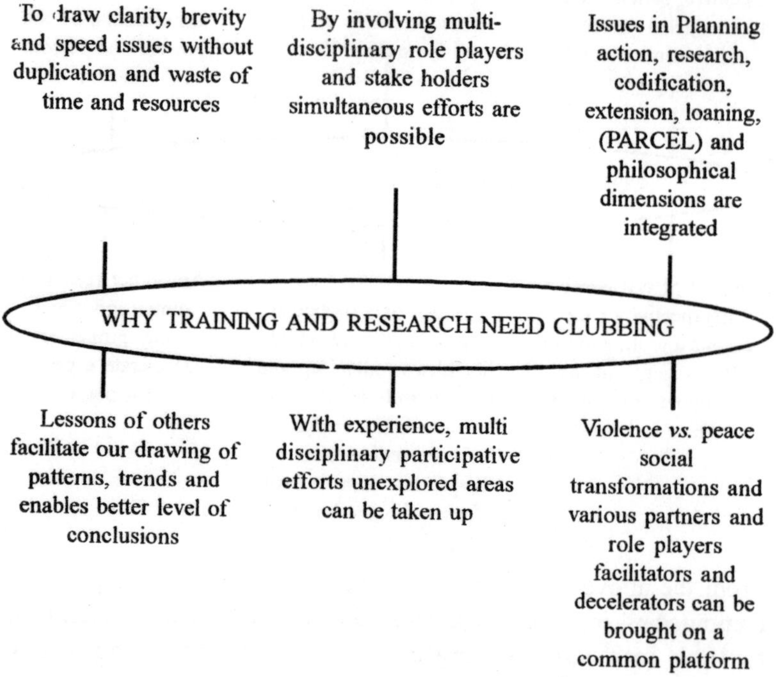

Since compartmentalised approaches by various institutions, professionals, religious and human rights bodies or peace builders are economists, nationalists, financiers have hardly bothered to come on a common platform and look at the issues holistically. Some of the words like sustainability, strategy, development, quality of life, gross domestic product, vis-à-vis per capita income, satisfaction and happiness, community, nationhood, State and inter-State relations etc. etc. need to be explored with different priority. As challenges of time keep changing as per region, religion, level of appreciation and knowledge, environmental and locational compulsions etc. one would find that the issues of clarity, brevity and speed with some other fundamentals of behaviour, satisfaction etc. needs to be churned and galvanised.

Working with Individuals and Institutions in New Context

One feel imperative of improving skills, working together, lessons of the past are clearly understood in the new context. The fellow and the society have to look into issue of working with individuals and institutions. The concept of gaining new insight, new data, new theory, new research method or even modes of enquiry for extensively and intensively enriching the conclusions then the pursuit of peace for the masses may become clearer and clearer. The concept of working in the new context also has many many new and unique dimensions. Needless to say there can be no static parameters for judging the success of this effort. But certainly, some oxygen like parameters for the success of these efforts can be drawn by asking certain questions like the following.

1. Depending upon the biodiversity, aspirations and level of knowledge of holistic livelihood how do the individuals and the society perceive development, peace, training, enterprises and also policy making instruments.
2. What are the practices in the community and the society to provide best opportunities for every member of the society. The opportunities may be through training, skill upgradations, employment, arts and crafts, business and culture or even information technology and by utilising cadre of self-employed mobilisers?
3. What is the communication gap between the organised and unorganised, urbanites and ruralites, those in well paid services and in self-employed sectors, those working with international bodies and the masses on whose names the linkages are framed, gender issues, children and the aged and how does the religion and spiritual dimensions of living affect the practices of society?
4. How do the professionals perceive their relevancy to their profession and also to their society.
5. How do scholars, journalists, editors, media and policy makers both at micro and macro level perceive issues of coordination, linkages trade, politics, sports and overall sustainability of higher level of quality of life.

6. In the era of globalisation, free trade, borderless state, rising aspirations of the masses, very fast communication and information sharing how the information technology and decentralised systems of governance with policy options will be able to contribute for the welfare of the masses on a sustianable basis.

Expected Benefits

With the active collaboration and working with seemingly conflicting partners and with thrust on self-employment and participative investment, the issues of peace, social transformation and conflict remove, avoidance will definitely get clarity.

It is only after the clarity that issue of dissemination, training and further improvement for better systems development and management is possible. The role of NGO as a complementary civic institute has hardly been utilised in the third world countries. The NGOs can transform the dormant lowest level political institution into vibrant agencies of social and economic empowerment of the people. Globalisation and localisation issues can very well be treated with the active partnership of the NGOs. It is here the networking, global vision and local action could facilitate win-win situation for all resulting in peace, sustainability and development. It is also a fact that NGOs and other training institutions have been working in isolation. It is high time as resources become scarce and demand ever increasing these opportunities are utilised to provide cost effective self-employment oriented extension and replication systems. It is here the organisations of community, society of professionals and bureaucracy learn to produce churn and disseminate knowledge and skills with speed and effectiveness. Needless to say seminars workshop brain storming sessions, case studies local area planning and resources mapping with conflict resolution and peace stabilisation efforts could be very useful.

Once these efforts are on the right path and widely accepted then certain additional efforts are required to make these efforts widely known through edited volumes, news media, conferences, web sites, policy workshops and also sensitisation of policy makers and leaders at various levels.

How the Training Research, Initiatives Contribute to Newness or Plan of Action

1. As mentioned earlier various isolated dispersed initiatives has been taken to compartmentalised and look into issues of social transformation, peace and conflict. Hence by bridging of different bodies of knowledge and theory produced by researchers and by involving various NGOs and role players.
2. We have to encourage performance by local initiatives, recognition and incentives with rewards.
3. Learning to working together on area basis with transparency, viability and win-win situation.
4. Panchayat, community NGO, IT and marketing led compulisions have to be involved.
5. Role of Vegetarianism, health food, broadening of mind-set and attitude development has to be converged.
6. Issues of Self-employment, rural investment and business like principles of good governance, accountability and value for money needs cost effective treatment.
7. There is overstaffing, very poor work culture, lack of transparency in most of the institutions both in Government and outside Government. Even private sector has been miserable failure. Hence a climate or an environment or an overall thrust has to be galvanised for better performance oriented systems.
8. Greatest problem is of the leadership at every level whether it is permanent or temporary, rural or urban, economic or social, developmental or regulatory, HRD or any other field, the whole motive seems to be root each rather than fruit eating. It seems whole system is under stress and holistic disaster seems to be the only outcome.
9. The utter frustration, cynicism and hopelessness and purposelessness and lack of direction prevalent all around needs to be converted into an opportunity by accepting the challenge.

Small initiatives should lead to policy changes and better public administration and governance.

10. Stereotyped workshops conferences of brain storming sessions must shift to result oriented output, based churning based upon previous codified level of knowledge. Entire scheme of things seem to be budget utilisation oriented. This has to undergo radical change through I, We, They initiatives.
11. Need to encourage example setting processes by reducing the gap between the precept and practice.
12. Innovations in thinking and implementation needs to be made a part of annual report of all departments. This should also include the areas of weakness and how societies, NGO, IT, community and entrepreneurs could forward to remove bottlenecks.

INDEX